Sam!
appreciate
our friendship!
Mike

The Entrepreneurial Spirit of Aggieland II

Tales of Success from Texas A&M Former Students

RUSTY BURSON

The Entrepreneurial Spirit of Aggieland II
Tales of Success from Texas A&M Former Students
All Rights Reserved.
Copyright © 2022 Rusty Burson
v3.0

The opinions expressed in this manuscript are solely the opinions of the author and do not represent the opinions or thoughts of the publisher. The author has represented and warranted full ownership and/or legal right to publish all the materials in this book.

This book may not be reproduced, transmitted, or stored in whole or in part by any means, including graphic, electronic, or mechanical without the express written consent of the publisher except in the case of brief quotations embodied in critical articles and reviews.

Outskirts Press, Inc.
http://www.outskirtspress.com

Paperback ISBN: 978-1-9772-4867-1
Hardback ISBN: 978-1-9772-4882-4

Cover Photo © 2022 Rusty Burson. All rights reserved - used with permission.

Outskirts Press and the "OP" logo are trademarks belonging to Outskirts Press, Inc.

PRINTED IN THE UNITED STATES OF AMERICA

This book is dedicated to my wife, Vannessa (Class of 1991), and to our children, Payton (Class of 2021), Kyleigh (Class of 2022) and Summer (Class of 2027). I am the only one in the family without an Aggie ring, but we all bleed maroon. This is also dedicated to my longtime and trusted transcriber, Tara Corder-Pizzino (Class of 2015). Thanks for all your wonderful work through the years. I challenge you to write your own book soon!

Table of Contents

Introduction..i

Chapter 1   Kent Moore..1
                   Moore's Path to Texas A&M...1
                   Moore's Path to Entrepreneurial Success..............................6
                   Moore's Most Challenging Obstacles..................................12
                   Moore's Advice to Young Entrepreneurs............................17

Chapter 2   Jon Acklam...20
                   Acklam's Path to Texas A&M...20
                   Acklam's Path to Entrepreneurial Success............................26
                   Acklam's Most Challenging Obstacles.................................29
                   Acklam's Advice to Young Entrepreneurs...........................34

Chapter 3   Lyle Milstead..36
                   Milstead's Path to Texas A&M...36
                   Milstead's Path to Entrepreneurial Success..........................42
                   Milstead's Most Challenging Obstacles................................47
                   Milstead's Advice to Young Entrepreneurs.........................51

Chapter 4   Monty Davis..54
                   Davis' Path to Texas A&M..54
                   Davis' Path to Entrepreneurial Success................................57
                   Davis' Most Challenging Obstacles.....................................63
                   Davis' Advice to Young Entrepreneurs...............................65

Chapter 5   Terrence Murphy..71
                   Murphy's Path to Texas A&M...71
                   Murphy's Most Difficult Challenge.....................................77
                   Murphy's Path to Entrepreneurial Success..........................81
                   Murphy's Advice to Young Entrepreneurs.........................85

Chapter 6   Jeff Schiefelbein..89
                   Schiefelbein's Path to Texas A&M..89
                   Schiefelbein's Most Challenging Obstacle..........................92
                   Schiefelbein's Path to Entrepreneurial Success....................99
                   Schiefelbein's Advice to Young Entrepreneurs..................105

Chapter 7	Mike Shaw	108
	Shaw's Path to Texas A&M	108
	Shaw's Path to Entrepreneurial Success	112
	Shaw's Most Challenging Obstacles	118
	Shaw's Advice to Young Entrepreneurs	123
Chapter 8	Leslie Liere	125
	Liere's Path to Texas A&M	125
	Liere's Path to Entrepreneurial Success	130
	Liere's Most Challenging Obstacles	132
	Liere's Advice to Young Entrepreneurs	136
Chapter 9	Jay Conner	140
	Conner's Path to Texas A&M	140
	Conner's Path to Entrepreneurial Success	145
	Conner's Most Challenging Obstacles	151
	Conner's Advice to Young Entrepreneurs	156
Chapter 10	Scott Polk and Emily Huskinson	159
	Polk's Path to Texas A&M	159
	Polk's Path To Entrepreneurial Success	161
	Huskinson's Path to Texas A&M	164
	Huskinson's Path to Entrepreneurial Success	167
	Huskinson's Most Difficult Challenge	170
	Huskinson's Advice to Young Entrepreneurs	172
	Polk's Advice to Young Entrepreneurs	175
Chapter 11	Chris Dailey	178
	Dailey's Path to Texas A&M	178
	Dailey's Path to Entrepreneurial Success	183
	Dailey's Most Difficult Challenge	188
	Dailey's Advice to Young Entrepreneurs	193
Chapter 12	Hendler Family: Barry, Laura, Hollie, BJ and Joe	197
	Hendler's Path to Texas A&M	197
	Hendler's Most Challenging Obstacles	202
	Hendler Family's Path to Entrepreneurial Success	207
	Hendler's Advice to Young Entrepreneurs	211
About the Book		215
About the Author		216

Introduction

Timing is everything in life, and God's timing is always perfect…and sometimes quite astonishing. This book is proof of that.

For many years while working at the 12th Man Foundation on the Texas A&M campus, I pondered how I could possibly connect the fabulously successful entrepreneurs I had the privilege of meeting because of my role with the organization and the bright, goal-oriented and ambitious students who strolled the sprawling campus in College Station. In fact, I pondered that possibility so many times that I knew God had placed it on my heart. He was calling me to do something, but I wasn't sure how I was going to answer that call.

In the meantime, I was blessed with the opportunity to write quite a few books: biographies on A&M legends like linebacker Dat Nguyen, NFL referee Red Cashion, World War II hero Roy Bucek and women's basketball coach Gary Blair; compilations on Texas A&M's football history, the history of hockey in the Lone Star State (it's deeper than you think) and the Texas Rangers' baseball history; business books with my good friend and insurance agent extraordinaire Warren Barhorst; and tradition-detailing books on Reveille and the yell leaders. Still, I had this calling to go deeper and to tackle a project that would fulfill my own entrepreneurial desires and inspire others to follow their dreams.

My wife has joked that I have written more books than I've read. That's not true, but it is true that I had not been reading as much as I should. So, in the summer of 2013, I vowed to read more meaningful pieces of literature than what I found in *Sports Illustrated*. A friend recommended an easy-to-read, thought-provoking book called "The Traveler's Gift," and I figured, "Why not?" I went to the bookstore, picked up a copy and carried it with me for a month or so while I crisscrossed the state with my son and his travel baseball team. I should emphasize the word *"carried."* I brought it everywhere, but I didn't open it until I attended one of my son's games, and he was not in the lineup. Quite frankly, I was disappointed he wasn't playing, which gave me the perfect opportunity—or excuse—to finally open the book while sitting in the stands of a ballpark.

Once I started reading, I couldn't put the book down. It was such a great read that I bought another book by the author, Andy Andrews. While reading *"The Noticer: Sometimes, All a Person Needs is a Little Perspective,"* one of the quotes I read practically leapt off the pages: "**Remember, young man, experience is not the best teacher. Other people's experience is the best teacher. By reading about the lives of great people, you can unlock the secrets to what made them great.**"

I read it again and again and again. Then I highlighted it. It was my eureka moment, as I knew I needed to write a book that spotlighted some the great entrepreneurs and business people I had befriended while with the 12th Man Foundation.

Still, there was something missing. There needed to be another element. My vision for the book was clear, but the purpose was cloudy. That's when I picked up a copy of *The Battalion*, the student newspaper on the Texas A&M campus. Honestly, that's not something I normally did. But for whatever reason, on that particular day in the fall of 2013, I picked up the paper and clearly found my purpose and heard God's calling. On the front page of that particular edition was a story about a new business incubator and accelerator on campus called Startup Aggieland. I had never heard of it before, but as I read about its mission— helping students nurture their entrepreneurial dreams—I knew I had been called to write the book and to donate all proceeds to Startup Aggieland.

That's what I did, and in 2017, I released *The Entrepreneurial Spirit of Aggieland,* focusing on 12 entrepreneurs who attended A&M. I donated all the proceeds from sales to Startup Aggieland.

The response to the book was overwhelmingly positive; not just from Texas A&M students, but from the children and grandchildren of the people featured in the book because they had never fully understood the legacy that their parents and grandparents created. Most of the successful entrepreneurs have never detailed the struggles they conquered. Their children and grandchildren never previously knew such stories.

Ultimately, I felt called to write another book, picking up where the first one left off.

Writing this book was a long journey—longer than I had envisioned, as we were delayed by a global pandemic and other factors. But interviewing and working with the remarkable subjects in this book has blessed me beyond belief. All their stories are different, but they are also essentially the same. There is no secret recipe for success, and the term "overnight success" is typically made for fairytales.

Business or entrepreneurial success is about courage, self-discipline, vision, belief, capitalizing on opportunities, overcoming obstacles and, most of all, hard work. These stories inspire me. They will inspire you, too.

These men and women have walked in your shoes across the Texas A&M campus. They were at one time where you are. And if you want to go where they have gone, it is possible. They are living proof.

As you begin reading their stories, keep one thing in mind, young man or young woman: **"Experience is not the best teacher. Other people's experience is the best teacher. By reading about the lives of great people, you can unlock the secrets to what made them great."**

Here's to unlocking your greatness. Gig 'em, God bless and go for it

CHAPTER 1
Kent Moore

President & Founder
Kent Moore Cabinets
Texas A&M Class of 1972

MOORE'S PATH TO TEXAS A&M

In many social settings, one of the first questions people tend to ask each other upon first being introduced is: "Where are you from?" While that's a fairly simple question for many to answer, I always feel a bit like Hank Williams Jr. singing his 1982 hit "A Country Boy Can Survive" when I begin answering. In case you're not familiar with the song, the lyrics include the following lines:

We're from North California and South Alabam'
And little towns all around this land…

We came from the West Virginia coal mines
And the Rocky Mountains and the western skies…

I am not actually from any of those places, but I am from all over this land. I was born in San Antonio on January 16, 1950 while my father was attending Trinity University and pursuing a career in ministry. From there, my family moved to Louisville, Kentucky, where my father attended seminary, and then it was on to Big Spring, Tennessee, where Dad was the minister of the small community's Presbyterian church. I attended three different schools in the first grade alone, and I spent second grade in a Census-designated place (it's not even a town) called Tok Junction, Alaska. The temperature was minus-60 degrees Fahrenheit on Christmas Day the year we were there. My father felt called to be a missionary, and Tok was the wild frontier. For perspective's sake, according to the 2010 Census, the population of Tok was 1,258 residents. While that may seem miniscule, it represents a significant amount of growth from less than 130 when we were there in the late 1950s. What I remember most vividly was the long, dark stretches of time in winter when the sun disappeared for days and the continual, around-the-clock sunlight in summer. A softball game is played in Tok without lights on the longest day of the year...at midnight. My older sister, Cerene, and I were not particularly fond of Tok, but my mother absolutely hated it. That's why we only stayed for a year.

We returned to Texas, where my parents had grown up in the small community of Snyder, which is roughly 85 miles southeast of Lubbock. When we left Alaska, we stopped in Idaho with my uncle's family for a short time and then drove back to Texas. My father initially took a job as the Director of Christian Education for a church in Abilene. We then bounced around Texas, stopping in Hamilton, Meridian, Vidor and back to Abilene. My parents bought a house in Abilene during our first stint in the community, and we circled back in an attempt to clean it up and sell it the second time. My father didn't have a job at a church the second time in Abilene, so the plan was for both of my parents to become Fuller Brush Company salespeople. The Fuller Brush Company, founded in 1906, began with door-to-door sales of brushes of various sorts, including hairbrushes with a lifetime guarantee, for which the company became famous. For many years, the company was an industry leader in the sales of branded and private-label products for personal care, as well as commercial and household cleaning merchandise. Many salespeople made a great living as Fuller Brush Men and Women.

Unfortunately, my parents were not among the fortune-earning salespeople, primarily because neither of them were natural salespeople. My mother was not even what you would describe as a "people person," which makes door-to-door sales quite challenging. To make a long story short, we wound up in Italy, Texas, which is about 45 miles south of Dallas. Dad was going to serve three churches in the area: Italy, Forreston (five miles north of Italy) and Milford (six miles south of Italy). I remember my mother commenting about how my dad's combined salary at all three of the churches was still below the national poverty level. I don't know how much he earned, but I do recall that when the television we hauled from Alaska died, my dad went to the local furniture store and bought a black and white portable TV for about $35 or $40. He had to make payments in order to afford it. Here's the point: I never lacked any necessity, but finances were always a struggle.

On the other hand, the opportunities for a skinny high school football player were far greater at Italy High than they were at Abilene High, where I had gone through spring football drills my freshman year. In the 1950s, Abilene High became a football dynasty under Chuck Moser. From 1954 to 1957, the Eagles won three state championships and 49 consecutive games. Abilene captured six district titles in a row in a rugged West Texas district that became known as the "Little Southwest Conference." In all honesty, it was going to be extremely difficult for me to ever make much of an impact at a place like Abilene High.

It was much easier for me to make a difference (and to make the team) at Italy High, which at that time was a Class B school. Italy was the 12th different school I had attended, and it may have been the best fit. During my sophomore year (1965-66), we became somewhat of a trendsetter among local schools because a young African-American student named David Henderson attended school with us to prepare Italy for full-scale integration the following year, moving us up to Class A. David was the perfect ambassador, as he was outgoing, funny, always smiling and a tremendous athlete. David was eventually killed in Vietnam, but I have thought often about what a wonderful person David was and what a great friend he was to me. The other thing I still think about is how I was able to attend Texas A&M, while David was not afforded such an opportunity during that timeframe. Thankfully, times have changed for the better in that regard.

Back in the mid-1960s, however, many schools in Texas were reluctant to make the move to full-scale integration. I can only speak for the athletes at Italy, but we loved integration. During my sophomore year we only had 18 athletes on the football team. After integration prior to my junior year, we had many more kids on the team and many more good athletes. For me, football provided an escape from my normal existence. Being a preacher's kid, football was my opportunity to hit somebody and get away with it. I liked it. I probably shouldn't have liked it as much as I did, but I really liked to play football.

My junior season was my best year. I played five games where I never came off the field. On special teams, I once kicked a 52-yard punt, and I played several positions on offense. But it was on defense where I really thrived. I possessed a nose for the ball and a high pain threshold, which made me a pretty good Class A defender. I was essentially a free-roaming linebacker, lining up at different spots on the field and stunting on virtually every play. From 1975-1988, the Dallas Cowboys featured a Hall of Fame defender named Randy White, who was nicknamed "The Manster" (half man/half monster). Long before White's debut in Texas and on a much smaller scale, I was the "Monster Man" of our defense.

I would have been perfectly content to play nothing but defense as a senior, but following my junior season, the head coach stopped me in the hallway and informed that I would be playing quarterback as a senior in the fall of 1967. That meant he wouldn't let me play defense, which I viewed as a major sacrifice. We ended up my senior season tied for the district lead, and we played Cedar Hill in the final game for the championship. Unfortunately, it rained the entire week before the game, and I wasn't much of a passer in the best settings, let alone the muddy, messy and miserable field conditions. The mud and the opponent managed to shut us out, 8-0. Still, playing football and helping our team to play for the district championship were significant accomplishments during my high school career that helped to shape me for future challenges.

Football, however, was not the most significant challenge I tackled during high school. My mother was an avid subscriber to *Reader's Digest*, and in one of the editions she read an intriguing article about the Colorado Outward Bound School, which ran the first Outward Bound course in America in 1962. The Colorado Outward Bound School was a spinoff from the original that was opened in Aberdovey, Wales in 1941. As World War II broke out in Europe in 1939, Lawrence Holt, a partner in a large merchant-shipping enterprise, insisted that faulty training was the cause of many seamen's unnecessary deaths in the Battle of the Atlantic. Hahn proposed starting a new kind of school in Aberdovey: a one-month course that would foster "physical fitness, enterprise, tenacity and compassion among British youth." The training at Aberdovey was based on a philosophy that training through challenges produced better outcomes and greater impact than training *for* challenges because it created transferable character traits. The sea, mountains and desert provide training that no institute or university can offer. These landscapes, in tandem with Outward Bound principles, teach the difficult, technical skills necessary for survival, but also teach relevant skills necessary for life.

As my mother read the story in *Reader's Digest*, she handed it to me and essentially challenged me, insinuating I wouldn't be tough enough to handle it. I read the article and applied to attend the Colorado Outward Bound School (COBS). I was accepted, along with two other high school friends (they went to different courses), and I went about the process of seeking the necessary funding. A businessman in Dallas provided me with a scholarship, which was roughly $350. My parents drove me to Denver, dropped me off and 40 to 50 of us boarded buses for Lake City, in the northeastern corner of Colorado's San Juan Mountains.

I recall looking out the window of the bus when the driver pulled to the side of the road and made an abrupt stop seemingly in the middle of nowhere. We were told to exit the bus and we dumped our luggage into a truck. "We will meet you over there," someone hollered as he pointed toward a barn in the distance. "That's the camp. We'll drive the luggage over there. Here's your first challenge: Make it to the camp without using the bridge. Good luck." Then the bus and the truck drove out of sight. The only way to make it to the camp without using the bridge was to cross the mountain river in front of us. This was summertime in Colorado, which means the river was filled with water that had recently been snow, so it was frigid as it raced across boulders and down the mountain. The river was about 75 feet across, and every one of us was soaking wet in a matter of moments. It was a treacherous journey across the river, but at least I was not wearing dress clothes, unlike some of my fellow COBS attendees. Once we crossed the river we were shivering during the mile hike to the campsite, where we were issued a sleeping bag, a compass and cooking utensils.

During our first few days, we were taught how to read maps, how to use a compass and how to travel from one spot on the map to another. We also spent a significant amount of time problem-solving, which was especially beneficial for me. We were then divided into groups of nine, and we were given assignments. Most of our assignments were three-day journeys, where all the groups took off in different directions and we were told to rendezvous in a particular place on the map. We cooked dehydrated potatoes and whatever else we were supplied that could easily be carried in a bag. It was basically survival training without a military emphasis. Some of the kids were there because of their troubled past. Some attended because their parents were rich and tired of them. Some like me and my two buddies were looking for the adventure of proving we were up to the challenge.

COBS was a significant event in my life. I had not previously believed I had been called to be a leader. After moving so many times in my childhood, I became quiet and introverted, fearful of making new friends and then having to leave again. COBS brought me out of my shell in many ways. There were times when each of us within the group were required to be leaders. When you come to a fork in the trail and you are trying to interpret the map, a mistake could take you 10 or 15 miles in the wrong direction. I became good at making those decisions. When others were put in charge, I noticed that it didn't take long for weaknesses to show up or for the natural leaders to step forward and to be assertive.

Toward the end of COBS, we made about a 150-mile journey on foot around Lake City. Then, one of our final challenges was a three-day solo trip where I was completely by myself with no food, no sleeping bag and only a handful of matches. The intention was for each of us to experience three days-worth of hunger. That was the hungriest I have ever been in my life, before or after. There were two or three guys who snuck back to camp for food and were caught. They didn't receive their certificate of completion (our only reward for completing COBS). In my three days alone, I read the Gospels of Matthew, Mark, Luke and John, wrote my parents a letter thanking them for being great parents and loving me, wrote a thank you letter to the businessman in Dallas who sponsored me and spent many hours of introspection, asking myself what I wanted to do and who I wanted to be in the future? I didn't have all the answers, but I came to the conclusion that I could accomplish much more than I originally thought, which was the point of attending COBS.

When it was all said and done, I spent 26 days at COBS, waking before dawn each of those days, dusting the frost off my sleeping bag and taking on challenges. During that month, I ran a marathon, not a full 26 miles, but a long way in the thin mountain air. We climbed to an elevation of 13,000 feet several times, which is when I learned the value of the "mountain pace." When you are climbing into the thin air, you must learn to take a step and then to take a breath. If you try to climb the mountain too quickly, you will run out of oxygen and energy. The mountain pace is all about taking one step after another, climbing higher and higher by plodding with consistency. I can't tell you how many times that has helped during the hard times of my career. Likewise, COBS taught me the value of choosing the right path. I learned on that mountain the consequences of making a bad decision and going in the wrong direction. I went for adventure, but I came home with some extremely valuable learned lessons that have benefited me throughout my life.

I also returned to Italy, Texas in great shape, which was important because I missed a few of our two-a-day football practices while attending COBS. As I previously noted, I had a good senior year on the football field except for that final game, which still bothers me somewhat. I graduated from Italy High School in the spring of 1968, which was the year that the number of U.S. deaths in Vietnam peaked at 16,899 casualties, roughly 5,500 more than any previous year. Richard Nixon had campaigned in the 1968 presidential election under the slogan that he would end the war in Vietnam and bring "peace with honor." But most of us realized there was no easy way out of Vietnam, which was proven by the fact that the American commitment continued for another five years. It has been estimated that more than 58,000 Americans were killed, which is about nine times as many as the Iraq and Afghanistan wars combined.

As an 18-year-old in 1968, going to Vietnam did not appeal to me. Texas A&M was not as popular then as it is now, and my plan was to use my student deferment until it ran out. By that time, my hope was that the war would be over. If not, I would serve my duty. But instead of going directly to Texas A&M, I spent my first semester of college at Southwest Texas in San Marcos. But even back then, Southwest Texas (now Texas State) seemed like a party school, and I was not a partier. So, after attending a football game at A&M with one of my best friends from Italy, I decided to transfer to Texas A&M in the spring of 1969. It was a wise decision and placed me back on the proper path.

MOORE'S PATH TO ENTREPRENEURIAL SUCCESS

Making cabinets was not my vision for the future when I enrolled at Texas A&M. My initial plan for my long-term future involved becoming a football coach and biology teacher. I loved football so much that I decided I was going to be a walk-on at Texas A&M. Yes, the skinny kid from tiny Italy, Texas became convinced that he could play football in the Southwest Conference. Not the Little Southwest Conference, the real one. I set up an appointment to meet with A&M head coach Gene Stallings, who played for the legendary Bear Bryant at Texas A&M in the 1950s and then became the Aggies' head coach in 1965. Two years later, the Aggies lost the first four games of the season by narrow margins, but then quarterback Edd Hargett engineered a late comeback against Texas Tech that kick-started a seven-game winning streak, including a 20-16 win over Alabama in the Cotton Bowl. Until Johnny Manziel led the Aggies past the Tide in 2012, Stallings' 1967 team had been the last A&M squad to beat Bama.

The point here is that Gene Stallings, who would ultimately lead Alabama to the 1992 national championship, was a larger-than-life figure at Texas A&M in the late 1960s, and walking into his office to inform him of my desire to play for the Aggies was probably the most intimidating thing I had ever done (COBS included) at that point in my life. I walked into that office with my knees practically knocking into each other and managed to speak the following words: "Coach Stallings, I want to play for the Aggies." He looked up from his desk, glanced at me quickly, sizing me up, and somewhat reluctantly said, "OK. Go talk to Billy Pickard."

At that time, Mr. Pickard was the head athletic trainer under Coach Stallings. He provided me with my equipment, and I proceeded to serve as a life-sized tackling dummy for the next couple of weeks. Because of my size (or more precisely, my lack of size) I figured my only chance to make the squad was as a wide receiver or defensive back. The biggest issue however, was that not only was I undersized, but I was also as slow as erosion. Seriously, the linemen were faster than me, so after about two weeks, I returned my gear to Billy Pickard and hung up my cleats for good. Rumor has it that nobody shed a tear or even noticed when I stopped coming to practice.

I tell that story whenever I hear somebody tell a young person that you can be anything you want to be when you're an adult. That's an irrefutable lie. There are some things that are simply out of the realm of possibility…like me playing wide receiver, defensive back or anywhere else at a place like Texas A&M. No, it's true I probably could have stayed on the scout team for four years and had my body mangled by teammates who were bigger, better, faster and physically superior to me in every way, but I wasn't going to make an impact for the Aggies. I made the realization that God did not bless me with all abilities. I think most people would be wise to understand both their strengths and their weaknesses before embarking on far-fetched journeys that are designed to fulfill implausible dreams. For example, none of my grandchildren should set their hearts and minds on playing in the NBA.

Despite my lack of ability to play football, I still had my mind set on being a coach and a biology teacher. I liked the science of biology. I often recall looking at my hand and wondering how things worked. I knew God created us in His image, and I really enjoyed learning how God designed our bodies to move, adapt, fight diseases and so forth. My friend from Italy, Bob Windham, and I both were intrigued by the opportunity to be a coach, a thought that was reinforced when we left A&M for the summer break and coached the Little League team in Italy. The kids enjoyed us, and we certainly enjoyed them, although I remember questioning whether or not I really wanted my paycheck to be based on the whims and performances of young people. When I was informed one evening that one of our top players, Little Joey, was not going to be playing that night because he was on vacation, I asked about where he had gone on vacation. I was told that he was at his grandmother's house in Avalon, which is only about eight miles to the east of Italy. Maybe he had to walk to Avalon.

Of course, I also worked some back-breaking, sweat-producing jobs in the summer that reinforced my desire to continue pursuing a college degree. During one summer in Italy, two of my friends and me were working for a contractor who was building conservation dams around Italy. We were working in the bottom of a large hole, pouring concrete. It was so hot that we had to pack blankets with ice around the concrete to keep it from setting too fast. It was miserably exhausting work in oppressive heat, but we were being paid. During another summer, I worked with two carpenters who built houses by the hour. They did everything. I remember being amazed at how quickly and accurately they could drive a nail flush without leaving a mark. They started writing my initials on the hammer marks that I would inevitably leave because they wanted everyone on the construction site to know that I was the one leaving marks. After working the summer days in those kinds of sweltering settings, coaching—even just coaching a Little League team—seemed like a dream job.

It was also during one of those summers back in Italy when I first really noticed—really noticed—Debbie, my future bride. Debbie, who is two years younger than me, lived all her life in Italy, and her family attended the Italy Presbyterian church where my father was the pastor. I knew her, but I didn't pay too much attention to her when we were younger. I was taking an algebra class at Navarro Junior College in Corsicana, and I was coming through town each day to go to work. She saw me and happened to be crossing Main Street in Italy at the same time I came back through town, which I later learned was not an accident. I stopped and talked to this attractive young woman, and I asked her if she would come and keep the scorebook for us for the Little League baseball game that night. What can I say? I obviously know how to sweep a girl off her feet by inviting her to keep score for a bunch of 11- and 12-year-olds.

Debbie and I actually began dating (going to places even more romantic than the Italy Little League Ballpark) during the first semester of my sophomore year. She was valedictorian of her high school class, and she decided to attend Sam Houston State in Huntsville. On virtually every Wednesday night, I drove to Huntsville to see her and to seek her assistance in trigonometry. Attending 12 different schools in my childhood did not help me master advanced mathematics. We would also see each other on the weekends, as Bob and I would drive home from A&M to see our girlfriends in Italy. We weren't the partying type so hanging out at Northgate on the weekend was not my thing. I would much rather spend time with Debbie.

In fact, I enjoyed spending time with Debbie so much that after dating her during my sophomore year, I asked her to marry me. When we went home to Italy to tell our parents, my parents were fine with it, although they were less than enthusiastic. Her parents, however, were not pleased with our decision. They were obviously concerned about how we were going to be able to make it work financially. Debbie's father wrote her a letter—the only letter he ever wrote her in her life—and sent it to her at Sam Houston, saying he had no confidence that I could provide for her and that marrying me was a mistake. She did not immediately share that letter with me, but when she finally did it became my inspiration to prove to him that I could provide for her. Years later, it was quite satisfying when my business had taken off and I was able to prove my ability to provide as a husband. In hindsight, though, I can now understand his concern. When Debbie and I were married on New Year's Eve in 1970 (there's always a party on our anniversary), I had $23 in my checking account, while

Debbie had over $300 in her account. So yes, I did marry her for her money.

Following our New Year's Eve wedding, we moved into a mobile home on the first day of 1971. I figured it was better to make a purchase rather than rent because mobile homes are such incredible investments. That's a joke! Real estate is a good investment. Mobile homes, on the other hand, often depreciate rather quickly. And unlike an apartment, I quickly discovered I was responsible for all the repairs in the mobile. Debbie transferred to A&M, and we both went to school that spring semester. Meanwhile, I took a job working on a framing crew for a local builder, who was building a home for a prominent lawyer in the community. The builder had me carry sheetrock from upstairs of one four-plex he was building to the upstairs of another four-plex across the street, I guess he was trying to run me off. My next job was doing trim work, starting by putting in baseboards in closets. As my skills improved, I advanced to begin working on door jams, door stops, paneling, installing beams in vaulted ceilings and working on the cabinets that they were building on site. I learned plenty on that job, but when winter slowed down construction, I found myself looking for another job.

For whatever reason, construction seemed to be a good fit for me. I like to draw; I enjoyed piecing things together; I liked working with my hands; and I enjoyed seeing progress each day on the construction site. It was during that timeframe that I came home one day and asked Debbie if she would be happy married to a full-time carpenter as opposed to a coach and biology teacher. She basically told me that she was fine with whatever I decided. So, I decided to move full-speed ahead with my trim work while still going to school.

As I began to search desperately for work, I found an architecture professor at Texas A&M who was building two speculative homes (spec homes) not far from A&M Consolidated High School. This was so long ago that there weren't houses around the school; it was just new streets being constructed and paved. The professor didn't really know what he was doing, and I didn't either. But we made a deal for me to trim the two houses, build the door units and build all the cabinets for a set price. To that point, I had been working by the hour, but I had an idea of how much others were charging per square foot and I bid a comparable amount. It was pretty brave of me to bid for the job since—unbeknownst to the professor—I didn't have the equipment necessary to do the work. It was close to Christmas, and practically everyone was slowing in the industry. So, after I struck a deal with the professor, my former employees loaned me a table saw. That was nice, as they didn't have to do that, and I couldn't have done the work otherwise.

I trimmed those houses and kept track of how long it took me to complete the cabinets and all the trim. I discovered that I had made about twice what I was making by the hour in my previous jobs. So, I quickly concluded that I needed to go into business for myself. I just needed to go find more houses to do. Fortunately, Texas A&M was beginning to grow, and as a result, so was the community at large. In order to go into business for myself, however, I needed my own equipment. After completing those first two homes, I went to Central Texas Hardware in downtown Bryan and bought a Delta nine-inch contractor's table saw on 30 days credit. I went home and told Debbie about the purchase. She promptly started crying. It was about $235, and she was convinced that I was never going to be able to pay for it. Once I made that purchase, I was bound and determined to find more work, which is exactly what I did.

I also purchased a Honda 90 dirt bike, because Debbie and I only could afford one car at that time. I'd be driving down Texas Avenue with an extension cord, circular saw and a nail apron strapped behind me. My friend, Robert Owen from my hometown bank in Italy, financed that bike for me, and my mother didn't appreciate it. One of my uncles had a serious, head-on accident on a motorcycle, so my mother was scared of all motorcycles. She told me that if I was doing well enough to finance a motorcycle that we obviously didn't need any more financial help from them, so my parents cut me off. I kept records of every penny that I borrowed from our parents, because I was determined to pay them back. Debbie dropped out of school her senior year and worked as a checker at Skaggs Albertsons grocery store, while I finished up at A&M. Then Debbie went to summer school while I worked.

I knew I wasn't going to use my degree to become a teacher/coach as I had originally planned, but I was convinced that a college education would give me an advantage. I still had to do my student-teaching in order to earn my diploma. Speaking of my diploma, back in the early 1970s, it was a requirement that every student was actually present at the graduation ceremony to receive the diploma. But I really didn't believe I needed to spend hours upon hours listening to names being called when I had work to do. I needed to install cabinets in a couple of duplexes on Dominic Drive in College Station instead of attending the graduation ceremony. I was afraid someone else would get the jobs if I fell behind. I claimed that I needed to be at a wedding in Lubbock on the same day as graduation. That's how I received my diploma without walking the stage.

I actually graduated on time, although I lost some hours after transferring and had to take 19 hours and 20 hours my last two semesters at A&M. I was also working full-time as a subcontractor at that point and trying to find some time to spend with my wife. It was quite a grind those last two semesters. After I graduated, Debbie went to summer school and ultimately not only graduated on time, but also as magna cum laude. Those words certainly didn't appear on my diploma. I think my professors and I simply declared a truce.

Once I graduated, I really kicked things into another gear. I was fortunate that there was work around Bryan and College Station, and I could talk and hustle enough to earn some of that work. I ended up purchasing a white, short wheelbase Econoline van that featured a driver's seat and nothing else. There was no passenger seat. Just a box. There was also no heater, so I bought a heater from the auto parts store and bolted it down to the floor. It didn't have any bells or whistles, but it allowed me to continue to build my operation, as I purchased more and more equipment from Central Texas Hardware in downtown Bryan on 30 days' credit.

With my own van and no more school to worry about, business began to pick up to the point that I realized I was going to need to hire some help or I would begin to lose jobs. I was fortunate that Bryan-College Station was entering a rapid growth period at that time, and there were many duplexes and small houses being built. The homebuilders needed somebody to build cabinets on-site, and more and more began to take a chance on me. I knew they would be happy with the finished product, and I managed to become the B team or C team for two or three builders. I finally hired a helper, and I realized that once you hire one person, you might as well hire 10 because of all the paperwork that must be done. I was more of a craftsman and entrepreneur than CEO, but I figured things out as time went along and business continued to increase. As a site-built cabinet company, Kent Moore and Trim (as it was known at the time) quickly featured myself and two employees, who moved equipment from job to job in the early years. Normally, we could complete a small house in a week or two. By January 1976, we'd grown to the point where the first shop was completed on Longmire Drive in College Station. It was a 1,500-square-foot metal building near Brazos County Lumber, which was significant because we could take a forklift across the street for the materials we needed. At that time, all site-built cabinet doors were essentially just a piece of plywood with some molding on the outside of it.

I wanted to do more. I decided to purchase some shapers, which are bigger machines that you really can't haul around in a truck, because I wanted to build cabinets with raised-panel doors. This was a distinguishing, eye-catching furniture look that I knew would set me apart from the competition. That was my motivation to build the shop, and instead of doing all the work on-site inside a home, we were able to purchase supplies from Brazos Valley Lumber and to do much of the work in the shop. Within a year, I was talking to the bank about expanding, and we added another section to the shop, increasing it to 2,700 square feet. Then at the end of the next year, it was still too small so we added another section. I ended up buying the lot next door and building on it. We had four or five expansions to the shop on Longmire in a short period of time. It wasn't too long after we started making raised-panel doors that it struck me that it made more sense to build the whole cabinet and take it to the job. That required much more room in the shop. At that point, my prime responsibility became going job to job ahead of time and measuring the exact dimensions of the cabinets we needed to build. After I drew it up, I would have to go through and calculate all the parts needed. Customers were buying our raised panel doors, and it took longer to build the doors than the boxes. I had to calculate what the openings were going to be and to know how big the door needed to be built before we ever built the box. That took some doing. There wasn't any calculus involved. You needed to get it right. The box was built, and if the door didn't fit, one or the other had to be redone.

My system was working for me, and our business was most certainly growing. But we were limited in just how much we could grow by our total lack of technology. I was measuring and drawing all of my plans, but a friend of mind introduced me to Bob Smith in the early 1980s. Bob was truly a genius, and he had taught some of the first astronauts how to use computers. Bob was running a computer center at Texas A&M, and he began working with me, although I certainly could not pay him what he was worth. We began meeting once a week, and he began to develop programs based on my measurements and specifications. This was way before there were any personal computers, so Bob built a computer for our company. We would enter the cabinet sizes and specifications, and Bob developed programs that allowed us to create cabinet parts on the fly. Today, we still do it exactly that way. Now we have our own programmers who are working on it all the time and expanding it. Now, we have routers that cut the flat parts. It is an amazing automated system of routers. Bob Smith translated what I had in my head to something machines now understand.

MOORE'S MOST CHALLENGING OBSTACLES

It is absolutely impossible for me to accurately portray how much God has blessed me throughout my life in the limited space I have in this publication. I could write an entire book on that subject, and in fact, I did that for my grandchildren. But please allow me to provide a few examples here. I once caught both of my thumbs in a coyote trap while it was nailed to the ground. But I escaped without having to chew my thumbs off. When my small bass boat was sinking on massive Lake Guerrero in Mexico with waves breaking over the bow I promised God if my life was spared I would never be caught in that situation again. I have kept my promise. I was once in the eye of an EF3 tornado…and I lived to tell about it. In case you don't know an EF3 tornado features winds between 136 and 165 mph. All the way back when I was in first grade, I saved family and friends from burning up in a house fire. And I once climbed to the top of the Italy, Texas water tower with a policeman.

I won't go into all the details of those events, because it would take up too much space. The point is that I have been so blessed—immeasurably—by my Lord and Savior, Jesus Christ, who has carried me through some extremely treacherous times, including dire financial straits.

During the late 1970s and early '80s, we had grown from $1 million to $2 million in sales, and then from $2 to $3 million in sales in a three-year period. We developed numerous lines of business, and we were expanding rapidly. In fact, during the earliest parts of the 1980s, we expanded to $1 million in sales in a single month. But things were about to change dramatically across the Lone Star State in 1982. For various reasons, oil prices begun to fall in '82, and it has since been estimated that each $1 drop in the price of crude resulted in a loss of roughly 25,000 jobs in Texas. Declining oil prices had significant adverse effects on the entire state's economy. When coupled with a weakening national economy, the oil price declines led to significant declines in employment in Texas. The first wave of layoffs began in the oilfields, but were followed by job losses in related fields (geologists and engineers) and next in service companies (motels, restaurants, retail stores and so forth). As more Texans lost their jobs, commercial and residential construction began to slow dramatically. The "oil bust" of the 1980s was underway.

I first began to notice in 1982 that it was becoming increasingly difficult to find jobs. And then it also became increasingly difficult to receive payment for the work that had been completed. It's all cyclical, and if people aren't buying homes, builders are not receiving income. Furthermore, the federal government began making significant changes in depreciation allowances. Prior to the mid-1980s, much real estate investment was done by passive investors. It was common for syndicates of investors to pool their resources to invest in commercial or residential property. Investors would then hire management companies to run the operation of the property. Tax reforms in the mid-1980s reduced the value of the investments by limiting the extent to which losses associated with them could be deducted from the investor's gross income. This value reduction, in turn, encouraged the holders of loss-generating properties to try to sell them, which contributed further to the problem of sinking real estate values. Throughout Texas, the real estate market was flooded with more and more real estate that nobody needed. The changes contributed to the end of the real estate boom of the early 1980s, as well as the banking collapses.

Kent Moore and his wife, Debbie, with their children: Casey, Lindsey and Dana.

Meanwhile, subcontractors like me were not being paid. We managed to make a little money in '82, but by 1985, we had lost what little working capital we had managed to accumulate. We had even fallen behind with our withholding payments owed to the federal government. At that point, two remaining members of my management team would sit down with me on Fridays and figure out if we were going to make payroll the next week. I told them I don't want our people to work for a week and not be paid. But the economy across the state was growing bleaker. During the 1980s, for example, 425 Texas commercial banks failed, including nine of the state's 10 largest bank holding companies. And by September 1986, it was estimated that more than 743,000 Texans were unemployed. I was so focused on my own problems I didn't realize how much I had in common with my fellow Texans

In the midst of those extremely difficult times, I tried two or three times to sell the company. It was a futile effort. We were behind in our payments to our suppliers, to the banks and practically everyone else. I remember during that time period making a desperate trip to Dallas to another cabinetmaker in hopes of selling my business to him. In the middle of my pitch, he stopped me and said, "We can't buy anything else. We're in about as bad of shape financially as you." I was truly afraid the IRS would show up one day and lock our doors shut. With few other options, I decided to file Chapter 11 bankruptcy. It was not one of my proudest moments. In fact, it was an extremely humbling moment. If I could have collected what was owed to me we would have been fine, After losing money for three years in a row, there was no other choice.

A Chapter 11 case begins with the filing of a petition in bankruptcy court. I will never forget sitting in the hallway of a federal courthouse in Houston as one of the court officials came out and announced, "The United States vs Kent Moore Cabinets." I promised myself then that this was never going to happen again, and I also vowed to pay back everyone whom I owed money. I didn't know how we were going to survive, but I was going to find a way.

I went to Houston in 1985 to begin the case. In most Chapter 11 cases, no trustee is appointed. Instead, the debtor (me in this case) continues to operate the business in the ordinary course as the "debtor in possession" (or "DIP"). But by filing Chapter 11, you lose control over certain major decisions to the bankruptcy court. Again, this was not one of my most glorious memories as a business owner, but at that point, the only thing I could actually afford to buy was time. Filing Chapter 11 bought me some time to propose a way to pay our creditors. Unlike many Chapter 11 cases, our creditors did not show up for the bankruptcy hearing. I guess they saw it as hopeless and a waste of time. Against my attorney's adamant advice, our proposal was to repay 100 percent of the debt over a 10-year period. "Nobody does that," my attorney told me. You need to say you are going to pay them 30 cents on the dollar. That is how this works."

That may have been how it worked in most Chapter 11 cases, but I was intent on paying everyone, especially my suppliers who provided me with materials in good faith, 100 percent of what I owed them. The bankruptcy judge looked at the proposal and was probably laughing at me for being naïve or foolish. He then approved the plan as it was proposed. The IRS demanded we pay them first. None of the suppliers received any payments for a couple of years. After we finally paid off the IRS, we would write these checks and send them to our suppliers. Because of the overall economic conditions in the state, some of those checks were returned to us because the suppliers had gone out of business, so we held onto those checks and tried to find them. We just continued marching along slowly, but steadily. Here again, I go back to the mountain pace I first learned by spending 26 days at the Colorado Outward Bound School. Sometimes, all you can do in life is take a step at a time, take a breath and plod forward.

By 1987, we were five years into the climb out, but I was beginning to feel more hopeful about our long-term future. We still encountered our fair share of obstacles; all companies do. But I have learned to trust God in good times and in tough times, especially the tough times. It's easy to praise God when things are going well, when all the bills are paid, all your employees are happy and there is some money in the bank. But I have found that it is especially important to focus on God's sovereignty in times of difficulty, as God uses the most difficult and humbling times in our lives to grow our faith. Adversities will come your way. Trials will stop you in your tracks. Road blocks and detours will blindside you. But as I've encountered difficulties throughout my life, I have gained a perspective and appreciation for Job in the Bible. For those unfamiliar with the Biblical story, Job (pronounced "Jobe") is a wealthy man living in Uz with his large family and extensive flocks. He is "blameless" and "upright," always careful to avoid doing evil. Job eventually loses everything—his children, his flocks, his health. Job did not reject God in the midst of his losses, but Job did challenge and accuse Him. God quieted Job decisively when He finally thundered His own perspective on the situation. God overwhelmed Job and his friends with the truth of His majesty and sovereignty. Consequently, Job came away with a deeper sense of God's power and splendor, trusting Him more. Humbled, Job goes back to his work, and eventually God gives him double what he had at the outset.

Here's my takeaway: Pain inevitably afflicts each of us. Suffering is unavoidable in this life. But will your relationship with God be enough when trials come? Will you trust Him through your suffering? I've learned to trust Him in all things. I learned it during the worst parts of the bankruptcy journey; and I was reminded of that when two of our driver's had wrecks (one in Dallas and one in San Marcos), ruining the inventory the trucks were carrying, as we were emerging from bankruptcy. By 1989, we had essentially put the bankruptcy in the rearview mirror, moving into a new, larger location in Bryan, where we still produce all of our parts. Something else happened in 1989 that made a profound impact on me as a leader and the future of Kent Moore Cabinets. I received a flyer in the mail from two Baylor professors who were promoting a seminar based on the "Theory on Constraints." The flyer also referenced a book called "The Goal" by Eli Goldratt, which I highly recommend to anyone who wants to increase efficiency and productivity. I ordered the book and ultimately insisted that my entire management team read it and write me a summary. Reading the book inspired me to define KMC's goal and to identify what was constraining our efforts toward realizing that goal. We had a mission statement, but our goal was not clearly defined. With Goldratt's help, we stated our goal as: "To make more money now, as well as in the future." That may seem simplistic, but it helped me to focus on what was most important.

I also attended the two-day seminar in Houston—twice, as a matter of fact. Other attendees and I were given a hands-on, simulated project that involved making three products on three different machines. On the first run, we all lost money, because there were setup and delay times whenever we switched from one machine to the next. We then identified the constraint (one machine was slower than the others) and ran the simulation again with slightly better results. In other words, we increased "throughput."

Throughput (also known as the flow rate) is a measure of a business process flow rate. Essentially, it measures the movements of inputs and outputs within the production process. It is an important metric in the operations management of a company. This variable primarily indicates the efficiency of operations that are vital to the overall success of a business. The maximization of throughput levels can be the key driver in maximizing a company's revenue. Our small group at the Houston seminar, led by the two professors, continued to make improvements on our throughput in further simulations. And we continued to make more money.

When I returned to Bryan-College Station, I vowed to apply the Theory of Constraints to every department, and I decided to attend the Goldratt Institute in New Haven, Connecticut for a two-week course that further solidified my belief that the Theory of Constraints could vastly improve KMC. After spending $10,000 on the course, I felt like I absolutely had to experience a return on investment.

When I returned from the course, we began the hunt to find our constraint. Our plant was divided into five departments. Our procedure had been that each department was required to stay until the day's work had been completed and was ready to be handed off to the next department. An eight-hour buffer existed between the departments, which meant it took five days for anything to make it through production to shipping. We initially decided to cut the buffer to six hours, expecting that job parts would pile up in front of the constraint, which would obviously allow us to identify the constraint. After a couple of days, however, nothing happened. Then we cut the buffer to four hours, and discovered that there was still no pile of parts in front of any machine or department. Finally, we cut the buffer to zero. Still no pile of parts.

By removing the buffers, we had cut the manufacturing time in half, which ultimately reduced our labor costs. It no longer required five days to take a cabinet from beginning to end. We increased our throughput per hour by accelerating the flow of parts. We were moving from the cost world (which most businesses focus on) to the throughput world, which allowed us to reduce labor costs. We also began to apply the Theory of Constraints to other aspects of the company, which further helped us improve our overall operations.

By June of 2001, we purchased 38 additional acres in the Brazos County Industrial Park for continued expansion. In 2004, we added a 47,000-square-foot facility at the industrial park site that features a finishing system that has allowed for an increased capacity along with a high-end, water-based furniture finish that is environmentally friendly.

For many years, the Bryan-College Station area was the market for us. Whether we had a good year or not depended on whether Texas A&M was growing or not. Nowadays, A&M is still the monster in the room, but there are other things going on locally, and Bryan-College Station represents only about 5 percent of our annual sales. Statewide cabinet sales have spurred the growth of the company, and we now have showrooms and sales offices located in Dallas, Austin, San Antonio, Georgetown and three facilities in Houston. In 2009, we added another 77,000 square feet of new manufacturing space for a total of 360,000 square feet. As I write this we have roughly 550 employees with annual sales well in excess of $75 million. Not bad for a company whose founder never even earned a business degree, wrote a business plan or had any investors. Kent Moore Cabinets has grown to be the largest custom-cabinet company in Texas

Please allow me to clarify this point here: Just because my name is also the company name doesn't mean that I am solely responsible for any of the accomplishments I've noted. My wife and my children have stood beside me and encouraged me throughout my career; God has blessed me with amazingly uplifting friends and allowed me to hire some remarkable men and women who have made this company what it is today; and God has guided me through each and every step of this journey, opening my eyes to things such as the Theory of Constraints.

I am not merely a lucky man; I am a blessed man. God has blessed me with a family, a purpose and perseverance, and he has allowed me to turn over the day-to-day operations of Kent Moore Cabinets to my own children. Few businesses make it to the second generation and very few survive to the third generation. My hope is that my grandchildren will eventually take over and continue the family legacy. Not just a legacy of making cabinets, but a legacy of perseverance, understanding the mountain pace and honoring God.

MOORE'S ADVICE TO YOUNG ENTREPRENEURS

During the early days of our bankruptcy issues, there were many times when I looked into the mirror and felt like I was probably the only stupid person who couldn't figure out how to make a business work. That was obviously a short-sighted and self-limiting viewpoint. In reality, all I had to do was look around and take the focus off of me. There were plenty of smart businessmen and businesswomen who went out of business in those difficult days.

Now, don't misunderstand me. I am not suggesting that I should be included in the list of "smart" businesspeople. I am completely convinced that you don't need to be a genius to be a successful entrepreneur. And if you consider me to be even remotely successful, I am living proof of that. I wasn't a great student at any point in my life. I didn't earn a business degree from Texas A&M. As I look back in time, what Debbie's father didn't know about me was that my father told me the most important thing his father taught him was how to work. I learned how to work, too.

Maybe that's just another way of saying I am hard-headed or too stubborn to quit. Whatever the case, I don't feel too comfortable sharing a bunch of advice for many reasons. I am not an expert on entrepreneurism, marketing, computer technology, mathematical equations or anything of the sort. But I do consider myself somewhat of an authority regarding how much you can achieve in life by never quitting, never wavering off the path and never failing to put one foot in front of another. If you remember only one thing from my story I hope you recall how much I have benefitted from being taught the mountain pace. I didn't build the cabinet company overnight; I didn't emerge from bankruptcy right away, either; but I just kept plodding forward for years.

So, here's my simple advice: If you don't quit, you will succeed. Period. Exclamation point, too.

There will be times in your business or entrepreneurial career where you will be tempted to quit. I practically guarantee it. Your lawyers, advisors and even family members may even encourage you to quit. Don't. Not now. Not later. Not ever.

According to *Bartlett's Familiar Quotations,* Winston Churchill's most famous speech was delivered on October 29, 1941, as he was recounting Great Britain's progress during the first 10 months of World War II. In the midst of a longer speech, Churchill uttered these famous words: "Never give in, never give in, never, never, never, never—in nothing, great or small, large or petty—never give in except to convictions of honor and good sense."

I wholeheartedly and emphatically agree. Whether it's in business, sports or practically any other endeavor, many times the key to success is simply persevering longer than most other people would normally last. Legendary Alabama and one-time Texas A&M football coach Paul "Bear" Bryant said it this way: "If you believe in yourself and have dedication and pride—and never quit—you'll be a winner. The price of victory is high, but so are the rewards."

I could quote many other people much wiser than me about the benefits of never quitting, despite being in the midst of even the most difficult circumstances. But I think you understand the point by now. Everyone fails, but not everyone understands how beneficial failing can be. You learn from your failures and mistakes as long as you keep on moving forward.

I believe it's also important to point out here that if you want to be successful in business or in any other area of life, develop your people skills and focus on building meaningful relationships with people. To quote former President Ronald Reagan: "Surround yourself with great people; delegate authority; get out of the way." God has blessed our company in many ways, but especially by allowing me to assemble a terrific team of employees. We have definitely invested in equipment and technology through the years, but we have also poured our resources into our people. We've been blessed to hire great people, and for the most part, we have kept them with us by making them realize they are vital to our successes. They are not merely employees. They are extended members of our family.

The way you treat your people will go a long way toward your success. That doesn't merely apply to treating your employees with great respect. My goal is to treat all people the right way. Not just friends. Not just customers or prospective customers. I strive to treat everyone around me the way I would like to be treated. That's the biblical "Golden Rule," and it should be a top priority for any entrepreneur or business owner. To clarify, the Golden Rule is often expressed as "Do unto others as you would have them do unto you," which is one translation of the Biblical verse Luke 6:31. We all know the difference between right and wrong. For me, it is simple to do what I know is right. It may never be the easier path, but it will always be in the right direction. Some people can't handle success. I am convinced God expects me to be the same whether times are good, bad or really bad. Doing what is right is always right.

That's probably enough "pearls of wisdom" from me. Somewhere along the way in your life, no matter what you choose to do for a living or what path you choose to take, you will encounter challenges. Maybe even overwhelming odds will be stacked against you. I hope my story of perseverance helps you overcome your challenges. I hope you commit to plodding forward with consistency and purpose, as if you are journeying toward the top of your mountain.

CHAPTER 2

Jon Acklam

President & Founder
Acklam Construction
Texas A&M Class of 1969

ACKLAM'S PATH TO TEXAS A&M

In 1989, a little-known country music artist from Oklahoma released his first album through Capitol Nashville—a self-titled debut that was simply called "Garth Brooks." The debut album, which included hits like "Much Too Young" and "The Dance," was a chart success, peaking at No. 13 on the Billboard 200. But there's another, little-known song from that album that best describes my rather humble beginnings, which was called, "Nobody Gets Off in This Town." That song, which was also the B-side on the 1990 hit single "Friends in Low Places," sarcastically describes an extremely small town where people board buses, but no one ever disembarks. Brooks paints a lyrical picture by singing, "It's a one-dog town and he's old and mean; There's one stoplight, but it's always green; nobody gets off in this town."

I can relate, although the town where I actually grew up—Bushnell, Illinois (population 3,000)—was such a small and rural farming town that we didn't even have a stop sign, let alone a traffic light. Everybody knew everyone else, and everybody knew the rules of the road, regardless of whether you were driving a pickup, a tractor or a bicycle. Bushnell, a map dot that is about a four and one-half hour drive to the southwest of Chicago, was a great place to grow up in the 1950s and early '60s because, while it was obviously small, it honestly felt like one big and extended family. My mother, Kathryn Acklam, had grown up in Bushnell, too, so my family was rooted as firmly in McDonough County as the old Burlington Northern Santa Fe Railroad.

I was an only child born to two only children, so our family gatherings were even more intimate than town meetings. Both of my parents possessed a great work ethic, although they came from much different backgrounds. My father, George Acklam, had grown up in Colorado under less than ideal circumstances. His parents were also from a farming community in the Centennial State, but they had lost everything financially and emotionally during the Great Depression. Losing the farm was tough, but what was more difficult on my father was watching my grandfather practically give up on life. He didn't actually take his life, but the Great Depression led to his deep depression, breaking more than his bank account; it literally broke his spirit.

Based on witnessing that heartbreaking transformation in his father, my dad was determined not to quit on anything in his own life. Moreover, he instilled in me a never-give-up determination to always finish what I started. My father, who was the manager of my maternal grandfather's lumber yard in Bushnell, strived to be a much more positive role model to me than his father had been to him. I didn't know my paternal grandparents extremely well because they lived out their lives in Colorado, and we simply didn't see them as often as we would have if they lived closer.

My grandfather's brokenness, however, was quite an inspiration to my father to approach life, marriage and parenting in dramatically different perspectives. In numerous ways, he measured his success as a father by making sure that I was equipped with intangible qualities that would enable me to persevere through even the most difficult circumstances in life. If I started something, my father expected me to finish it. Period. End of discussion. He was a strong disciplinarian, but he was fair. If I misbehaved or broke a rule at school or while participating in athletics, I feared facing my father much more than being disciplined by a principal, teacher or coach. Even though he could be extremely tough at times, I had a tremendous amount of respect for my father, and I know he took great pride in watching me achieve my goals and dreams. In spite of his physical absence since 1989, my memories of Dad and the values he instilled in me continue to influence my life today in so many ways.

Likewise, my stay-at-home mother was a powerfully positive inspiration to me. She was a self-starting, energetic dynamo and the living, breathing definition of a bundle of energy. Not only did she mow our yard, but she also mowed the apartment complex that my parents owned. When she wasn't cleaning, cooking and caring for me, she would bicycle with friends and tackle virtually any task that came her way. When I started school, she also added volunteer work with the hospital, church and various community organizations to her weekly to-do list. Her enthusiastic and lively motto was, "I am going to wear out, not rust out." She lived out her final days in that spirit.

Her enterprising and spirited personality traits were part of her DNA. In addition to the positive impact my parents had on my development, my maternal grandfather, Neil Hummel, made a major impression on me and my future. He lived one block away from my parents' house, and he was an extremely successful commercial building contractor. He built schools, churches and several of the buildings on the Western Illinois University campus in Macomb (roughly 20 minutes to the southwest of Bushnell). My grandfather never met a stranger and never viewed any job as impossible. He was a visionary with a resolute determination. He also loved to take me with him as he visited construction sites when I was a young boy, which undoubtedly planted the seeds of passion for my future career in life. Unfortunately, my grandfather suffered a debilitating brain hemorrhage when he was just 58, and he was forced to retire at that point, but he and my maternal grandmother, Gladys Hummel, both loomed large in my life.

Some people in Bushnell suspected that my grandmother would struggle to cope with daily chores and responsibilities once my grandfather endured the hemorrhage and later died. Perhaps that was because she was so petite, feminine and gracious, and she was always so content for my grandfather to lead the way in their marriage and family decisions. Those who predicted her downfall, however, were pleasantly mistaken. She was so strong in her Christian faith and convictions that no problem was insurmountable for her to tackle. In absence of my grandfather, she took charge of her life, and she made us all quite proud. I was blessed with numerous family role models in my childhood.

I also was fortunate to have one friend who lived in Bushnell, in particular, who meant a tremendous amount to me. As an only child, I often longed for a sibling. That never happened, but Fred Bertolino was essentially the older brother that I always wanted. He was four years older than me, and I idolized him. He was a terrific athlete and student, and he took me under his wing, so to speak. I was a pretty good athlete, especially in baseball, but Fred was at an entirely different level altogether. He was sensational, and he was undoubtedly the "Big Man On Campus" during his senior year (my freshman year) at Bushnell. It was no surprise to me or anyone else who knew him that Fred was selected as one of the 807 young men who arrived at West Point in 1962. Across the country, more than 5,000 people had applied that year to West Point, but less than 20 percent were accepted.

The ones who were accepted were the elite of the elite. Four years later, 579 of those men had graduated in West Point's Class of '66. And less than five years later, as documented by Pulitzer Prize-winning author Rick Atkinson in the book, "The Long Gray Line," 30 members of that class had been killed in Vietnam, with another 100 wounded. Unfortunately, my dear friend Fred Bertolino was one of the deceased, but there's no doubt that Fred played a role in my patriotism and my overall sense of duty to eventually serve in the military.

While my father did not serve in the military, Bushnell was a patriotic small town with many residents who were veterans. I have many fond memories of listening to those veterans tell vivid stories of defending our country in World War II, and I knew that God had placed on my heart a desire to serve in the U.S. Armed Forces, as well. That desire was only heightened when I watched Fred Bertolino depart for the United States Military Academy on the west bank of the Hudson River. As my own high school career began to progress toward graduation, the idea of attending an institution with a military heritage appealed to me. The idea of leaving Bushnell appealed to me, as well.

Many of the residents in that Illinois farming community naturally assumed that I would follow in the family footsteps that led to managing the lumber yard. While that may have been the safest path to a career, it was important to me to carve out my own identity and to create my own destiny. Another natural—and perhaps logical—collegiate destination would have been at the University of Illinois, located in the twin cities of Champaign and Urbana, which is roughly 150 miles to the east of Bushnell. Coming from such a small town, however, I was somewhat apprehensive about attending a school with such a sizable enrollment as Illinois.

With the assistance of my high school guidance counselor, I narrowed my possible college destination selections to Georgia Tech, Clemson and Texas A&M. In the summer following my junior year in high school, I visited the schools with my mother and some of her friends, and A&M just felt right to me. With an enrollment of about 9,000 students, Texas A&M was small enough that it felt comfortable, and with a storied military history, it certainly appealed to my patriotic side. I was also extremely impressed—if not in complete awe—that World War II hero General James Earl Rudder, the commander of the historic Pointe du Hoc battle during the Invasion of Normandy, was the president of the university.

I had no ties whatsoever to A&M, a school some 1,300 miles from my hometown. In fact, I had no ties to any university, as I was the first person in my family to attend college. I will never forget the sense of pride, honor, satisfaction and pure elation when I received my acceptance letter from Texas A&M University.

When I arrived in Aggieland in the fall of 1966, a couple of things made a strong impact on me right away. At that time, A&M was still predominantly a male school, and roughly half of the students were members of the Corps of Cadets. Corps participation was no longer compulsory at A&M, but the entire school was probably still best-known and identified regionally and nationally because of the Corps of Cadets. As an aspiring member of the U.S. Armed Forces, being a part of the Corps was a no-brainer for me, but it was still rather intimidating during Freshman Corps Orientation when we were all told to look to our left and our right. "In four years," said the Company G-1 First Sergeant, "only one of the three of you will still be here." The picture was clear to me right away: This was going to be tough. Fortunately, my father's most prominent instructions to me—words that will forever be a part of me—about not quitting anything I started provided me plenty of motivation, especially during that extremely difficult freshman year.

The corps—like Texas A&M itself—features plenty of unique traditions. One of the most memorable traditions that served me well when I entered the business world was called "whipping out." All freshmen (or "fish" as youngsters were commonly called) were required to learn the name, hometown and academic major of every upperclassman in the corps. If a freshman cadet encountered an upperclassman or a group of upperclassmen on campus, the fish was expected to extend his hand—or "whip out"—stand in an upright, military posture and, while looking the upperclassman in the eye, to loudly and respectfully shout, "Howdy, sir. I am Fish Acklam, sir. I am majoring in architectural construction, sir. What is your name, sir? Where are you from, sir? What's your major, sir?"

According to tradition in the corps at that time, upperclassmen had earned the right to look down upon the lowly fish. Upperclassmen rarely stopped to carry on a conversation with such bottom-feeders, but the fish was expected to follow in step with the upperclassman as this one-sided whipping out interaction transpired. I find myself chuckling still today when I think about how ridiculous we fish looked and sounded, especially if another upperclassman passed by and said "howdy." At that point, the fish was expected to turn and follow the other upperclassman while repeating the same drill. I have many memories of chasing upperclassmen all over campus and throughout the four levels of the dorm. But it served me well. When I entered A&M, I was shy and reserved. Whipping out allowed me to grow in my social skills. Later when I started a business, I felt confident when I met strangers and had no problem initiating conversations in social or business settings. Whipping out gave me a much more outgoing personality.

My other immediate realization upon starting school at A&M was that life in the Corps of Cadets was not the only part of the college transition that was going to seriously test me. I had been a good student during my public school years in Bushnell, Illinois, but I was no longer a big fish in that type of small pond. It was sink or swim time for me in the classroom environment, which was much more difficult and competitive on an intellectual level than I had ever experienced. I looked around the classrooms at A&M, and I quickly deduced that 100 percent of the class was equal or superior in scholastic ability to what the upper 25 percent had been in my high school class. I was determined to become the first college graduate in my family, and I quickly learned how to better manage and prioritize my available time. I discovered that meeting deadlines on my papers and projects was absolutely vital to my survival and success academically. Once again, these lessons proved to be invaluable to me when I opened a business. Deadlines are non-negotiable and excuses are not accepted in the business world. Thanks to A&M, I possessed that do-it-now, make-the-most-of-the-moment mentality right from the start of my business career.

I was also inspired by so many former students who came back to the university to speak. I can't overemphasize the importance of successful role models, and they were readily available to me then—and to you now—just by being on campus. From my perspective, I have so many fond memories of attending Aggie Musters, commissioning ceremonies and Corps of Cadet gatherings in which military Generals from Texas A&M spoke and inspired those who attended. Most of those men served in World War II, and they truly were part of what has become known as "the greatest generation" in terms of the sacrifices they made and the heroic courage they displayed in defending not only our country, but democracy and freedom. They were heroes in every sense of the word, and I encourage all current A&M students and recently graduated former students to tap into the resources you have at your disposal. Military leaders, business leaders, political leaders and so forth still return to Texas A&M today to inspire the current students and recent graduates. Their experiences and teachings can inspire and propel you toward achieving your dreams.

As I look back, the distinguished group of military leaders who spoke to my peers and me set an extremely high bar for what it meant to be an Aggie and how to live as a person of the utmost character and principles. Even to this day, I feel truly inspired beyond description. I also feel extremely fortunate that the corps experience and the military sciences classes inspired me to be a leader. With leadership, comes confidence, and confidence is critical to achieving any level of success in any endeavor.

Perhaps more than anything else, though, my time as a student at Texas A&M provided me with some especially meaningful friendships and lifelong bonds. As an only child, I absolutely cherished the camaraderie on campus and the overall sense of brotherhood we possessed within the corps. While I was blessed with many terrific friendships, there were two special Aggies who were instrumental advocates on both a personal and business level, not only during my collegiate days, but also later in my business career.

When I was a freshman in 1965, the corps assigned incoming fish to units based on the cadet's academic major. I was assigned to Unit G-1, which was comprised primarily of architectural and engineering majors. The first impactful person was Jim Holster, who was one year ahead of me, and the second was Jim Kirkpatrick, who was two years older than me. During my freshman year, each one of those upperclassmen doled out an unmitigated amount of harassment in my direction, as they were entitled to do because of their "elder" status. After that first year, however, they became my most respected and admired mentors/friends. Jim Holster, Class of '68, opened an architectural business in College Station, and he generously provided me with tremendous support and encouragement. In my first year of business, for example, Jim asked me to build several of his designed projects. The first "professional project" was a remodeled garage. Not exactly rocket science, but it was a start. As the years progressed, I was honored to build numerous Holster & Associates projects, including schools, churches and office buildings. His premature death after being diagnosed with brain cancer left a profound void in the Bryan-College Station community, as well as in my life.

The other lifelong friendship that was initially fostered at A&M was with Jim Kirkpatrick, Class of '67. He is also an extremely successful architect with a family-owned business in Denton. His commitment to integrity and maintaining the highest standards in everything he does has been quite inspirational to me. Jim saw something in me many years ago, and he took a special interest in helping me succeed at A&M and later in life as a general contractor. Fate shined on me, and I had the opportunity to serve briefly with Jim in Vietnam. Jim and I continue to follow each other's business pursuits and involvements, and I am truly blessed to call him a lifelong friend.

ACKLAM'S PATH TO ENTREPRENEURIAL SUCCESS

My road to entrepreneurism from Texas A&M took me first across the country and then across the Pacific Ocean and into Southeast Asia, where the United States' military involvement in the Vietnam conflict had continued to escalate throughout the 1960s. American involvement probably peaked in 1968, the year before I graduated and the same year that the communist side launched the Tet Offensive, which failed in its goal of overthrowing the South Vietnamese government. Nevertheless, that became a major turning point in the war, as it convinced a large segment of the U.S. population that its government's claims of progress toward winning the war may have been misleading despite many years of massive U.S. military aid to South Vietnam.

When I graduated from A&M, the Vietnam conflict certainly loomed large in the consciousness of America, especially at a patriotic and proud institution like A&M, with its long military ties. Following my commencement ceremony at A&M, I was immediately commissioned as a Second Lieutenant in the U.S. Army, where I had a two-year commitment. The experiences I faced and endured in the military were definitely the most defining and maturing two years of my life. I was tested and challenged beyond my wildest expectations. As I look back on that period of my life—with the benefit of a "golden years" perspective—I realize those years were pivotal and extremely valuable to my overall development and my self-confidence.

Upon leaving the security of Aggieland, I attended a 10-week engineer basic training school at Ft. Belvoir in Washington D.C. Apparently, graduates of Texas A&M (and specifically those who had been part of the corps) had established an impressive record at the school, and it was assumed that all Aggies were well-prepared and expected to excel. Regrettably, I put a black eye on that sparkling reputation by partying and drinking on a nightly basis. After three weeks of classes and tests, I received a much-needed wake-up call when each of the 125 students was provided his grades and class ranking. To my utter shock and disbelief, I ranked dead last in the class. I was so embarrassed, as I felt like I was not only tarnishing my reputation, but also the established perception of Texas A&M University. I buckled down and cleaned up my act from that point forward, and I managed to climb into the upper half of the class (graduating 62 overall) once we completed the 10-week school.

From that point, my next assignment took me to Fort Leonard Wood, Missouri, where I was a platoon leader overseeing 30 soldiers. I arrived in the "Show Me State" looking to prove myself right from the start, as opposed to my initial approach in Washington D.C. That's when my military service confidence improved significantly, which was important because my next assignment was in Vietnam, where it has been estimated that more than 58,000 Americans were killed and as many as

2.5 million total lives were lost from 1954 to 1975.

We were all aware of the danger and all at least a little nervous as we boarded a plane for Southeast Asia. But I was comforted somewhat and certainly surprised when all 125 engineer officers whom I served with at Fort Belvoir were reunited for the flight overseas. We were all serving in the U.S. Army Corps of Engineers, and while there was definitely a sense of apprehension, there was also a tremendous amount of pride. Upon arriving in Vietnam, I initially served as a platoon leader in a remote area of the country where I was charged with the responsibility of completing the seven-barrel culvert project. The road project consisted of constructing seven six-foot tall culverts with concrete headwalls and wing walls. The culvert project was critical and necessary before the planned road could be completed. The road was essential, as it would be used to transport troops and supplies. Three prior lieutenants had previously been given this same assignment, but had failed to complete it due to heavy flooding following the monsoon season. Fortunately, my extremely dedicated and talented platoon was successful in the completion of the project.

At the seven-barrel culvert site, I was promoted from Second Lieutenant to First Lieutenant by General Cooper, the commanding General of the Corps of Engineers in Vietnam. Photos were taken at the promotion by the General's aide and later signed by the General. It's especially rare that a General-grade officer promotes a Lieutenant, which made that day particularly memorable to me. The memory of that honor was made even sweeter when the photos were eventually presented to me. Those photos still hang in my office today, serving as a constant reminder of the importance and gratification of a mission accomplished.

Four months into active duty in Vietnam, I was awakened in the middle of the night and told to pack my belongings for a change in assignment. I boarded an awaiting helicopter and flew to Engineer Command Headquarters, where I learned I was replacing Lieutenant Pace, who was killed in an artillery fire base attack earlier that evening near the Cambodian border. I received a 90-minute briefing on the situation at the fire base and surrounding area. The meeting was conducted by three commanding staff officers, and they didn't mince words in explaining to me the numerous problems and addictions that plagued the platoon I was inheriting. In addition to rampant drug and alcohol abuse, the platoon was infected by a pessimistic, negative and overall disconsolate attitude.

As the meeting ended, the three commanding officers informed me that General Cooper wanted to

Jon Acklam in Vietnam

speak to me privately. It was approximately 2 a.m. when I entered General Cooper's office, and I was pleased when he shook my hand and told me it was good to see me again. I took a seat in his office—a casual and relaxed setting—but the somberness of the situation that reunited us loomed large and ominous. He asked me if I wanted to join him for a drink, and I gratefully obliged. He began to talk about how undesirable and difficult this assignment would be, even apologizing for placing me in this situation. "I know you don't like this," he said, "but if it's any consolation let me tell you how you were selected."

He then explained to me that, following the death of Lieutenant Pace, he instructed his staff to perform a review and search to recommend the most qualified engineer officer available with six months or more of tour duty left in Vietnam. I was humbled and honored when he told me I was their selection. At that point in the conflict, replacement officers were not regularly arriving in Vietnam. Furthermore, in addition to the tragic loss of Lieutenant Pace, the company commander for the fire base engineer unit—Lieutenant Pace's superior officer—would soon be leaving. General Cooper was uncertain if a company commander would be arriving, so he needed a strong and trustworthy leader to fill that potential void, as well.

The selection process for Lieutenant Pace's replacement included, among others, all of my fellow Fort Belvoir engineer officers with whom I attended Engineer Basic Training School. Considering where I once ranked in that class, imagine the odds of me being selected in front of all those other qualified officers. Although I certainly wasn't excited about my new assignment, my confidence and self-esteem skyrocketed as General Cooper spoke to me. I experienced a renewed belief in myself and my capabilities, which represented a defining moment in my life, not just my military career.

After my tour of duty was completed in Vietnam, I thankfully and gratefully returned to my home state, where, at the age of 24, I landed a job at Williams Brothers Construction in Peoria, Illinois. It was in Peoria that I met and ultimately married a wonderful, vibrant, beautiful and delightfully engaging woman named Dawn Detwiler. That's the name that was on her birth certificate, but Dee Dee is her nickname, which is far more fitting of her fun personality. Never did we imagine as we recited our wedding vows that life would lead us on the adventurous road we have traveled. That was the beginning of quite a journey, and Dee Dee remains the most important and respected person in my life.

Ten years after I returned to my home state from Vietnam, I returned to College Station accompanied by my wife for a Class of '69 reunion in Aggieland. I was 34 at the time, and even though Texas A&M's campus had grown and changed in many ways, it still felt like home to me. We had a 5-year-old daughter (Jenny) and a 3-year-old son (Shawn), and I began to ponder the possibility of raising my family and starting a business in the Bryan-College Station community, which was filled with great schools, youth activities, wholesome virtues and opportunities. Besides, the opportunity to return to Aggieland was irresistible. My wife says Aggies are typically like homing pigeons, because no matter where they go after graduation, many of them ultimately desire to return to College Station to roost.

I am a case in point, and my wife was totally supportive of the move. So, in 1981, we packed up our belongings, moved to Aggieland, sharpened a pencil and started Acklam Construction Company.

ACKLAM'S MOST CHALLENGING OBSTACLES

I never took this class in school, but perhaps there is no better education than an "obstacle course." Think about it. Adversity tests and sharpens you; resistance makes a muscle stronger; and as an old proverb eloquently stated, "smooth seas do not make for skillful sailors."

Like virtually any other new business owner, I certainly faced some challenges when beginning Acklam Construction. First, I was new to the area and had no business or construction contacts. I began addressing this issue by developing relationships with architects, engineers, subcontractors and suppliers. The Aggie network was invaluable in this endeavor, as one contact led to another and another. I do not know of any other alumni group that even comes close to Texas A&M's former students in terms of the willingness to help one another, even if you happen to be in the same industry.

My second challenge was that, while I knew the construction trade reasonably well, I lacked business experience and knowledge. I knew I could build a project, but could I manage to bill it, receive payment, document it and so forth? At that point, I couldn't afford to hire someone on a fulltime basis, so I turned to my fulltime partner in life, my wife. Dee Dee took control in this area, serving as the bookkeeper and account supervisor for our upstart construction firm. Her father had been the vice president of purchasing for John Deere in Moline, Illinois, and he had always preached to Dee Dee that if a businessperson took care of the pennies, the dollars would take care of themselves. We had to watch every penny at that point, and we still live according to that mantra today, which leads to our third major obstacle: Minimal cash. Very minimal.

The solution to this issue was not easy, and it did not resolve itself quickly. We didn't go out and incur a great amount of debt, nor did we strike it rich through the lottery (there wasn't a lottery in Texas at that point). We simply pinched pennies and made the most of every dime we made. Our home also doubled as the office. That was partly because Dee Dee was taking care of the books and financial matters for the company, but she was also adamant about being home for our two young children. So, we juggled the demands of parenthood and the stresses of starting a business right in our living room and on our kitchen table. It was not an easy juggle, and we were not in a financial position to even purchase health insurance for our family. Thank God for no catastrophic illnesses that could have ruined us financially, not to mention what it would do to our family dynamics. Those were nerve-wracking times—probably even more harrowing for me than serving in Vietnam—because we were so dependent on God, our neighbors and friends. I can't tell you how many times neighbors and friends lifted us up with support, a meal or whatever we needed at the time.

Many challenges presented themselves to my wife and me as we attempted to wear multiple hats each day. From 8 a.m. to 3:30 p.m. each school day, for example, we were strictly business partners. While the kids were at school, we were completely devoted to company business. We each had the welfare of the business at heart, but our thoughts and approaches were often on opposite ends of the spectrum. It can be extremely stressful to be in disagreement—sometimes volatile disagreement—with your business partner, while still attempting to maintain a loving and affectionate relationship with your spouse. I am sure there is no marriage counselor who would advise a couple to enter into such a partnership, but we knew that if it was to be, it was up to Dee Dee and me. So, when the children came home at 3:30, we shifted into husband and wife/father and mother mode. Dee Dee would greet the kids at the bus stop every day, and no matter what the stresses may have been at work, we were committed to making sure our kids enjoyed childhood. That meant making time for Girls Scouts, Boy Scouts, sports, swimming, karate, piano lessons and so forth. It was quite difficult to cast aside pressing work issues and problems the moment the kids walked in the door, but it was also absolutely necessary to maintain balance and to foster positive and healthy family relationships.

Jon and Dee Dee with their children, Jenny and Shawn

Of course, you might hear a different version of that story if you asked my kids to recall their childhood memories, because owning a family business often meant "all hands on deck." One vivid memory stands out in my mind—and probably in the memories of my son and daughter—involving the construction of Sadie Thomas Park in Bryan. It was shortly after we had started our business, and in an effort to maximize job profit, I enlisted the entire Acklam family, ages 5 through 35, to participate in a clean-up activity at the construction site. All of us donned boots and gloves and picked up construction debris from Sadie Thomas Park. Our daughter was not particularly entertained by such activities, but from an early age, our son became fascinated by the concept of building something, a precursor of things to come.

Because of our limited funds and because summertime is often the busiest season of the year in the construction industry, we did not take as many family vacations as I would have liked. To this day, that is probably one of the biggest regrets I have of my kids' childhood, but in hindsight, I doubt we could have done things much differently. Instead of taking those dream summer vacations, we'd take long weekend trips to Galveston, the San Antonio River Walk, Schlitterbahn and other easily drivable destinations. We did manage to take the family to Disney World during one memorable Christmas holiday season, which was a magical memory. We would have liked to have done more, but the reality is that if you are going to build a business, you are going to need to make sacrifices.

You are also likely going to have plenty of moments when you are overcome with self-doubts and question whether you are doing the right thing. Euphoric moments, when you experience a tremendous sense of satisfaction, will be counterbalanced with the lows and angst that a business owner is destined to face. Many outsiders who may look upon an entrepreneur's career accomplishments with envy only see the tip of the iceberg or the finished product. What they don't see are the years and decades of sacrifices and sack lunches. I always chuckle when well-meaning but misinformed associates say something like, "You have been so lucky." From my viewpoint, luck is simply seizing an opportunity, working hard to capitalize on it, possibly risking your personal/business finances, all while maintaining your ethics and principles.

So many examples of that come to mind when I look back to our early years. I remember that our first accountant drove from Houston to meet with us, as we followed the advice of our initial bonding agent. In our business, a bond is essentially equivalent to a life insurance policy on a specific project. Basically, if a general contractor goes "belly up" during the course of the project, the bonding insurance company will ensure that the project is completed for the owner as the contract dictates. In other words, the owner is guaranteed that the project will be built with no additional costs. Our accountant met with Dee Dee and me at our kitchen table, as we informed him of our financial situation. He was supportive, but I will forever remember his parting words before he drove back to Houston.

"I have talked to many people who believe in you and your capabilities, and they truly believe you will be successful," he said. "However, I have never seen a start-up company take off with as little capital and financial resources as your company." His message was clear: The odds were not in our favor, but we took those words—and any other doubts—as a challenge, fueling our motivation to succeed.

Largely because of our meager beginnings, I also vividly recall those instances when we turned the corner and proved ourselves. One of our first really big opportunities was to build Rock Prairie Elementary School in the early 1980s. The timeframe we were provided was small, and there were concerns whether or not we could complete the project in time to begin the school year. It was a challenge, but we finished the job and began building a strong reputation.

I will also never forget our first construction project on the Texas A&M campus. We were hired in 1984 to build a state-of-the-art complex that would be jointly shared by the A&M athletic department and the physical education department. On one hand, the Physiology Research and Conditioning Lab—later named the Netum Steed Laboratory—would serve as the strength and conditioning home for all Aggie athletes. But it would also be an academic center of sorts, dedicated to physical education research and the study of sports medicine. The gross square footage of the entire facility was 27,300—a massive structure and probably the finest athletics training facility in the country at that time. Working on a project at A&M means that there is no shortage of people who are willing to provide input regarding the dimensions, finish-outs and overall look and feel of the facility. Perhaps the most vocal person sharing his thoughts and ideas about Netum Steed was head coach Jackie Sherrill, who made national headlines in January 1982, when Texas A&M hired him away from Pittsburgh to replace Tom Wilson. Sherrill signed a record six-year contract that was valued at over $1.7 million, a salary that was practically unimaginable for a college head coach at that time.

Sherrill's first two teams at A&M struggled, but the Aggies turned the corner at the end of the 1984 season and began a streak of winning three straight Southwest Conference championships from 1985-87. It's probably not coincidental that 1985 is also when Netum Steed opened its doors, giving the program a recruiting and performance shot in the arm. Before it was completed, though, Coach Sherrill toured the facility several times. On one occasion, he was adamantly opposed to how many interior structural support columns were located throughout the training facility. "One of these posts needs to be removed," he said. "I don't care which one, but I need to be able to assemble my entire team in this room and be able to look each one of my players in the eye. When I am speaking, not one of them is going to be able to hide behind a post." The "posts" were an integral part of the structure of the entire facility, and to remove even one of them could have caused the building to collapse. As much as I wanted to grant Coach Sherrill his wish, I could not. The project engineers and design team would not consent to eliminating a column anywhere, and much to Coach Sherrill's chagrin, the plans were not altered.

Another time, though, we were able to accommodate Coach Sherrill's visions. We were nearing the completion of the project and were wrapping up the interior painting. Jackie looked around the room, and was absolutely livid about the color scheme. "Who picked these colors?" he asked in an agitated and animated demeanor. "You've got red paint here, purple there, blue here…these are the colors of our rivals in the Southwest Conference. No Aggie maroon anywhere!" Fortunately, we were able to maroon-out the entire interior, winning the favorable approval of Coach Sherrill and many other Aggies. And even more satisfyingly, we finished the project six months ahead of schedule, allowing the football team to begin using it during the 1985 season, a full year ahead of schedule. Everybody was happy, and I gained a tremendous sense of satisfaction knowing that the team's conditioning in that facility led A&M to three straight titles.

Throughout Acklam Construction's history, the company has completed many other notable projects on campus, including the first two privately owned office buildings in the Texas A&M Research Park, the George Mitchell Tennis Center, Military Walk, the Davis Player Development

Center, the Lohman Lobby and the R.C. Slocum Nutrition Center. We have also done additions to the Bright Football Complex. Construction of the College Station Cemetery and the Aggie Field of Honor are especially meaningful to me for a couple of reasons. First, I know that will be the final resting place for my wife and me. Secondly, my son and I worked so closely together on the development of the project. Shawn has been interested in construction ever since he helped us clean up Sadie Thomas Park in Bryan. As he aged, he helped clean up many construction sites and became enamored with all facets of construction. He earned a construction science degree from A&M in 2000, and he spent many years as an Acklam management employee, supervising the job site, project managing and overseeing the day-to-day operations of the company.

At the age of 34 in 2011, Shawn approached me one day to speak to me about his vision for the future. "Dad, you started your business at the age I am now. I feel quite capable and prepared to either take this company to the next levels or start my own company." His statement caught me a bit off guard, but it was a well-planned vision for the future. At about that same time, Shawn had made our company's presentation for the Davis Player Development Center project as the construction manager at-risk contractor. The presentation was given under dire circumstances as Shawn had just been informed that morning that his beloved grandmother had unexpectedly died in Bushnell, Illinois. Shawn was certain that his grandmother would have wanted him to make the presentation, and sure enough, we were awarded the project. Without a doubt, that was one of my proudest moments as a father. Watching Shawn meet his professional obligation under extremely difficult circumstances signaled to me that he had the maturity, experience and professional demeanor to run the company. Besides, it just seemed like the right time. It was symbolic to me that Texas A&M was planning the demolition of Netum Steed, while my son had constructed the buildings successor (the Davis Player Development Center). Maybe it was time, I concluded, to step aside and allow him to take the reins of the company. In 2012, I officially passed the baton to Shawn and retired.

I was blessed to ease into retirement. In the corporate world, a longtime employee is typically told to pack his bags and turn in his keys. If he's lucky, he may receive a gold watch. But my retirement was much less cold. I was still able to go to the office on a regular basis, drink my cup of coffee (or two), catch up on current events (mostly through TexAgs.com) and leave whenever I decided.

Then, on a certain January day in 2019, a business proposal changed the future. Acklam Construction was located adjacent to a massive, Texas-sized, Christmas-themed park called "Santa's Wonderland." The park's ownership was ambitiously expanding its property, and negotiations began to acquire the Acklam Construction property. Since starting our business was a family decision, dissolving the business was also a family decision. After prayerful thought and discussion, Shawn, Dee Dee and I decided that it was the right time to dissolve Acklam Construction. It was a decision that brought great happiness and satisfaction to our family, as well as to the owners of Santa's Wonderland. It is with great pride that the property once known as Acklam Construction will now become part of many joyous Christmas memories for families and children for many years to come.

My wife and I have three grandchildren (Christian, Ryan and Kate), and they all live in College Station, which allows us to spend ample time with them. I am at a great stage in life, and all of the struggles we endured have made reaching this comfort level quite satisfying. It certainly wasn't easy, but the sacrifices were definitely worth it.

ACKLAM'S ADVICE TO YOUNG ENTREPRENEURS

Reflecting back on 35 years as a businessman, I believe that one of the most succinct "pearls of wisdom" I can share is this: Sacrifice and setbacks are inevitable. You must expect them. No matter how prepared you may be for business, setbacks will arise, and you will be forced to alter your plans, make sacrifices and adjust to the situation at hand. Business owners do not have the luxury of scheduling obstacles, planning for hardships and arranging the calendar for setbacks. The sacrifices I've made have made me truly appreciate and value the good times and positive experiences even more. The difficulties have taught me that the sun will rise tomorrow, so it is imperative to move forward. There is no greater fallacy than to believe that success in business will be a steady ascent, no matter how meticulously you've made your plans.

I also believe that a leader must treat every person in his organization with dignity, respect and appreciation. Each employee has his own thoughts and ideas, and it is important for everyone to have an opportunity to provide input. Treating your employees right not only creates loyalty, but it is also the right thing to do. It is prudent to bring employees in the inner circle of your thoughts, plans and goals for the business. Instill in them a sense of aspiration, ambition and pride. Your people are truly the heart of your business and its future.

As an employee for a family business and then subsequently launching a family business of my own, I can wholeheartedly attest to the fact that there must be balance between family and business. Children in families grow up, mature and usually build their own independent nests. Businesses, on the other hand, are in constant need of attention. Businesses are somewhat like children who never grow up and become independent. A businessman must be ready at all times to tend to situations as the need calls for it. My business was a true family operation in every sense, as it started with my wife and me at the kitchen table. Making the company work, while also building a family and a relationship, can be quite difficult. We faced plenty of hardships, but in the process, we built some strong marriage muscles that only fortified our commitment to one another.

I'd also encourage aspiring entrepreneurs to minimize financial risks and be prepared for the competition to attempt to intimidate you. If you are a start-up company with big business ambitions, the larger companies in your chosen industry—no matter the industry—will attempt to discourage you and bully you. They don't want the competition, so be prepared to handle whatever may be tossed in your path. Keep your nose to the ground and persevere through anything.

As a second verse to the family business anthem, passing down the family business to the next generation can also present unforeseen hurdles. Each successive generation has a different vantage point, a different perspective and a different outlook regarding how business should progress. For example, when I started Acklam Construction in 1981, computers and technology were not integral components of the construction industry. By the time Shawn became a major player in our company, computers, software programs and technology were essential elements in the construction arena. I felt like a dinosaur living in a modernized world. My son's emergence in the business brought immediate value, knowledge and an upgrade of technological skills to Acklam Construction.

The sports jargon, "You win some, you lose some," is also applicable to businesses. Some business plans and deals will go awry. The wheels will fall off a seemingly solid plan. My advice is simply this: *Move forward*. Living in the past is, for the most part, a total waste of time. Forward thinking and onward movement is a better option. Live and learn, but don't live in the past.

Stay connected to your principles and values, and listen to your heart. At the end of the day, you must have a sense of contentment and peace within yourself. Business is not trickery, and if you attempt to run your business with anything but honesty and integrity, you'll probably find yourself out of business. No matter the times, integrity, honesty and genuine ethics will persevere and prevail. Business decisions should be based on the long-term impact, not on short-term gratification.

I look back on my life, family and business with great pride and a sense of accomplishment. It has been a great journey, although it has taken me on a meandering path at times. I hope there are many days ahead of me, but whatever the case I am eternally grateful because God has blessed me in so many ways, including with the opportunity to share my story with you.

As a final thought, I offer the eloquent words of the great leader Winston Churchill, who once said: "Success is not final; failure is not fatal. IT IS THE COURAGE TO CONTINUE THAT COUNTS."

CHAPTER 3
Lyle Milstead
President
Environmental Improvements, Inc. (EI²)
Texas A&M Class of 1990

MILSTEAD'S PATH TO TEXAS A&M

From my earliest childhood memories, I knew beyond the shadow of a doubt that I wanted to follow my father's footsteps to Texas A&M University. What I didn't know as a child or even as a student at Texas A&M was that I would one day follow my father's trendsetting footsteps into the business world, as well.

Our family is rooted as deeply in the soil at Texas A&M as some of the massive oak trees that line the sprawling campus in College Station. Likewise, Texas A&M is an absolutely integral part of our company's past, present and future. As such, this chapter isn't really about me; I'm merely the storyteller. This chapter is about a maroon-blooded family with a family business that has been built, buoyed and boosted by the same core values that define the university we love: excellence, integrity, leadership, loyalty, respect and selfless service. You don't have to be an Aggie to work for us, but you absolutely must be committed to those core values that distinguish Texas A&M…and Environmental Improvements, Inc. (EI²).

In a different era, I may have never become part of this family business because in a different time, my dad would not have needed an off-season job. Long before quarterbacks selected in the draft were awarded seven-figure signing bonuses, my dad, Charles Frank Milstead (Charlie), signed a professional football contract with the Houston Oilers in 1960, which included a $1,000 signing bonus. While that may sound like a paltry sum compared to today's bonuses, it was actually more money than he had ever seen. According to my mother, Jill, Dad met with the owner of the expansion Oilers, K.S. "Bud" Adams, inside the colorful oilman's office near Main Street and Holcombe in downtown Houston.

Mr. Adams opened a desk drawer and pulled out a handful of $100 bills. He started counting the money and said, "Charlie, tell me when to stop." My father stopped him when he reached $1,000, which represented his signing bonus. The Oilers also provided him a contract worth $18,000 per season, which was a sizeable amount in 1960, especially for an AFL team. This was before the NFL-AFL merger, and he had also been selected by the NFL's Washington Redskins and the AFL's Los Angeles Chargers in the expansion draft.

Obviously, my dad was a prized prospect coming out of Texas A&M, and he was way ahead of his time in terms of his overall passing skills. Growing up in East Texas, he quarterbacked Tyler to the 1955 state championship game against Abilene. During that distinguished season, he was chosen as the 1955 Texas High School Player of the Year, was named to the all-state team for the second consecutive year and was selected to play for the West squad in the 1956 Prep All-America Classic held in Memphis, Tennessee. Additionally, he was the MVP of the 1956 Oil Bowl All-Star Game, which was played annually between squads from Texas and Oklahoma. Dad could have gone to practically any school in the country, but he chose Texas A&M for two primary reasons: First, his older brother, James, had already become the first member of the Milstead family to attend school in Aggieland. Secondly, he was being recruited to A&M by then-head coach Paul "Bear" Bryant, a legendary figure in the history of college football.

My dad was born on November 21, 1937, which means he was two years old when Texas A&M won the 1939 national title. A&M also shared a SWC championship in '40 and won an outright conference crown in '41. Even during the height of America's involvement in World War II—A&M's enrollment had been greatly reduced by the military draft—the Aggies remained competitive, producing seven-win seasons in 1943 and '44. Beginning in 1946, however, lean seasons began occurring regularly. In 1948-49, for example, the Aggies were a combined 1-17-2. So, Bear Bryant was lured from Kentucky to return the Aggies to their glory days of the late 1930s and early '40s. Bryant accepted the A&M job without ever visiting the campus—perhaps because he was so eager to be out of the shadows of Adolph Rupp, the revered basketball coach at Kentucky. While Bryant enjoyed plenty of success at Maryland and then at Kentucky, he realized he would never truly be viewed as the top dog on a basketball-first campus. He took a chance on Texas A&M sight unseen. "At first glance, Texas A&M looked like a penitentiary," Bryant wrote in his 1974 autobiography. "No girls. No glamour. A lifeless community. A&M is a great educational institution, but at that time it was the toughest place in the world to recruit to because nobody wanted to go there."

Nevertheless, Bryant immediately began beating the streets and the odds in recruiting, signing what would become the senior class of '57. The impressive class featured names such as John David Crow, Charlie Krueger, Bobby Joe Conrad and many others who would help reshape the image of A&M football. Bryant's first A&M team in '54 went on the well-documented, 10-day preseason journey to Junction. Bryant took approximately 115 players to Junction, but he returned with only 35 survivors. The depleted Aggies endured a miserable 1-9 season in '54, which was the only losing season in Bryant's 36 years as a head coach. The following year, however, the hardened survivors of Junction and the super sophomore class began to turn things around. The '55 Aggies went 7-2-1, losing only the first and final games of the season. That was my dad's senior year in high school, and it was obvious to practically everyone in the state of Texas that A&M would be a force to be reckoned with in 1956…and as long as Bryant stayed at A&M.

That certainly played a big role in my dad committing to A&M. Bryant was building a program capable of winning a national championship, and he wanted to be part of it. Freshmen were not eligible to play on the varsity back then, but in '56—my father's freshman year in Aggieland—the A&M varsity went undefeated (9-0-1) for the first time since the national championship season of 1939. NCAA probation kept the Aggies out of a bowl game, but big things were on the horizon.

Midway through my dad's sophomore year, A&M climbed to No. 1 in the *Associated Press* poll released on October 28, 1957. Unfortunately for the Aggies, the biggest challenge of all would not be from any opponent, but rather, would be a news item. During the week of the A&M-Rice game in Houston, officials from Alabama arranged to meet Bryant on Wednesday morning at the Shamrock Hotel in Houston. In that meeting, Bryant agreed to return home to become the head coach at Alabama. But he also specified that no announcement should be made until after the season. It didn't happen that way, as the *Houston Post* dropped a bomb on Aggies everywhere the day of the Rice game. When the team woke up on Saturday morning, the game had become secondary in importance. A&M lost the game to Rice, 7-6, lost to Texas the following week, 9-7, and lost to Tennessee in the Gator Bowl, 3-0.

"Looking back on it, I think the article had a big impact on that game and the rest of the season," my dad recalled. "A lot of us came to A&M because Coach Bryant had told us to come. Some guys

Lyle Milstead's father and role model, former Texas A&M quarterback Charlie Milstead

may have been happy he was leaving because he was so tough. But we all knew he was special, and that he was the one who wouldn't let us lose. So, certainly, the news that he was leaving was a big distraction. We were No. 1 in the nation going into that Rice game and on top of the world. The next thing you know, we lose three straight games and lost our coach, who was more responsible for us being No. 1 than any of the players. To this day, I can't explain how it all fell apart so quickly, but it did."

The rest of the story is that Bear Bryant really wanted my dad to transfer to Alabama with him. Who knows how different our lives might have been if he had followed Bear to Tuscaloosa? Bryant won the first of his six national titles at Alabama in 1961. My dad could have been a big part of building the Crimson Tide juggernaut, but it was never a serious consideration because he had given his word to A&M. Although his final two years were played on some less-than-stellar squads under the direction of head coach Jim Myers, my father was selected as an All-SWC quarterback in '58 and was an Academic All-American in 1959, the same year he was chosen as team captain and MVP. Despite the team's lack of success, he finished his A&M football career with nine school passing records. He also proved his versatility, as he finished among the top three in the SWC in 1958 and '59 in rushing yards and passing attempts and among the top four in total touchdowns.

More than all the honors he received or even the degree he earned at A&M, perhaps the most valuable asset my dad took from A&M was the connections he made. Many of his teammates and classmates became lifelong friends and colleagues, including his future business partner, Joe Schmid. Joe was an entrepreneurial-minded manager for the football team at A&M when my dad was in school. The NCAA didn't have the same rules and regulations back then that are enforced nowadays, so it was permissible for players to sell the tickets they received to home games, although the players often didn't have the time or connections to find buyers. That's where Joe saw an opportunity. He would collect the tickets from the A&M players, sell them to fans, give the money to the players and keep a commission for himself. Joe's resourcefulness impressed my dad, and they became good friends. Joe graduated a year before Dad and landed a job with a company called Doug Toole & Company, a manufacturers' representative based in Houston. According to historical documentation, the company started in the early 1950s, establishing a reputation based on quality service, integrity and "pull through marketing." The foundation for success from the beginning was to sell and promote "through" the customer rather than "to" the customer. Searching out opportunities to bring profit-building products and services to the customers was always a priority, but the primary focus was to deliver the manufacturer's market penetration goal.

Once my father graduated, turned down the Redskins, rejected the Chargers and signed a contract with the Oilers worth $18,000 per season, Joe Schmid also encouraged his buddy to take an off-season job with Doug Toole & Company, which would pay him $12,000 per year. Making

$30,000 a year placed my dad in rather elite financial company in 1960. He didn't receive a great deal of playing time with the Oilers because he was the backup quarterback to future Hall of Famer George Blanda, who was in the midst of his amazing 26-year career in pro football in the early 1960s. Nevertheless, he handled the punting duties for the Oilers, and Houston defeated the Los Angeles Chargers 24-16 in the first American Football League title game on January 1, 1961 at tiny Jeppesen Stadium on the University of Houston campus in front of a near-sellout crowd of 32,183. In comparison, the 1961 Cotton Bowl between Duke and Arkansas—played on the same day—attracted 70,500 fans, and the 1960 Bluebonnet Bowl (played two weeks earlier at Rice Stadium in Houston) drew 68,000 fans to see Alabama and Texas. Obviously, pro football still had a long way to go to become king of the sports universe in the Lone Star State, which was a big reason he only played two seasons with the Oilers.

After the 1961 season—a year in which the Oilers again defeated the Chargers in the AFL title game—my dad was traded to the New York Titans. At that time, though, my mother was pregnant with my older brother, Mark, and my oldest brother, Charlie, was two years old. Mom didn't like the idea of raising a family in New York City, and Dad figured he could make a good living by going full-time with Doug Toole & Company. My father never started a game as an NFL quarterback, but he completed four passes for 43 yards in his NFL career and recorded two interceptions while playing defense. More significantly, he'd already begun to carve a niche in the business marketplace at Doug Toole & Company by implementing a simple philosophy that is still our company's motto more than 50 years later: *The true definition of success is when a customer becomes a friend.* Or, as Joe Schmid often said: *Everyone needs friends, so you might as well make them the people you work with.*

Once my dad made the decision to retire from football, my parents planted permanent roots in Houston, paying cash for a home not too far from where Royal Oaks Country Club is today. Things went extremely well for him and Joe, and my dad bought half of Doug Toole & Company in the early 1960s, while Joe bought the other half in 1966. They changed the name first to Mil-Toole and Company for a short time and then to Environmental Improvements, Inc. (EI^2). The EI^2 logo was created by Joe.

Doug Toole, who was known as the "King of the Martini Lunches," had built a solid foundation as a manufacturer representative by treating his customers the right way. He had offices in Houston, Dallas and New Orleans, making many lasting friendships and earning the trust of customers over long lunches and strong martinis. My dad and Joe, however, took things to an entirely new level. Both of them were pilots, making it much easier for them to build even stronger customer bases in multiple locations because they could fly the company plane whenever they needed it. But the primary reason they were able to transform a good company into a great one is the simple philosophy of turning every customer—or prospective customer—into a genuine friend. Practically everything we did, from our family leisure time to my father's weekly routines, involved our friends/customers.

When Dad first began working with Doug Toole & Company, the organization represented about 10 different manufacturers. Doug Toole and Company had the exclusive rights to sell those products, so my dad and Joe began working closely with more and more engineers and contractors, using their Aggie connections to develop new leads. Obviously, they loved Aggie football, and they both thoroughly enjoyed taking their families to College Station for games. Instead of merely building family memories, however, they also used A&M football games to build their business. With so many Aggie contractors and engineers that were prospective customers, my father decided to invest in a recreational vehicle and group tickets, filling the RV each weekend with family and friends to travel to College Station. Joe had three daughters, and my parents had three sons. We each were allowed to bring a friend, and some of my favorite childhood memories throughout the 1970s and '80s involve packing the coolers with beverages and thick corned beef sandwiches as we made the drive to Aggieland. We'd all tailgate before the games while the kids traversed the parking lots and campus. Meanwhile, my parents and the Schmids networked with their guests.

One of the truly great lessons I learned from those memories was simply to value and cherish every relationship. My parents never, ever wasted an opportunity to make a connection or to build upon that relationship. It was never a burden to mix business with pleasure, because my dad loved to build relationships. When it wasn't football season, they would take friends and prospects on hunting trips or golf excursions. Dad would invite contractors, engineers and customers to his kids' ballgames, and he'd also attend the games and events of those contractors', engineers' and customers' kids. And when those prospects and customers visited from out of town, my parents welcomed them into our home instead of staying in a hotel.

As you've probably already realized, my mom was an integral part of everything because it was her role to make sure the wives of those prospects felt like they were welcomed and at ease to be themselves. She made sure the wives and children had a great experience at all the various outings, which made just about everything a family affair. It wasn't rocket science or a secret formula, but as I watched my parents, I could tell they genuinely enjoyed making friends and developing relationships. As a result, those friends wanted to do business with them. Nurturing those relationships allowed the company to grow exponentially over the years. Today, EI^2 is one of the largest water and wastewater equipment reps in the entire country.

Naturally, I admired my parents, as well as the Schmids. In fact, Joe was like a second father to me in so many ways. He was at the hospital when I was born, and he regularly attended my ballgames and family events throughout my childhood. His passion for Texas A&M, along with my parents' devotion, was yet another reason I never even considered attending another university other than A&M. It's not a stretch to say that I idolized my father and genuinely wanted to make him proud. In hindsight, I probably placed him too highly on my parental pedestal. I remember at one point in my life that my dad sat me down and said that, while he appreciated the amount of respect I gave him, I needed to reserve such admiration and gratitude for my Heavenly Father, not my earthly one. Of course, even that piece of advice made me respect my father even more because his priorities have always been focused on his Christian faith, his family and his career—in that order.

I realized Dad had built quite a legacy at A&M long before I ever enrolled in 1985. Not only had my dad enjoyed a tremendous football career in Aggieland, but his success as an entrepreneur had enabled him to donate significant amounts of money to many organizations on campus. As I made my way through A&M, I realized that being the son of Charlie Milstead was probably much easier on me than being my oldest brother, Charlie Jr., because he literally had my father's full name to carry. It was also easier for me to uphold the family name at A&M because I wasn't trying to follow in my father's football footsteps. I would have loved to have played for A&M, but I didn't have the size or athletic ability to suit up for the Aggies.

One of the great things I accomplished at A&M, however, does involve the football term "outkicking my coverage." Among the many key contacts I made while attending school at A&M was meeting a beautiful young woman from Missouri City named Trish Bramlett. I knew from the moment I met her that she was my dream girl, and remarkably, I sold her on me, as well. We have the same birthday—four years apart—and we share the same values: faith, family and career ambition. In January 2021, we celebrated our 28th wedding anniversary, and God has truly blessed us in so many ways. We have two wonderful children, daughter Alex and son Michael, and I thank the Lord regularly for allowing our paths to cross. Without a doubt, Trish is the most important lifelong connection I made at A&M, but some other relationships I developed in College Station were quite meaningful, as well.

From left, Trish, Alex, Charlie, Jill, Michael and Lyle Milstead

MILSTEAD'S PATH TO ENTREPRENEURIAL SUCCESS

Thanks to the vision of my father and Joe Schmid, EI² was already an established and respected multi-location company by the mid- and late-1980s. Like even the most successful sports dynasties, though, great companies must never remain stagnant. To grow and prosper over the course of decades, a business must always be looking to expand its products and/or services, to adapt to changing times and to add outstanding individuals to the corporate team. Although none of us could have predicted it at the time, a large part of the future leadership of EI² was enrolled in classes at Texas A&M at one point or another during the mid- and late-1980s.

Louisiana native Bucky Richardson was part of a monster 1987 football recruiting class, and he made an immediate impact in College Station. While Craig Stump was viewed as A&M's primary passing quarterback, Richardson started five games and eventually earned SWC Offensive Newcomer of the Year honors. In the final game of the regular season in his freshman year against Texas, with the score tied at 13-13, the SWC title on the line and the fans inside Kyle Field whipped into a feverish pitch, Bucky kept on a speed option play and scored on a 7-yard run that helped the Aggies to secure a 20-13 win. It was A&M's fourth win in a row over Texas, and it gave us a third consecutive conference title. It also sent us to the Cotton Bowl where we faced Heisman Trophy winner Tim Brown and Notre Dame. On a chilly afternoon in Dallas, Bucky and the Aggies thoroughly whipped Notre Dame, 35-10. An Aggie legend had been born.

At the end of a disappointing 1988 season, Richardson blew out his knee, as A&M went 7-5. He missed the entire 1989 season to rehabilitate from major knee surgery, but during that time, A&M head coach Jackie Sherrill had introduced Bucky to my father. In a testament to the old cliché "it's a small world," Bucky's college roommate was Brian Payne, who was a backup quarterback and the holder for the football team.

Many years earlier, my dad and Brian's dad, Buddy Payne, had been roommates. Consequently, Brian and I were like cousins growing up, and I even referred to his father as "Uncle Buddy," although we weren't actually related. Anyway, that's how Bucky and I also began to become close friends. By the end of the 1990 season, Bucky was back in prime form, finishing up the season with a magnificent performance in the 1990 Holiday Bowl against BYU. Then in 1991, Richardson led the Aggies back to another SWC title, just as he did as a freshman. After that season, he was drafted by none other than the Houston Oilers in the eighth round and spent the next three years playing in Houston. For many reasons, I was elated that he was picked up by the Oilers. First and foremost, it meant that we could stay in touch and remain close.

When I graduated from A&M in May 1990 with a degree in industrial distribution, I went to work for an organization called Sisco (Service Industrial Supply Company), which sold high-yield fittings to businesses in the oil and gas pipeline industry. I started in the warehouse, learning the products, which proved to be great training for my future with EI² because I was calling on buyers, sending quotes and building relationships. I worked with Sisco for about two years until I received a call from Joe Schmid, who wanted to meet me for lunch. It wasn't necessarily unusual that Joe called me, but I could tell there was something pretty significant on his mind. Many years earlier, Dad and Joe had made an agreement not to hire any of Joe's three daughters or any of my dad's three sons—nor any in-laws—because it would be practically impossible to fire a relative. Somewhere along the line, though, apparently Joe changed his mind in regard to hiring me, and since it was Joe's idea, my dad didn't have a problem with it, either.

I started in 1992, and because I was practically raised to build meaningful relationships one person at a time, I was able to hit the ground running in our Houston office. At the time, we had six or seven employees in the Houston office. Dad and Joe had weathered difficult economic times in the 1980s—specifically in the mid-1980s when the world price of oil fell in 1986 from $27 to below $10—and had turned the corner in the 1990s under more promising economic terms. Then in the mid-1990s we received another shot in the arm when Larry Kelm finished his NFL career following the 1993 season. Kelm, a solid and steady linebacker for the Aggies from 1983-86, was a fourth-round selection by the Los Angeles Rams in the 1987 NFL Draft, playing for the Rams from 1987-92 before finishing his career with the San Francisco 49ers. Larry, a native of Corpus Christi, returned to the Lone Star State, moved his family to Houston and tried out with the Oilers. He made it to the final cut before being released. With his football career over, Larry called Texas A&M in hopes of utilizing the Aggie network to find a new career path. He was a civil engineer, and he was eventually connected with Paul Wahlberg, who owned an architectural firm in Houston and was a member of A&M's Class of 1950. For over four decades Wahlberg was also a volunteer for the Houston Golf Association, with most of that tenure spent as the chairman of HGA's Charity Selection Committee. Wahlberg suggested that Larry should meet with Charlie Milstead, and my dad happily obliged.

Dad initially met with Larry and gave him the names of several Aggie-owned engineering firms, encouraging Larry to use his name to begin interviewing. Several weeks passed, Larry went on various interviews and my dad and Larry met again. To make a long story short, Larry liked the idea of working with one of those firms, but he really liked the idea of working with my father and Joe at EI². After some discussions between Joe and my dad, it was announced that Larry was going to start making some calls with me. I was delighted because I had loved watching Larry play at A&M, and I had admired him and his work ethic from afar for many years.

We went on that initial sales call in Orange, Texas, and we hit it off right away. Dad and Joe hired Larry, and they sent us to numerous factories for training over the next couple of years. Larry and I probably went on 15 business trips together over the next couple of years as we began to extend beyond the company's roots as purely a manufacturer's representative. As the years progressed, we grew and expanded to become involved in manufacturing and system integration. Additionally, we also have a preventative maintenance program that follows the manufacturer's service requirements for its clients, and we have an expansive and qualified service department to address the service needs of the contractor and end user.

Larry was a big part of our growth in the '90s, as he really taught all of us to have fun. We'd go on business trips, meet with customers, contractors, prospects or engineers and take them to dinner. Other times we'd go to ballgames or to play golf. Larry was such a personable man's man that people loved to be around him and to listen to his stories. He was a great addition to EI², as was Bucky

Richardson a couple of years later. Bucky and I had stayed close during his three years with the Oilers (1993-95), and I remember numerous times after an Oilers home game in those years, Bucky would call and invite Trish and me to meet him and his teammates at this restaurant or that one around town. I met plenty of Oilers back in those days, and we had plenty of good times. Following his three years with the Oilers, Bucky had short stints with the Patriots, Cowboys and Chiefs. When he left football for good following the 1996 training camp, he asked my dad to introduce him to some business people in Houston. Like Larry Kelm, my dad didn't intend on hiring Bucky right away, but after several other things didn't quite work out the way Bucky or my father anticipated, Bucky came to work for us in 1998, allowing us to continue building our staff with high-quality, top-flight men and women.

I am fully convinced that it takes at least five years to completely comprehend all of the working parts that make EI² what it is today because we have grown exponentially since the early 1990s. Today, we have offices in Houston, Lewisville, Buda and Oklahoma City. We have about 40 staff members, and we have assembled a tremendous management team, which also includes Brian Phenegar in our Austin office and fellow Aggie Eric Fields, who is in the Dallas office. In early 2020 our management team grew with four "third generation" employees joining THE TEAM, another fellow Aggie and Big 12 shot putter Jeff Houston, Curtis Cathey, Joey Brown and Jeff Adams.

From our four office locations, we service a customer loyalty base that covers every square mile of the Lone Star State and the Sooner State, ranging from McAllen, Texas to Tulsa, Oklahoma, and from as far west as the Rio Grande River to the Golden Triangle along the Texas-Louisiana state lines. While we have evolved tremendously as a company since Joe and my dad first bought out Doug Toole & Company in the 1960s, we have continued to grow with the same family-oriented, customer-focused philosophy that Joe and my dad instilled more than 50 years ago.

That philosophy, along with the numerous perks we provide our employees, has resulted in a 23-year average for employee tenure. That's a phenomenal statistic that has enabled us to build and maintain a level of continuity that most companies could never duplicate. Joe and my dad believed in hiring great people and keeping those people happy because they understood that your employees are your No. 1 asset. Watching my father operate as an entrepreneur—first as a child and later as an employee—I was always amazed at how hard he worked to fulfill the requests of his employees. If the request was ethical and legal, my father wanted to make the answer "yes." He taught me to be a great provider. If his employees came to him in need of a loan or required assistance in practically any endeavor, the answer was yes. If an employee needed a loan, he would give it to him/her and never even ask for it back. He truly believed in the principle that it is more rewarding to give than to receive. He is a man of great faith, and he practiced what Jesus preached about giving and loving others. Most of his employees didn't just like working for my father; they loved him like a family member. Even when he had to let one woman go who was stealing from the company, he did so with compassion and tried to make the incident a teaching moment. Joe and my dad also provided staff members with bonuses, flexible vacation plans, continuing education opportunities and tremendous benefits programs, creating a sense of camaraderie and team unity.

The continuity of our staff is matched or surpassed only by the stability of our customer base and the manufacturers we represent. Today, we represent more than 60 companies that manufacture all types of equipment for the municipal water and wastewater treatment market. Many of those relationships with the manufacturers are 20, 30 or even 40 years old. And when we celebrated our 50th anniversary as a company in April 2016, we held a party during a manufacturer convention in Fort Worth. More than 400 people attended that party, including so many of our customers. We understand that customers have a choice, and we are honored and humbled to maintain such long-standing relationships with our customers.

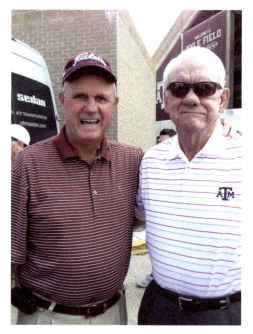

Charlie Milstead and 1957 Heisman Trophy winner John David Crow

Another key to our success is the relationships we maintain with engineers because there are always issues on construction projects. Many of our competitors will back away from such issues, claiming that this or that is not our problem. My dad and Joe, however, taught not to point fingers, but to instead figure out solutions. If one of our customers has a $15,000 problem that we are aware of, we will help solve the issue even if it's not our fault or responsibility. Typically, we'll go to the contractor and the manufacturer and discuss the issue and offer a proposal, for example, of dividing the cost of the issue into three different payments of $5,000 that will be paid by the contractor, the manufacturer and EI^2. My father taught all of us that solving issues like that for a customer is not a $5,000 cost, but rather, it's a $5,000 investment in a relationship that will likely stand the test of time. That's how we have been able to so successfully maintain our customer relationships for decades upon decades.

In 2004, Larry Kelm, Bucky Richardson, Brian Phenegar, Fred Willms, Eric Fields and I made the bold decision to approach Joe and my dad about purchasing EI^2 from the two founders. They had grown the company and trained us to run it with professionalism, principles and integrity. We could tell that the time might be right for them to step back, and we initially borrowed enough money from the bank to buy out Joe. My father was onboard, and he even co-signed for the loan to pay Joe. But he refused to allow us to borrow the money to pay for his portion of the company. Instead, we paid him monthly over the course of 10 years as he assisted us in making the transition. He was pleased with the arrangement, and we were delighted in playing less of a role in the day-to-day operations. Nevertheless, he guided us through our early years of ownership. I remember one time, in particular, when a contractor in the Austin area owed us a significant amount of money, and my dad advised us how to handle the situation. He also encouraged us in numerous situations and gave us many valuable lessons. Dad always encouraged us to borrow as much money as we needed and to pay it back quickly. He preached integrity and being true to your word.

In some ways, it was daunting to take over the company because Joe and my dad had done so much with it. But as the years passed, we could tell that they were pleased with how we were running the business the right way and building upon the legacy that they had started. Now, it's an honor to oversee the business and to still be representing what they started.

MILSTEAD'S MOST CHALLENGING OBSTACLES

One of the great things about the work environment at EI² is that it has always been a family atmosphere…and not just because I once worked for my dad, as did my wife (Joe Schmid broke his own rule again when he hired Trish to work for EI² in 1993). Like virtually any other company, we've experienced lean financial times. When I was in high school, for example, I recall some particularly stressful times during the 1980s oil glut. The world price of oil, which had peaked in 1980 at over $35 per barrel, fell in 1986 from $27 to below $10. Because we work with so many municipalities in the water and wastewater industry, that segment of our business is practically recession-proof. After all, everybody needs drinking water and wastewater cleanup, and the funding will always be there from taxes. But we also work with plenty of other companies in various industries, including the oil and gas business. The mid-1980s were tough at EI², and there have been plenty of other difficult decisions, circumstances and times that we have encountered. But as the bible points out in James 1:2-4: "Consider it pure joy, my brothers and sisters, whenever you face trials of many kinds, because you know that the testing of your faith produces perseverance. Let perseverance finish its work so that you may be mature and complete, not lacking anything."

Nobody seeks adversity or difficulties, yet we know that a muscle grows when it meets resistance, diamonds are formed under intense pressure, towering trees take deeper root in the midst of storms and courage is only developed by overcoming your fears. Christian author C.S. Lewis said: "Hardships often prepare ordinary people for an extraordinary destiny." Walt Disney put it this way: "All the adversity I've had in my life, all my troubles and all my obstacles have strengthened me. You may not realize it when it happens, but a kick in the teeth may be the best thing in the world for you." And the legendary playwright William Shakespeare said: "Let me embrace thee, sour adversity, for wise men say it is the wisest course." It's a fact of business, personal development and practically every other endeavor in life that our greatest growth is often a result of our toughest tests. I'm not suggesting to look for difficulties or to create tough times, but I am guaranteeing that practically every business, every entrepreneur, every family and every individual will experience character-building, resolve-testing and strength-building times. EI² has endured plenty of those times, but we have always relied on each other to move past the difficulties. That's what is so great about our working environment: It's more than just a pleasant situation where we get along with each other; it's really more like an extended family.

Like any family, though, we have been tested by the loss of family members. On July 16, 2012, Joe Hunter Schmid died after battling cancer at the age of 74. Like I had mentioned previously, Joe was like a second father to me, and he was beloved by so many. He was a great businessman, who also formed Gaylord Investments after he and my dad took over EI². Beyond all his business accomplishments, however, Joe was simply an all-around great guy with a huge heart for others. He and his wife, Judy, first joined Pines Presbyterian Church in 1967, where he was an elder and served on the stewardship and Christian education committees. He loved cooking barbecue for our staff, the Aggie golf team and the Granada Cookers, which became the Emerging 9 Cooking Team. He was a Lifetime Director of the Rodeo and was chairman of the Breeder Greeters Committee. He was also extremely active with Camp Blessing, Texas, a camp for special needs children founded by his daughter and her husband, Jodi and Charles Ferguson. Losing Joe was tough on many of us, but he lived a full life and it wasn't unexpected when he breathed his last breath.

The same cannot be said about the shocking death we endured as a company on November 22, 2014. As I noted previously, Larry Kelm was one of the greatest additions that we've ever made as an organization. Not only was he a tremendous leader, but he was also the fun-loving, prank-pulling, adventure-seeking catalyst of EI² who infused our staff with a contagious zest for life. After our new executive team bought out dad and Joe in 2004, Larry was the natural choice to replace Joe as the president of EI². Just as he had been on the football field, he was just a great leader.

As a player at A&M, Larry was never the biggest, strongest or most talented player on the field, on the defense or even among the linebackers. Yet, he was such an intelligent player and a student of the game that he still holds the records (through the 2017 season) for the single most tackles in a game (24 against SMU in 1985, which is tied with the 24 Larry Horton compiled against Baylor in 1990) and the most tackles in a season ever by a senior (152 in 1986). At 6-4, 236 pounds coming out of A&M, Larry wasn't projected to be much of an NFL linebacker, but he played seven seasons, made 49 career starts and led the Los Angeles Rams with 105 tackles in 1991. One former Rams coach, John Robinson, referred to Kelm as "a master of managing the defense." Another Rams coach, Chuck Knox, called him a steady influence. I am just grateful that I was able to call him a close friend.

So many stories come to mind when I think of Larry and his impact on EI² and our staff members. More than anything, though, the stories of his playful personality come to mind. I remember one time, in particular, when Larry and I were on a training trip to a factory in Pittsburgh in mid-January

1996. The trip had been planned months earlier, but as fate would have it, the hometown Steelers were playing host to the Indianapolis Colts in the AFC Championship Game on January 14 at Three Rivers Stadium. One of the stars of that Pittsburgh team was future NFL Hall of Famer Kevin Greene, who had been a fellow linebacker and teammate of Larry's when the two played together with the Rams. Larry and Kevin had not seen each other in years, but Larry took me with him to the team hotel and the front desk attendant called Kevin Greene's room, asking him if he knew Larry Kelm. This was the day before the game, and I really didn't know what to expect, but Kevin appeared quickly in the lobby of the hotel and escorted us both past security and up to his room. Understandably, Kevin Greene really wasn't interested in hearing from me, but he and Larry shared great stories, and Kevin volunteered to arrange for the two of us to receive tickets for the AFC Championship Game. We received two tickets on the 40-yard-line on the fourth row up from the Steelers bench to a terrific showdown that has been voted among the best Conference Championship Games in NFL history. The Steelers were big favorites, but the outcome was not decided until the last play of the game when Colts quarterback Jim Harbaugh threw a Hail Mary that was dropped in the end zone by the intended receiver Aaron Bailey, allowing the Steelers to advance to the Super Bowl with a 20-16 win. Attending that game was fantastic, but the vivid memory I have is of the night before when Larry and I left the Steelers hotel and went to dinner together.

We arrived at the restaurant together, were seated at our table and Larry looked across the room and spotted legendary 49ers quarterback Joe Montana, a four-time Super Bowl champion and three-time Super Bowl MVP. Like Larry had told me regarding Kevin Greene, he said, "I haven't seen Joe Montana in years." I knew they had played together in San Francisco for one year, and I also knew that Montana was born in New Eagle, Pennsylvania and had been raised in Monongahela, a coal-mining town 25 miles south of Pittsburgh. I knew quite a bit about Montana because my wife happened to be a huge fan. Larry also knew that, and he encouraged me to introduce myself to Joe Montana while Larry made a quick trip to the restroom. "Tell Joe you are my friend," Larry said as he made his way to the restroom. "Tell him I will stop by the table in just a moment."

As Larry excused himself to go to the restroom, I quickly called Trish from my cell phone and excitedly told her that I was about to meet Joe Montana. She was equally excited when I told her I was going to see if he would say hello to her. After the visit with Kevin Greene, I was feeling quite confident about name-dropping Larry Kelm. I approached Montana's table, told him I was a close friend of Larry Kelm's and asked him if he would say hello to my wife. As I reached to hand him my phone, the manager of the restaurant grabbed my shoulders and apologized to Mr. Montana as he whisked me away toward the front door. He threw me out of the restaurant, and the first person I saw was Larry Kelm outside the restaurant, laughing hysterically, and admitting that Joe Montana didn't have the slightest idea who Larry was, because he had been a backup linebacker in his one season with the 49ers. That was fun-loving, prank-pulling Larry at his finest. He just had a way of making practically anything memorable.

Unfortunately, I will also never forget the day I received the tragic and shocking news regarding Larry's death. During the afternoon on November 22, 2014, I received a call from Bucky Richardson, whom I knew was on a hunting trip near Laredo with Larry and several other friends and co-workers. I didn't go on that trip because my son, Michael, was the quarterback at Stratford High School and the Spartans were facing Temple in a playoff game at Bryan High on November 23. It had been a great game, although Temple emerged with a close win, and I thought Bucky was calling me to receive an updated on the game. Instead, he broke the news to me that, one week shy of his 50th birthday and just five days before Thanksgiving, Larry was dead. He had fallen from a windmill that he was using as a deer blind. There was nothing anyone could have done, and it was nobody's fault. It was a freak accident, and I was in complete shock.

Nevertheless, I knew it was time to be assertive. Larry's wife, Lynann, and his children, daughter Ashley and son Drew, needed our prayers, condolences, help and support. Likewise, our entire staff needed to be notified and comforted. We'd just lost our leader, the president of our organization and the captain of our team. Our staff needed to be assured that everything would be OK despite the intense anguish and pain we were all feeling at that time. We called a meeting for that following Monday morning, gathered in a conference room, closed the doors and the first thing we did was to pray. I led that prayer, and I can honestly say it wasn't me speaking; it was the Holy Spirit speaking through me. It was quite an emotional meeting, but it was beneficial to all of us, as we told stories, cried, laughed and anguished together…as a family. Most of all, though, Bucky and I assured everyone that we were going to make it through this painful, shocking time together, leaning on one another and doing whatever was necessary to comfort the Kelm family. During that time together, I was also encouraged by others to take over as president of EI^2. Quite frankly, I had no interest in filling that role, but I was ultimately persuaded to take the job. I realized that Larry would have wanted me to step out of my comfort zone and into that role, and it was something I needed to do. It still pains me to even talk about Larry's death, and a part of me still longs to travel, laugh and spend time with my dear friend. But we have only had three presidents in the history of EI^2—Joe Schmid, Larry Kelm and myself. I consider it an honor to sit at the same desk in the same broken chair that they both used at one time while trying to build on the legacy that they left us.

Likewise, it is a tremendous honor to continue building upon what my dad and Joe started many years ago. And each day I am driven to lead our organization in the way that best reflects Jesus Christ's glory and the legacies of our past leaders. We all wish that there was some way to bring Larry back, but that accident did bring our team even closer together. Larry's death made us appreciate our lives and our times together even more, and we are all resolute about honoring those who have done so much to make the business what it is today. We don't know exactly what awaits us, but after all that we have been through, we're confident we can hurdle any obstacle that comes our way.

MILSTEAD'S ADVICE TO YOUNG ENTREPRENEURS

Never waste an opportunity to build a relationship. You may possess the greatest entrepreneurial idea or you may hold a patent or copyright for the most innovative invention in modern times. Regardless, your reputation as a businessperson/entrepreneur will ultimately be determined by the relationships you build and maintain. I've seen plenty of jerks build successful businesses. I've also seen unscrupulous men and women succeed in business. But ultimately, the way you treat people will come back to you and your company—whether it's in a positive or negative fashion.

One of the things I most admired about watching Joe and my dad grow their business was that they treated everyone they encountered with tremendous respect and made it a point to turn their business contacts into close friends. That doesn't mean that they never had to take a tough stance with someone or that they never had any conflicts. There were times when clients didn't pay bills or employees didn't perform up to their expectations or when tough calls and difficult decisions were made. The fundamental philosophy of the company for more than 50 years, however has been this: *The true definition of success is when a customer becomes a friend.*

I know many salespeople and businessmen who make finding contacts part of their daily goal. But business—even life—becomes so much more enjoyable when you make the fundamental shift to quit seeking potential leads and to begin developing meaningful friendships. Joe and my dad trained Larry, Bucky, me and many others involved with our organization that developing relationships is the most important aspect of the business. Sure, product knowledge is important. So is price, convenience, location and a litany of other things. But building friendships has been the key to our success for more than 50 years, and the best way to do that is to spend quality time with the people you are meeting and greeting in your business circles.

We spend that quality time taking friends to Aggie football games, the golf course, hunting trips, fishing trips, dinner gatherings and so forth. We get to know our friends' wives, their kids and their businesses. If a genuine friendship is developed and nurtured, those friends typically want to do business with us or will recommend us to their friends/associates. As I mentioned earlier, this is not rocket science. We love developing relationships with others, and we are grateful when those friends do business with us.

We cherish the relations we've made with customers, contractors and engineers, and we also treat our employees like family members. As an entrepreneur/business owner, your most valuable asset is your people. You can't build and maintain a successful business without great people. Here again, I've seen some business owners and CEOs run (or rule) their organizations with an iron fist, but that's hardly a recipe for long-term success. I am so proud of the fact that the tenure of our average employee is 23 years. That means that people love working with us, and that they genuinely love what they do. The Chinese philosopher Confucius is credited with the following quote: "Choose a job you love, and you will never have to work a day in your life." I absolutely believe that, and if you love your work you will be rewarded not only financially, but also by feeling fulfilled, accomplished and satisfied. And as an entrepreneur/business owner, your staff will tend to follow your lead.

If you make every staff member feel like he/she is a valuable part of your team, loyalty will define your organization. And if you make their spouses and children feel welcome and important, as well, you create chemistry and unity that will propel your company to great heights.

Likewise, if you provide your people with great benefits, incentives, bonuses and financial blessings, they will value your organization and will be grateful for the careers you provide. And if your work environment is a family atmosphere, your employees will value each other and support one another. My dad and Joe certainly instilled discipline within the organization, and everyone knew there were consequences if goals and objectives were not met. They also released some employees who were not "team players." For the most part, however, the reality is that the staff knew how much they cared about them. As a result, the employees always went the second mile to make sure the company thrived. It was a win-win situation for everyone, and that's still the way we run the EI^2 operations on a daily basis.

I know that I have been incredibly blessed with great business mentors in my dad and Joe Schmid, who was like a second father to me. But your mentor doesn't need to be a parent, an uncle or even a close friend. It just needs to be someone who is willing to guide you to greatness. As the son of one former legendary Texas A&M quarterback and the associate of another former legendary A&M quarterback, many of my analogies tend to be related to football. Now, can you imagine how difficult it would be for a quarterback to lead his team to victory without any coaching? No head coach to provide direction and discipline. No offensive coordinator to call plays. No coach in the press box to make adjustments for what the defense is doing. And no input from anyone else.

Not even my "dear friend" Joe Montana could succeed under those circumstances, and going into business or entrepreneurship without mentors would be every bit as daunting. Mentoring as we know it today is loosely modeled on the historical craftsman/apprentice relationship, where young people once learned a trade (like butcher or blacksmith) by shadowing the master artisan.

Nowadays, mentors or business coaches are one of the most valuable resources an aspiring entrepreneur should utilize. The idea of launching a business should no longer be a scary or daunting experience, riddled with unknowns. With the assistance of mentors, it should be a collaborative experience accumulating the guidance and advice of numerous entrepreneurs who have already traveled the road you are mapping out. Many successful entrepreneurs are happy to lend their guidance if you will simply ask, and the power of the Aggie network can most definitely lead you to find great mentors who can help you avoid plenty of heartache and hassles just by seeking their advice.

I believe it is also wise advice to not be overwhelmed by circumstances. As the leader of a business or the sole employee of a startup company, the daily to-do list can become so long and daunting that you fail to truly accomplish anything. Dad had a unique ability to handle the most important agenda item, one at a time. You cannot tackle eight responsibilities or meet with five different customers at once. Planning your day and executing your plan daily can be extremely important in accomplishing the most important things on your agenda. Maybe it was because Dad was a quarterback on some mediocre A&M teams and he was quite accustomed to being pressured from all sides, but whatever the case, he had the ability to stay composed and to focus on one agenda item at a time. As an entrepreneur, you will be pulled, pressured and blindsided by your responsibilities and unexpected challenges. Stay calm and composed, and handle what's most important right in front of you.

So many other pieces of advice come to mind from Joe and my dad's teachings and my own experiences. Dad always advised, for example, to develop great banking relationships and to be a person of your word when it came to repaying loans. And if there was ever a time you were going to be late with the payment, your banker should know well in advance. There's no substitute for banking integrity and good credit when starting or building a business. Likewise, many other business principles and lessons come to mind, but perhaps the best piece of advice I can lend is this: Don't take a day for granted.

When you are young, it's so easy to have a bulletproof mentality. It's easy to think that the accident will never happen to you or the tragedy that you see so often on the news will never hit close to your own home. Even as a middle-aged adult, it's easy to take your blessings, your family, your friends and your career for granted—not because you don't care, but because life can make you so busy that you don't truly appreciated the little things. Little things like waking up tomorrow and visiting with friends in the office.

Larry Kelm's death changed my perspective on life. Deep down, I've always known that we are not promised tomorrow, but Larry's death really brought it to the forefront of my mind. There's not a day that goes by that I don't miss him, but there's also not a day that I don't appreciate because of his memory. Larry's accident brought all of our partners and all of our employees across the state even closer. We were really three separate offices and now we are really one family. We do things a little differently. We communicate much better, and we talk every Monday on a conference call. We don't take each other, our business success, our friendships or our families for granted. I strongly encourage you to do the same. Make the most of every day, and make the most friendships you can. Success will inevitably follow.

CHAPTER 4
Monty Davis

Chief Operating Officer
Core Laboratories
Texas A&M Class of 1977

DAVIS' PATH TO TEXAS A&M

As a Baptist raising two sons in Killeen, Texas—the home of Fort Hood Army Base and roughly 60 miles southwest of Waco—my father gravitated toward the nearby Baptist university to occasionally spend some bonding time with his boys on Saturday afternoons in the fall. As a result, the only NCAA football games I attended as a child were at Baylor University. So, my choice of picking a university was wide open.

Thank God Baylor was not my pick! I wouldn't have fit at Baylor for a variety of reasons. Nor would I have met my wife, Becky, and there's no telling where I would be or how my business career would have evolved if I had not discovered my home away from home in Aggieland. Fortunately, when it was time for me to decide on a collegiate destination, I was led to Texas A&M because of the school's academic reputation. A&M turned out to be the perfect place for me. Perhaps it was the friendliness of the students on campus; maybe it was the conservative and patriotic culture that permeates the community; or possibly it was simply the colors that made me feel so at home. I attended Rancier Middle School and graduated from Killeen High School in 1973. Both of those campuses featured maroon and white as the school colors, so I didn't need to change any of my preferences (or any of my wardrobe options) when I arrived in Aggieland.

All I had to do was figure out a major and what I wanted to do with the rest of my life. I arrived at Texas A&M in the fall of 1974 after a year at Central Texas College. The campus and College Station were much different back in the mid-1970s than they are today. Women were first permitted to enroll at Texas A&M in unrestricted numbers in 1969, and women were admitted as members of the Corps of Cadets in '74. My first year at A&M was also when the women's athletic program was established. Primarily because of the addition of women, the enrollment began to grow significantly in that time frame. Back in 1963, A&M had an enrollment of only 8,000 students, but by 1974 the enrollment surpassed 18,000, including 4,000 women. As a result of the rapid growth, dorm rooms were not readily available to many incoming students, including me.

My brother and I lived at the Treehouse Apartments off of Marion Pugh Drive, which is just a stone's throw away from what is now known as George Bush Drive (it was Jersey Street when I was in school). My brother, Lloyd, is a year younger than me, and we lived together throughout our time at Texas A&M. My hard-working parents stretched and sacrificed for both of us to go to college, but we were also instructed not to waste time in securing our degrees. Our purpose at A&M, my father reminded us both, was to receive a top-flight education so that we could be in the best position for long-term career success. He was not opposed to us having fun, but he was not paying for us to experience the "college life." As such, his instructions to us were rather simple and straightforward: *Get it done in four years and get on with your career.*

When I initially enrolled at A&M, I thought a management major through the business school seemed like a good idea. I didn't possess a clear vision regarding my long-term career plans or what a management degree would do for me, but as I began taking classes in the business school, some things began to click for me. Ironically, I began to find my niche in a class (Accounting 101) that was designed to weed people out of the business school. While many of my classmates absolutely despised Accounting 101, it made sense to me and the way my mind worked. To me, accounting seemed quite logical, and halfway through my sophomore year, I made the decision to switch from being a management major to an accounting major. For numerous reasons, it was a good fit for me.

My brother and I both worked hard throughout our time at A&M, because we knew the expectations our parents had for us. Times were much different, and it was much easier to complete an A&M degree in four years back when we were in school than it is today. Don't misunderstand me. It wasn't easy, but it was easier than it is today. We kept our focus on our schoolwork, but we also managed to have some good times. Our collegiate days, for example, were especially good times for Texas A&M's football program.

The addition of thousands of females to the student body wasn't the only significant change at A&M in the 1970s. In, 1976 Fred McClure was elected by the student body as our first black president, which was two years after Gail Sedberry became the first black female member of the Corps of Cadets in '74. Also in 1976 Kim Tomes became Texas A&M's first Miss USA.

Head football coach Emory Bellard also arrived at A&M in that decade (1972), two years before my brother and me. Bellard's first signing class in 1972 helped A&M become a much more diverse university. That class marked the first time an A&M coach had actively pursued African-American athletes in large numbers. Bellard didn't specifically go after black athletes. He only instructed his coaching staff to find the best athletes. The end result was a 41-member signing class that instantly gave the Aggies a shot in the arm and eventually gave A&M a shot at the national championship. Some of the marquee names in that class include African-Americans like Edgar Fields, Pat Thomas, Bubba Bean, Jackie Williams, Skip Walker and Carl Roaches.

Prior to Bellard's arrival in '72, the Aggies had endured 13 losing seasons in a span of 14 years. And during Bellard's first two seasons, A&M struggled to records of 3-8 and 5-6. But by the start of the 1974 season, it was apparent that the class would form the nucleus of something special. The '74 Aggies posted the school's first winning season (8-3) in seven years. Then in 1975, things truly came together as A&M rolled to a 10-0 start and was ranked as high as No. 2 nationally, before losing the last game of the year at Arkansas. Nevertheless, the '75 Aggies were as loaded with premier players as any team in the school's history, as 21 of the 22 starters in '75 went on to play in the NFL.

My brother and I loved following Aggie football, as did my parents, who came to campus every Saturday in the fall to catch up with their sons and to watch Aggie football. My father died in 2010, but at the time of this writing, my mother is still alive and still in love with Aggie football. She will only occasionally attend a game, but she always watches the Aggies on television.

When my brother and I were not taking care of our coursework or following Aggie athletics, we did manage to meet two extremely significant women who would help shape our futures. My brother met his future wife, Caron, in 1976. Caron and her sister were our neighbors at the Treehouse Apartments, and Lloyd eventually asked Caron out on a date. Meanwhile, I took a liking to one of Caron's sorority sisters, the former Becky Woodruff, who was a member of Delta Zeta Sorority. Like so many other things that have changed over the decades at Texas A&M, the Greek life was so much smaller in the 1970s than it is today. There were only a half dozen sororities and two fraternities at that time.

Lloyd and I would occasionally meet Caron and several of our friends on campus between classes at the Memorial Student Center, where we would grab a cup of coffee or a snack. On the way to one of those meetings, Caron introduced me to an attractive young woman named Becky, who was an elementary education major from Cleburne. She was bright, engaging and captivated my attention. Unlike me, Becky was raised on A&M spirit and traditions, as they were passed down to her by many members of her family who were Aggies. She made quite an impression on me right away, although I obviously didn't make a similarly strong impression on her. To this day, she doesn't remember meeting me for the first time at the Harrington Education Center, as she claims we met later But that's not something I will forget.

Meeting Becky was obviously one of the defining moments of my time at Texas A&M, and it didn't take me long to realize she was *the ONE* for me. We met in 1976, and by August 1977—shortly after I earned my A&M degree—we were married. Not only did I have my partner for life at that point; I also had a foundation for success. Looking back on it now, my parents gave my brother and me guidance, a moral foundation and a strong work ethic before we went to A&M. But A&M was definitely the springboard that propelled me to accomplish some great things. Before I ever officially entered the workforce, I felt equipped to tackle any challenge. Becky was not just my better half, she was my partner, and we vowed to work as a team no matter where life might take us. Little did we know then that it would take us on a whirlwind adventure around the globe.

DAVIS' PATH TO ENTREPRENEURIAL SUCCESS

With a new wife and a fresh Texas A&M degree in hand, I accepted an accounting position with Dresser Industries Petroleum and Minerals Group in Houston in 1977. At the time, Dresser Industries was a multinational corporation headquartered in Dallas, which provided a wide range of technology, products and services used for developing energy and natural resources. The company traced its roots all the way back to when founder Solomon Dresser created a "packer," using rubber for a tight fit that he advertised and sold to oilfield employers as the *Dresser Cap Packer*. Then in 1885, he invented a flexible coupling called the *"Dresser Joint,"* which linked pipes together in such a way that they would not leak natural gas. The coupling was so successful that it permitted for the first time the long-range transmission of natural gas from the gas fields where it was extracted to the cities, which were the main gas consumers.

From left, Kelsey, Cristina, Monty and Becky Davis

In the ensuing decades, the company evolved tremendously and grew substantially, but when I came onboard in '77, Dresser Industries was still operating with plenty of old-school technology practices. Many companies, including Dresser, had a significant need for entry-level accountants because it required many more of us than it does today. The reason? Not many personal computers back then in the workplace or anywhere else. In 1977, the most popular personal computer was probably Radio Shack's TRS-80, which had an initial production run of just 3,000 computers. Then in 1978, the accounting world was introduced to VisiCalc, the first computerized spreadsheet program. Still, the business environment was an entirely different world than it is today.

Speaking of different worlds, Houston was a much different, eye-opening experience than Becky and I could have imagined, as we were both raised in small towns and attended Texas A&M in a much different community than it is today. We had no family in the Houston area, which forced us to rely on each other and to develop new friendships. Becky and I lived in an apartment off the Southwest Freeway, and we were both working, driving through traffic every day. She was initially teaching and then went to work for a construction company as an estimator. Looking back on those times, we didn't have much, but we didn't need much, either. We poured ourselves into our work, our marriage and eventually our first daughter, Kelsey, who was born in August 1981.

Things were going well for us, and I was eventually promoted to a comptroller position within Dresser's international group. As I continued to work my way up the Dresser corporate ladder, I heard about an opening for the North Sea comptroller based in Aberdeen, Scotland. During the 1970s, following the discovery of North Sea oil, Aberdeen became known as the off-shore oil capital of Europe. Geologists had speculated about the existence of oil and gas in the North Sea since the middle of the 20th century, but it wasn't until the mid-1970s that enough infrastructure was in place to tap into the North Sea's deep and inhospitable waters to produce major oil finds.

I didn't possess an extensive knowledge of Aberdeen or the North Sea's oil potential when I first learned about the opening, but I did believe it might be a good opportunity to prove my worth to the company and to further broaden my knowledge. Becky and I talked about the opening, and she was supportive of packing everything up (we didn't have much at the time) and moving to Aberdeen, Scotland's third most populous city and the home of more than 300 castles. With Becky's consent, I approached the Vice President of my division and volunteered to take the opening in Scotland. He initially believed that would be a lateral move for me, at best, and possibly a step backward. But a few days later he came to me and said, "The one thing I wish I had done when I was your age was to travel and to explore the world while building my career. If you want the job, it is yours."

I was thrilled. Becky was excited, as well. Our parents, on the other hand, were less than ecstatic about us taking their 18-month-old granddaughter to Scotland. Unfortunately, I was not yet an avid golfer, and I didn't take advantage of the historic courses. The sport was born on the eastern coast of Scotland (south of Aberdeen) in the Kingdom of Fife during the 15th century. The earliest players would hit a pebble around a natural course of sand dunes, rabbit runs and tracks using a stick or primitive club. Golf's status and popularity quickly spread throughout the 16th century due to its royal endorsements, as King Charles I popularized the game in England and Mary Queen of Scots introduced the game to France. But Scotland was the birthplace of the game, and I only wish I had played in Scotland back then, as I was not far from the Royal Aberdeen Golf Club, which was founded in 1780.

Of course, I probably didn't have the time or the money to play such a prestigious course back then anyway. Becky stayed at home with Kelsey, and I worked as diligently and relentlessly as possible. I was initially placed as the head of finance for Dresser Atlas' operations overseeing the Netherlands, Norway and the United Kingdom. In less than a year, we also added Algeria, four locations in the Middle East, Germany and the Netherlands. It was an unbelievable and invaluable learning experience for me, as I gained tremendous international business knowledge that ultimately proved to be instrumental in my overall career development. Once I had my foot in the international division's doorway, I made the most of it as I was extremely intrigued by international business and the way different cultures viewed commerce.

We enjoyed our time in Scotland, and it was obviously a move that paid off for me professionally because it began to open my eyes—quite literally—to a world of possibilities. Whenever I speak to college students and other young people today, I advise them to make calculated moves, especially early in their careers. If you want to grow as a person, a businessman, an entrepreneur, an employee, a spouse, a parent and so forth, it is often tremendously beneficial to leave the comfort zone of your familiar surroundings. There are so many reasons I encourage young, career-minded and ambitious people to venture out on their own, whether it's a new city, a different state or a new country. If you never leave your hometown, you'll always be contained within strictures not of your own making. At home you're always only an outgrowth of your perceived past. No matter what you do, many people will still perceive you as "Little Johnny," the high school jock or Joe and Debbie's kid. It's always been that way. Even the Bible reminds us of this in Mark 6:4, which states (New Living Translation): "Then Jesus told them, 'A prophet is honored everywhere except in his own hometown and among his relatives and his own family.'"

In a new location, though, you can define yourself, write your own story, be judged on your merits and establish your worth by your own productivity. On the other hand, it's difficult to discover yourself when you're defined so much by your heritage and the perceptions others have formed about your family and their place. Unfortunately, most Americans never venture too far from their hometown. According to a 2015 *New York Times* article, the typical American adult lives only 18 miles from his or her mother. Similarly, a 2008 Pew Research Center survey found that, with the exception of college or military service, 37 percent of Americans had **never** lived outside their hometown, and 57 percent had never lived outside their home state. Finally, an Allstate/National Journal Heartland Monitor poll found that 54 percent of respondents said that they lived in close proximity to where they grew up, and only 11.6 percent of the population moved between 2010 and 2011, the lowest rate of movement since such trends began being tracked in the 1940s.

Personally, leaving the Lone Star State and the United States was a wonderful period of growth in my life, my career, my marriage, my parenting skills, my faith and so much more. It forced me to grow up quickly, to meet new people from all different kinds of backgrounds, to step outside of my comfort zone and so much more. I think that is especially important to do today because we live in an increasingly global business environment where the connectivity of the world's economies and cultures grow rapidly and change regularly. Understanding different cultures and countries can be a huge advantage for you now and into the future.

We were in Aberdeen for a few years and then a bigger and better job became available in

London, so we moved on to England in 1985. We found a house to rent right next to the All England Lawn Tennis and Croquet Club, a private club that was founded on July 23, 1868. Since 1877, the club has also been the home of Wimbledon, which is considered the world's premier tennis tournament. The back fence of our rent home was also the fence line of one of the practice courts at the All England Club in Wimbledon. We had an opportunity to attend the tournament several times, and we once hosted a young player in our home from Australia, who was playing in Wimbledon and made it through a couple of rounds. We weren't necessarily seeking a home location near such a prestigious landmark; we were really just looking for a place with a backyard where Kelsey could play. But it certainly worked out for the best.

I held various positions with Dresser Atlas while in England, continuing to travel throughout Europe, Africa and the Middle East. People who know how much I have traveled throughout my career often ask me if I enjoy going to different countries, regions and continents. International travel is interesting, but it's not as exciting as many people would assume. It can be taxing and troublesome, especially when doing business. While many people around the world know English, it is sometimes quite difficult to understand everything they are saying because English is their second or third language. You really need to be able to read people and to truly understand what they are saying before shaking hands on an agreement or signing something. I've also learned to be cautious in my travels.

I have been to some dangerous places in Nigeria, Venezuela and Colombia when the drug wars were significant. And obviously, much of the Middle East seems to be on the constant brink of bloodshed and violence. Fortunately, I have never been in a situation where I felt extremely threatened, but you must learn to keep your eyes open wherever you go. You need to be aware of your surroundings wherever you go, as opposed to having all your attention on your smart phone, computer or even the scenery around you. Be alert to who and what might be surveying, monitoring or following you. The most nervous I ever was on a trip was in Algeria, when the country was having quite a bit of trouble with rebels. The oil company representatives that I was meeting with provided me with escorts and bodyguards. But as we were driving around, I realized I could have painted a big target on my back and been less obvious. I was not real thrilled with armed escorts everywhere I went, as they just drew more attention to me. I also knew that if the rebels came after me, they were just going to shoot my escorts before they kidnapped me. Fortunately, that never happened, but I've learned to be on guard…and not just in terms of my personal safety.

Situational ethics exist in America, but they are even more common internationally. Here's the bottom line: If someone mentions "situational ethics," it means he/she is trying to talk you into something you shouldn't do. Your ethics are your ethics. You don't steal from people, you don't cheat and you don't lie. You will never have a longtime successful business career or life doing those things. There is no such thing as situational ethics in my book. I've been asked to do things or to turn a blind eye away from things, but I've always been firm about sticking to my core values. We stress that all the time to our employees.

I've been successful with a company that does business with over 100 countries. That's because we are committed to doing things the right way. We may lose a contract, but we are going to stay with our ethics and our business practices.

Companies, technologies and times change, but your core values should never waver. Speaking of companies changing, in 1987, Western Atlas was formed through the merger of Western Geophysical (owned by Litton Industries) and Dresser Atlas. The resulting company was a joint venture of Litton and Dresser Industries.

Cristina Davis-Blackwood and her father dancing on her wedding day

By that time, Becky and I were ready to move back to the U.S., the Lone Star State and Houston, where Western Atlas was headquartered. We planned on planting some long-term roots in Houston, but as it turned out, we were only in H-Town for four and a half months before moving to Dallas. The person who was going to be the CFO at Western Atlas in Houston called me to his office three times one particularly memorable day. He called me once in the morning. Then he called me that afternoon, as I was planning a trip in the Middle East to establish a new company. I met with a gentlemen who was the president of a business unit called Core Laboratories, which had become a division of Western Atlas International in 1987. We talked about my trip, and I went on my way. But then my boss called me back later in the afternoon and asked me to visit with him for a third time. Usually, I didn't see him more than once a week, so I knew something was on his mind. The third time in his office was the charm, because he told me he wanted me to become the Vice President of Finance for Core Laboratories, which was in Dallas at the time. That sounded great to me because I really wanted out of corporate accounting and wanted back into the operations and financial management scene.

The only issue, he said, was that I would need to move to Dallas. We'd only been in Houston for four and a half months, so I called Becky later that day and asked her what she was doing. "I just unpacked the last box from the move," she said triumphantly. "How's your day going?"

I barely had the courage to tell her what was on my mind at that that moment. I asked her where in the house she was, and she said she was in the bedroom. "OK, I think you should sit down for a moment," I said. "An opportunity has come up, and we are moving to Dallas so I can become the Vice President of Finance for Core Laboratories. I believe it's a really good career move for us." Once again, we chose to make some personal sacrifice as an investment for our long-term future.

MONTY DAVIS | 61

We moved to Dallas in 1987, I started with Core Laboratories and we stayed in Big D…for a grand total of just nine months! That's how long it was before Core Laboratories moved us back to Houston. In hindsight, it would have been nice to know that we were only going to be in Houston for four and a half months and then in Dallas for nine months. We wouldn't have bought two homes for such short stints. It is not easy packing up everything and selling your house over and over again, but looking back, we wouldn't trade those experiences for anything. They shaped and strengthened us, and we grew because of those experiences. I served as Core Laboratories' Division Vice President of Finance from 1987 to 1991, and I then made the decision to return to Atlas Wireline Division (formerly known as Western Atlas) as Vice President of Finance and Administration from 1991 to 1993.

One of the keys to any amount of success that I have achieved has been making an impact wherever I worked and leaving a company on good terms. Although I am probably not an entrepreneur in the truest form, I have taken an entrepreneurial approach for each company where I have worked. As my late friend and fellow Texas Aggie Artie McFerrin often said, "Always think like a CEO because we are all CEOs of our own lives." I've always poured myself into every company where I've worked, attempting to make myself invaluable. The reality is that no one is irreplaceable, but I wanted my employers to think of me as a crucial part of the team. I also made sure that I never burned any bridges when I left a company for another job. That's why I was able to return to Western Atlas in 1991, and it's why I eventually returned to Core Laboratories. More on that later.

During our second stint in Houston (or third if you include the four and half months following our return from England), we adopted our youngest daughter, Cristina. We found Cristina through a contact with Core Lab's office in Colombia. Adoption was a lengthy process, but it eventually came together, and we adopted Cristina when she was about 18 months old. She had been in a true state orphanage. Her birth mother went into the hospital, delivered Cristina and left. They never heard from her mother afterward. According to Columbian laws, Cristina could not be placed for adoption until officials had at least one year to locate her mother. That never happened, which is why she was placed with us at 18 months old. When we first gained custody of her, she didn't really walk or talk. She was also a bit malnourished. We were required to stay in Columbia for 40 days and 40 nights before taking her back to Houston. So, we loaded up the family and took Kelsey, who was nine, to Columbia. Kelsey's school officials approved of the trip to Columbia, agreeing that a trip to a foreign country would be an educational experience for her.

We adopted Cristina and took her on her first day with us to a Colombian doctor, who added some nutrients and supplements to her diet to alleviate the malnourishment. Within a week of being part of our family, she was walking and started to talk. It was amazing to see what the power of love and some basic nutritional needs did for her. After 40 days, we returned to Houston. Shortly thereafter, another career opportunity sent us out of the country once again. The former president of the Core Lab Business Unit was working for a company in Canada called Bovar Inc. of Calgary, which was an environmental company. He asked me to come to Calgary for a visit, and I eventually accepted his offer to serve as Chief Operating Officer. I served in that role from 1994-95 and was then promoted to President and Chief Executive Officer of Bovar from 1995-98.

We spent about five years in Calgary, which is in the Canadian province of Alberta. Calgary is the center of Canada's oil industry, and it is steeped in the western culture that earned it the same nickname as Fort Worth, Texas: "Cowtown." We enjoyed living in Calgary, and as Kelsey neared her high school graduation, I began encouraging her to look at possibly attending the University of Alberta or the University of British Columbia in Vancouver. She just looked at me like I was from outer space and said, "I'm going to A&M." That's when Becky began encouraging me to find a way back to the Lone Star State. It turned out to be extremely good timing, because Bovar Inc. was 55 percent owned by another publicly traded company that made a decision to divest their affiliates. We were working through that when one of my former colleagues at Core Lab called me up and said there was a great opportunity back in Houston to serve as the Senior Vice President at Core Lab. I am convinced it was God's timing, and it was a perfect time to go back to Texas. Kelsey finished her senior year of high school in Cypress and started at Texas A&M in 1999, the same year I was promoted to Chief Operating Officer at Core. Obviously, watching our daughter attend our alma mater was a proud moment for Kelsey's mother and me.

Many more proud moments would follow. Kelsey earned her degree in International Studies in 2004. A few years later, Cristina also followed the family's maroon footsteps to Texas A&M, where she received a degree in International Studies and a Masters in International Affairs from the Bush School. Becky and I are so proud of both of them for so many reasons, and it delights us that both of our daughters majored in an international field after spending much of their childhoods seeing the world. Both of our daughters also married bright men. Kelsey is married to Mack T. Nolen, A&M Class of '04, who has a degree in Political Science and a Masters in International Affairs from the Bush School. Cristina, who graduated from A&M in 2012, is married to Simon Blackwood, who has a Masters in Quality Management from Robert Gordons University in Aberdeen, Scotland.

DAVIS' MOST CHALLENGING OBSTACLES

In retrospect, it's difficult for me to single out one or two specific obstacles that have really defined or stretched me as a business leader. In reality, there have been hundreds upon hundreds of challenges—some major, some fairly minor—that have tested, molded and strengthened me ever since I left Texas A&M and joined the staff at Dresser Industries in 1977. Quite frankly, the challenges have continued to grow as I have evolved as a business leader and my responsibilities have expanded. I've discovered that you get ahead taking those challenges head on and persevering through any obstacles.

As an entrepreneur or business leader, I can practically guarantee that you will be tested by personnel issues. Businesses are a multi-variable equation, and some of the most disappointing challenges I have experienced have involved people on our staff who behave in a way that is not loyal or expected. That happens. It's a fact of life and business. People who you trusted and relied upon will occasionally let you down and betray that trust. That is certainly a difficult situation, but you must be prepared to deal with that. I've often been disappointed by someone's actions or words, but I am no longer surprised. As President Ronald Regan once stated, "Trust, but verify." That phrase entered American consciousness when Reagan's adviser on Russian affairs, Suzanne Massie, was preparing the president for talks with Mikhail Gorbachev in 1986. Perhaps Reagan ought to learn a few Russian proverbs, Massie suggested, and the one he liked best was "Doveryai no proveryai" — trust, but verify. Reagan liked it so much, in fact, that Gorbachev expressed annoyance at the president for using it at every meeting. The line worked brilliantly for Reagan's purposes. The "trust" part suggested good faith toward the Russians; the "verify" part disarmed the president's domestic critics, who worried that the administration would commit the United States to a deal the Russians had no intention of honoring.

The phrase is still applicable today, and not just regarding foreign relations. It's a phrase that has crossed my mind many times with our own personnel issues. And your business success will likely be determined by how you handle your people and address personnel issues and read people. McDonald's founder Ray Kroc once said, "You are only as good as the people you hire." I wholeheartedly agree. You don't really build a business. You build people, and those people build the business. The issue for any entrepreneur or CEO is finding the right people. Practically everyone will be on his/her best behavior and will be impressive in the interview process. But the key is being able to read people, and you only develop that ability by studying people. Even the best leaders make hiring mistakes, but the better you hire, the more successful you will likely be.

At my level, the most important thing I can do is to put together the right team. Like a football coach putting together a championship-caliber team, it's not as easy as simply finding the most talented people. It is sometimes more important to find hard-nosed individuals who will be focused on the team's greatest interests. That's not easy, and as the leader of your organization, you must be constantly in search of the right people. And once you find them, it's imperative to keep them as long as possible.

That takes constant communication, whether that involves rewarding someone who is doing a great job or correcting someone who is failing to meet the team's standards. I don't want to mention any specific issues, but perhaps the best thing I have done as a leader is making sure that my executive team is focused, motivated and moving in the right direction. It's much like the football coach analogy in that if I don't hire the right assistant coaches, I am not going to be successful, and neither is the team. Making sure the right people are on the bus is not enough. You must also make sure that everyone is intent on going in the same direction. To do that, as a leader, you must constantly communicate and display the vision and mission of the company. It's not my job to accomplish spectacular things; it's my job to attract and inspire my people to do spectacular work. I have constantly been motivated to surround myself with the most talented people I can find. Our business would not have prospered like it has if we had not remained adamant about investing in high-quality people and coaching them to help them achieve their best results.

Success in leadership also requires learning as quickly as the world is changing. Technology is constantly developing, while the world is growing smaller and quicker every day. Communication is now instantaneous. When I started in this business, we were sending telexes, and you would receive a reply in a couple of days from the other side of the world. Now, communication is real time, whether it's across the country or around the world. But just because someone on the other side of the world receives my communication doesn't mean that he/she understands what I meant to say. One of the biggest obstacles in operating an international business is understanding all the different cultures and how they communicate. Some things are easily lost in translation, which can impact the bottom line in terms of millions of dollars in any given transaction. That's why it is still important for me to meet face-to-face with other business leaders in all parts of the world. No matter how technology evolves, there is no replacing human interaction and a handshake. You must learn as a leader when it's best to utilize technology and when it's best to take a long trip.

Ultimately, running a business is all about people. While there are many things out of your control, a leader must set the tone of his/her company's culture and must constantly nurture that culture. If you do not develop your corporate culture, it will develop itself…either positively or negatively. Establishing and maintaining the proper corporate culture is a major challenge for any leader, but it's worth its weight in gold. As management consultant, educator and author Peter Drucker once so eloquently stated, "Culture eats strategy for breakfast."

DAVIS' ADVICE TO YOUNG ENTREPRENEURS

One of my true passions in life is hunting. Not just any kind of hunting, though. The tougher the challenge, the better. The more adventurous the journey, the more enjoyable. And the more dangerous the mission, the more exhilarating.

First and foremost, I absolutely love nature and thoroughly enjoy traveling the world to witness and admire God's creations. From the mountaintops of America to the jungles of Zimbabwe, our world is a fascinating and breathtaking tribute to the artistic eye and creativity of our creator. I find it extremely relaxing to experience nature, and I tend to gravitate toward the extreme end of hunting because I love challenges. For example, I've had the opportunity to pursue and achieve the coveted North American Grand Slam of Sheep, comprised of four distinct subspecies. This is some of the most difficult and challenging hunting anywhere. While I realize some people disagree with hunting, the reality is that hunters are often the primary conservationists. At the Wild Sheep Foundation's convention each January, single hunting permits from various states, provinces and Indian reservations are auctioned off to the highest bidders. Most go for well more than $100,000. In 2013, a permit in Montana sold for $480,000, still a record at the time of this writing. That money is typically used to fund wildlife organizations and to protect endangered species and environments. Becky and I support the Wild Sheep Foundation as Marco Polo Members, and wildlife conservation is a major focus for me.

It is estimated that there were millions of wild sheep in North America 200 years ago. But by the 1950s, squeezed out by people and livestock and decimated by diseases (especially carried by domestic sheep), the wild sheep population dwindled into the tens of thousands. Conservation efforts saved the sheep and have expanded their territory again, often by transplanting herds and greatly limiting hunting opportunities. It is estimated that there are now nearly 200,000 wild sheep in North America…thanks in large part to hunters who are funding conservation efforts and protecting habitats. Habitat loss is the critical issue for wildlife conservation around the globe.

The United States Fish and Wildlife Service estimates that there are more than 10 million big-game hunters in the United States. But only about 2,500 wild sheep are hunted each year across North America, a fraction compared with nearly every other animal. This shows the difficulty, dedication and perseverance required to hunt rams.

Non-hunters often presume that the biggest prize in North America is something large or fierce—a bear, an elk or maybe a moose. But the widespread belief among serious hunters is that rams are the ultimate pursuit. For one, opportunities to hunt sheep are scarce, and they are often prohibitively expensive. Two, the hunts are among the most difficult in some of the most remote regions on Earth. That's part of the challenge I embrace. Taking the North American Grand Slam of Sheep involved learning about the animals and their behavior, preparing physically to climb mountains, tracking the rams and persevering some dangerous situations and terrain. I spent many days climbing mountains and many nights sleeping in a tiny little tent while eating freeze-dried foods. The hunt thrilled me, but it was overcoming the challenges that truly invigorated and inspired me.

In 2017, I also completed the "Big Five in Africa," which refers to the five most difficult animals in Africa to hunt on foot (I used a tranquilizer dart on the rhino and elephant). The members of the Big Five were chosen for the difficulty in hunting them and the degree of danger involved, rather than their size. One of the most interesting aspects of the Big Five hunt involved tracking the rhino. Both the black and white rhino are at risk of extinction due to the poaching epidemic caused by the demand for rhino horn in Asian cultures. It is estimated that there are around 5,000 black rhino and 20,000 white rhino left in the wild. Because of that, I used a tranquilizer dart and tracked a particular female rhino because her electronic tracking bracelet that protected her from poachers had stopped working. She was a smart animal, but we finally caught up with her and darted her. Rhinos don't often go down when they are drugged, so she was standing in a sedated state when my guide raced up to her to replace the electronic tracking bracelet with one that worked. I was holding the screws for the new bracelet with one hand on the rhino's hip. My guide cut the old bracelet off, looked up at me and said, "Don't let her fall on me." Since she weighed about 6,000 pounds, I told him that I would give him a warning if she started falling his way, but that was about all I could do. Fortunately, we didn't have any issues, and once the new tracking device was in place, he administered the drug to wake her up. Being that close to a 6,000-pound animal, however, was quite the adrenaline rush. It's one that I will never forget.

So, what do my hunting stories have to do with my advice to young entrepreneurs and aspiring business leaders? Everything. In practically any endeavor, the biggest rewards will be earned by taking on the biggest challenges. That's been true for me in hunting, and it has most certainly been the case in my life as a businessman. The key to any amount of success I have achieved has been my willingness to accept different challenges, whether that has involved uprooting my family for a new international destination or stepping out of my comfort zone into a new role with a new company and persevering in my endeavors.

I have always found that you will be better off in the long run by taking the most challenging assignment or role. Taking on a difficult assignment will make you grow and make you a better asset to your company or your own business. Taking on difficult tasks will also improve your ability to make tough decisions. Any successful entrepreneur or businessman must be capable of regularly making decisions. As the leader of your own company or even the manager of your business unit, your course will be determined by the decisions you make. And if you have not yet ventured into the business world, you would probably be surprised and quite disappointed by just how many people—even people in leadership positions—can't make a decision. It seems like so many people are so afraid of making a mistake that they avoid making decisions. Others are purposely vague or not outspoken because they are afraid of confrontation or offending anyone. Let me assure you that if you want to be a leader, you will offend people. You will also be involved in confrontations. And you will most certainly make mistakes. After all, the only person who never makes a mistake is the person who never does anything.

I tell all the people who work for me that if they are not making any mistakes, they are not doing near enough. So embrace failures, mistakes and shortcomings because they not only make us uniquely who we are, but also teach us powerful lessons. Mistakes teach us, through analysis and feedback, about what works and what doesn't. They also teach us to take responsibility. Sometimes our instinctive reaction to a mistake is to shift blame elsewhere. Taking responsibility for a failure may not be fun, but doing so develops personal integrity and causes others around you to trust you even more. And ultimately, your mistakes will inspire you and others to find better ways. I always tell our personnel to attempt to minimize the impact of mistakes and maximize successes. But if you are not making mistakes, you are not doing enough. Step outside of your comfort zone without fear of failing. And learn from every mistake and setback. As the New Zealand mountaineer, explorer and philanthropist Sir Edmund Hillary said after he scaled Mount Everest, "It is not the mountain we conquer, but ourselves." When we learn from our mistakes, we begin to move toward reaching our potential for greatness.

Besides, if you really want to attract positive attention from your employers or customers and to win rave reviews, it will be less about avoiding mistakes and more about solving issues. If you can develop a reputation as a problem-solver, you will receive great opportunities to grow and prosper as an executive. You learn so much more from those opportunities than what you may have been told by a professor or a boss.

Be known also as a person of impeccable integrity and character. While that seems like such common sense, it's really rare in the workplace. I am convinced that most people are not going to steal large amounts of money from your company, and they probably won't try to take off with big office furniture or expensive computers. But I am often disappointed by how many people will waste time at work on mindless tasks like socializing with fellow employees or visiting social media sites during their work hours. Speaking of social media, it is critical not to be distracted in a world that is full of distractions. Unless you're employed to handle social media at your company, work is not the place to post photos, to comment on other friends' posts, to hold political discussions or to provide commentary on last weekend's games. There's a time and a place for all of that, but it's not at work. If you are collecting a paycheck, especially early in your career, make sure you are proving your worth. Stick to the core values that Texas A&M instills in its students—excellence, integrity, leadership, loyalty, respect and selfless service—and the rest will often take care of itself.

Also, be willing to learn new things without compartmentalizing yourself. Your degree may have been in marketing, accounting, engineering, communications, economics or any other thing, but don't limit yourself to one area of expertise. Learn every aspect of your company, especially as a young businessperson. Whether you want to eventually start your own business or rise to the top of the corporate ladder, the more you know about the various departments, the more valuable you will be as a leader. Take on new tasks; ask questions; volunteer to work in other departments and always be curious. When you leave Texas A&M, you have a base education, and it is a dang good one. But understand as a recent graduate that there is so much about this world that you don't yet know. So treat every day as an opportunity to learn and improve. If you are just starting with a company, resolve to give that company your best effort every day. You probably won't be at that company forever, but as long as you are working for that company, be there, be on time and be invaluable every day. That is a critical mindset to getting ahead. Whether you think you are paid enough or not is not relevant to your career, especially in your early years. What is relevant is that you are committed to doing your best every day. It is difficult sometimes, but you will be recognized for it. And one day, you will thrive as an entrepreneur, CEO or anything else because of your consistent commitment to excellence.

Finally, I believe it is extremely important to document your goals and dreams. Throughout the course of history, studies have continually proven that those people who write their goals are much more likely to achieve them than those who don't. For example, in 2016, Dr. Gail Matthews, a psychology professor at the Dominican University in California, studied the science of goal setting, as documented in a story in the *Huffington Post*. She gathered 267 people—men and women from all over the world, and from all walks of life, including entrepreneurs, educators, healthcare professionals, artists, lawyers and bankers. She divided the participants into groups, according to who wrote their goals and dreams on paper, and who didn't. She discovered that those who wrote their goals were 42 percent more likely to achieve them, simply by writing them down on a regular basis.

There is scientific evidence to support this conclusion. The human brain has a left and a right hemisphere, and the bundle of neural fibers that connects the two hemispheres is called the corpus callosum. This is the conduit through which the electrical signals between the right brain, which is imaginative, and the left brain, which is literal, make contact. The electrical signals then move into the fluid that surrounds the brain and travels up and down the spinal column. The signals communicate with every fiber, cell and bone in your body to the consciousness that operates within us to transform our thoughts into reality. This is significant, because if you merely think about one of your goals or dreams, you're only using the right hemisphere of your brain, which is your imaginative center. But if you think about something that you desire, and then physically write it, you also tap into the power of your logic-based left hemisphere. Consequently, you send your consciousness and every cell of your body a signal that says, "This goal is important to me. It must be achieved."

Personally, I keep a desk diary. I always have, and it is the easiest way for me to prepare for the day, week, month, year and so forth. In the back of my diary, there are a bunch of blank pages where I set certain personal goals for the year. I set goals regarding how much time am I spending focusing on the family, how many days I want to play golf, how many times I want to go hunting, financial goals for the year and so forth. I also include business goals, targets I want to hit, how many customers I am going to visit a year and so forth.

Then I frequently chart those goals throughout the whole year so that I can determine how I am progressing toward those goals. Sometimes, I reassess my goals. Other times circumstances dictate that other objectives have risen to greater importance. But the bottom line is that writing my goals and charting them regularly helps me to stay focused on what is really important and what is not. If you really want to accomplish great things in your life, take the time to document those goals and objectives. You will often be amazed years later when you look back at those goals and realize how much you have achieved, how much you have grown and how powerful it is to simply document your dreams.

CHAPTER 5
Terrence Murphy
CEO and Founder
TM5 Team and Terrence Murphy Companies
Texas A&M Class of 2005

MURPHY'S PATH TO TEXAS A&M

Looking back on my childhood and my course to Texas A&M University, I probably didn't fully appreciate the difficulty of the journey. That's not a misprint. I know some people look back on their childhood as a carefree time, and they long for those simpler, easier times. I am not one of those people.

Growing up in Chapel Hill, a small rural community a few miles east of Tyler, and earning a scholarship to Texas A&M was not easy. Nor was it a particularly carefree time in my life. Not having a great relationship with my biological father, watching neighborhood friends fall victim to drugs and crime, seeing my mother battle for her life following a heart attack, starting my first lawn mowing job at the age of 12, flipping burgers at Dairy Queen, sacking groceries at Albertsons to help make ends meet and attracting college recruiters while playing on a football team that went 1-19 my first two years on the varsity did not make for an easy path to Aggieland. Besides, my high school had not produced a major, Division I scholarship player in almost 10 years, so the odds of being noticed were stacked against me. These are just a few obstacles I encountered, which combined to give me the chip on my shoulder at the time…and one I still carry to this day. It wasn't my choice to do things the hard way; it was just my only option. I would have changed some things about my story, but to be totally honest, that's life. It produced within me grit, substance and a never-ending desire to work hard at an early age.

I truly give thanks for obstacles now. A muscle grows stronger when it encounters resistance; diamonds are formed because of high temperatures and pressure; trees grow deep roots and develop the stress wood they need to remain upright in response to battering winds; and people develop strength, character and courage when encountering and overcoming challenges. Every person in this book and practically every successful person on the planet has faced adversities that have strengthened them. We all know that trials test, toughen and train us for greater triumphs. It's just that in the midst of storms and adversities, it is not easy or natural to embrace the difficulties. But once you see the rainbow after the storm, you can appreciate the journey.

Fortunately for me, I can clearly see now that the difficulties and challenges I faced in my past shaped me into the man I am today. Without a doubt in my mind, I wouldn't be where I am without all the difficult circumstances I faced. I say that not to pat myself on the back or to make my story seem more entertaining or heroic. I say that to encourage you if you are going through difficult times. Chances are that if you are not going through challenges and hurdling obstacles right now, you will be in the near future or may have already dealt with them in your past. That's just the nature of life and entrepreneurship. My hope is that my story can be a source of encouragement to you as you encounter inevitable struggles or if your blueprint for success doesn't go as planned. The bottom line is that—sooner or later—life is probably going to send you to the school of hard knocks. When you're there, make sure you earn your education. Learn from hard times, make the most of difficult circumstances and remember that the biggest challenges will ultimately prepare you for the biggest growth and success. I feel like I am living proof of that and I want to encourage anyone reading this chapter with this simple reminder: It's not where you start that matters; it's where you are going.

Throughout my life God has continually allowed me to face enough trials and tribulations to prepare me for greater triumphs than I could have imagined in endeavors that I could have never envisioned. I never fathomed, for example, that before my 39th birthday my start-up real estate brokerage, TM5 Properties, would go from $0 in sales to $1 billion in sales in eight years. Nor would I have ever believed that it would be possible for me to be among the top one percent among agents in the United States or that I would have personally closed more than 50 $1 million+ transactions as a real estate agent in Bryan-College Station. And I would not have possibly comprehended expanding into all 50 states and into 20 countries, while also building and operating other lines of business under the Terrence Murphy Companies brand where we own and operate over 20 companies. Quite frankly, my original plan never involved returning to Bryan-College Station or becoming an entrepreneur. In my 30s, I figured I would be enjoying my retirement from the Green Bay Packers after winning multiple Super Bowls en route to what would hopefully earn me a spot in the NFL Hall of Fame.

For reasons I will detail later, the Hall of Fame career in the NFL was out of the realm of possibilities before even the midway part of my rookie season. I had to find another way to achieve my dreams. In fact, I had to find entirely new dreams and passions for my life.

While I didn't have a biological father to lead, encourage or inspire me, I did have a great mother and teachers, coaches and principals who saw promise in me as child. I also had sports, and I channeled much of my energies and frustrations into becoming the best athlete possible. From a young age, I could do things on baseball diamonds, basketball courts and football fields that others could not. I also realized that talent alone could not take me where I wanted to go. So, I worked, trained, studied, prepared and prayed as if my entire future depended on the progress I made the next day.

Baseball was actually my best sport, but ever since my mother bought me a Doug Williams/Washington Redskins uniform as a young child—it was a Christmas present that she hoped could double the following fall as a Halloween costume—football became my primary passion. It also didn't hurt that that my older brother, Kendrick Bell, was an exceptional all-around athlete who led Chapel Hill High School to the 1989 Class 4A state championship, beating A&M Consolidated in the title game and rushing for more than 1,500 yards during the season. While Kendrick was admired by many football fans in the community, he was absolutely adored by me. Kendrick was more than just my brother; he was my first hero. When my mother was at work, it was Kendrick who would pick me up at the daycare after his football practices, take me home and feed me. On many of those nights before I went to bed, Kendrick would allow me to watch game film with him as he studied an upcoming opponent.

After his stellar high school career, Kendrick went to Baylor, where he was a running back his first two years and cornerback his final two seasons. From time to time, I was even able to hang out with Kendrick in Waco, spending a couple of nights at a time with him and his teammates in their apartment. I grew to love Baylor football and further admire and appreciate Kendrick. Watching my brother and my hero win a state championship and earn a college scholarship made me want to do the same thing. I knew collegiate athletics could serve as my ticket to a much brighter future.

My total focus on becoming a scholarship-worthy athlete helped me to avoid many of the pitfalls and temptations that derailed some of my friends and other teenagers in the area. Following my mother's heart attack—an ordeal that nearly took her life—I spent virtually all my time working, going to school, playing sports or working out. At 12, I started my first lawn-mowing business finding clients at offices for doctors and dentists, as well as other commercial properties. My mom would drive me 30 minutes into the city, drop me off and I would mow, weed-eat and pick up trash at my properties. Then I would sit under a tree with my water cooler and wait on my mom to come back and get me.

At 15, I was sacking groceries, flipping burgers and continuing to mow yards to earn my own money and ease the financial burden on my mother and step-father. But even then I wasn't just enduring those tedious jobs; I was paying attention and learning from everything and everyone around me. I knew then it was all a test and God had a greater plan for my life. Not once did I believe that I was destined for hourly jobs with little room for growth. I knew there was more. I just needed to be patient, pay my dues and be prepared for an opportunity if it presented itself.

I have always been a chameleon in my ability to blend into an environment and to learn as I watched others. Way back at Dairy Queen I figured out that there are people with an employee mentality, and there are people who are meant to lead. There is absolutely nothing wrong with an employee mentality, and I know many friends and colleagues who can/will happily spend 45 years in the workplace working for others. I think it is very important to realize that if you have that mentality, entrepreneurship is probably not right for you. But if you are a risk taker, believe in yourself at all times, are driven to control your own destiny and are OK with no guaranteed salary, then you're reading the right book.

Honestly, I didn't really know what entrepreneurship was at 15, but I knew I had something deep within me—a gene or something within the core of my being—that made me always step to the front of the line and to step out of the crowd, as opposed to following the "cool kids." Obviously, I didn't immediately demand to take over the managerial role at Dairy Queen, but I did figure out relatively early in my life that I wanted to eventually call my own shots and set the course of direction in the workplace instead of merely following instructions and working for someone else. While I couldn't immediately do that in the work setting, I found another outlet.

In the late 1990s, 7-on-7 football started gaining strong popularity across Texas. Nowadays, there is a Texas State 7-on-7 Association, and the whole process is a well-oiled machine. But during my high school days things began taking shape, and teams were competing around the state in the spring and summer. Because of various UIL rules, coaches from the high schools couldn't actually coach the teams, couldn't oversee practices and couldn't officially do many other things. Our coaches at Chapel Hill had designed some plays and a basic offensive system for us to run that we would then carry into my senior season at quarterback. But after glancing at the plays, I called a mandatory practice with all the skill position guys from the football team at Chapel Hill. We spent about 45 minutes to an hour running the plays our coaches had designed. After practice, I told the guys, "We are not running this crap." Instead, I had my own plan that would make our offense unstoppable.

I went home that night and designed a new offense, with new formations and a new system in which to call the plays. Then I called my top guys and told them on the phone the game plan. We had more than 30 new plays from scratch. I taught those plays to my guys; we practiced them regularly; and we set off to win games against other teams in East Texas in hopes of making it to the state 7-on-7 tournament at Texas A&M. Sound like a risk-taker to you?

Nobody figured we had a prayer because of how poorly the Chapel Hill regular-season football teams had been in recent falls. To make a long story short, though, we almost went undefeated through East Texas. We not only made it to College Station for the state tournament; we also made it to the final day of competition at A&M, and we were among the top 15 teams. My teammates were thrilled, but our regular high school coaches were essentially pissed off that I had changed their plays. My hope was that our coaches would see the effectiveness of my offensive system (it was similar to what Mike Leach was doing at that time at Texas Tech) and that we would implement that offense into the Chapel Hill system in the fall. That never happened, and we continued to stumble. All the success from 7-on-7 fizzled.

During my sophomore year—my first on the varsity—we went 0-10. The following year when I took over as the starting quarterback, we made some dramatic improvements, but we still went 1-9. During my senior year, though, we quadrupled our win total. While that sounds good, it actually means we went 4-6 and didn't have a single winning season in my high school career. During the final two years, I passed for more than 2,500 yards, rushed for over 1,100 yards and contributed to 25 touchdowns. Despite our win-loss record, those numbers helped me to win the District 16-4A Offensive MVP in 2000 in a district that produced over 20 Division I signees in one year.

I think those numbers and my overall play should have helped me earn the attention of many college coaches and recruiting services. But I didn't receive any help from my high school coaches in terms of promoting me to college suitors. I don't know what any of my high school coaches said or didn't say to college coaches, but I do know that I had to produce my own highlight films to send to college coaches… and this was long before the simplicity of digital video technology that allows practically anyone to compile a collection of plays. Fortunately for me, a teacher at Chapel Hill who ran "Bulldog TV" had all the audio and video equipment, as well as the actual footage from the games that I needed. I told her I would sweep her floors, clean her room and perform any necessary grunt work in exchange for some access to the video recorders. I was able to piece together my own highlight tapes. Then I wrote letters to college coaches, following up with phone calls and more phone calls.

The point is—and this also applies to entrepreneurship—that even if you don't know exactly what to do, take action. Doing something is far, far better than doing nothing. If I had merely waited on my high school coaches to take any initiative in my recruiting efforts, I might have never played big-time college football. I was not going to let my problems become bigger than my dreams. I could focus on the problems or focus on the opportunity at hand (a scholarship to a major university), which at the time was the biggest opportunity of my life.

Primarily because of my familiarity with Baylor, along with the school's knowledge of my brother's accomplishments in green and gold, I initially committed to play for the Bears, who were then coached by Kevin Steele. I had also taken a recruiting trip during my senior year to A&M to watch the 2000 game against No. 1-ranked Oklahoma, and even though the Aggies lost a close game to a team that eventually won the national championship, I was extremely impressed with the electric atmosphere of Kyle Field. I was not a five-star recruit, but this was the time where desire and a never-ending work ethic opened the door of opportunity.

Texas A&M head coach R.C. Slocum had commitments from many big-time recruits in that particular signing class and had only a few scholarships left. Assistant coach Tam Hollingshead convinced him to watch the highlight tape I had spent countless hours making, and it was an instant success. Coach Slocum called an immediate coaching staff meeting and they called me from a speakerphone to offer me a scholarship. When Coach Slocum offered me a scholarship after reviewing my highlight film, I took a few weeks to come around to make sure A&M really wanted me. Then I leapt at the opportunity to build a football future and to earn an education in Aggieland. This was truly a life-defining moment, and it was the opportunity I had spent countless hours dreaming about and working toward. The road to that successful moment in my life was quite lonely at times, because I was on a mission that no one around me thought was remotely possible. But I believed it was possible, and I did not let anyone talk me out of the dream. It may seem cliché, but looking back at the odds that were against me, it was only remotely possible with God's favor and a never-ending work ethic.

Once I received the opportunity, I vowed to make the most of it. I only thought I had worked hard in high school. When I arrived in College Station in the summer of 2001, I slept on a couch of some guys on the team, and I was a man on a mission. I busted my butt in the weight room and during voluntary workouts, and I made quite an impression on my teammates, including veteran quarterback Mark Farris, who had a spectacular season in 2000. The reporters asked Farris about the younger guys who had impressed him, and he mentioned me prominently.

The hard work paid off right away. In my first collegiate game, I caught four passes for 79 yards and a touchdown in a 38-24 win over McNeese State, a game we trailed by two touchdowns in the third quarter. I caught the game-winning touchdown in the fourth quarter and was overwhelmed with emotion because I knew the journey I had traveled to reach that point. That was the start of a strong debut season for me. Farris trusted me right from the start, receivers coach Kevin Sumlin mentored me, and I learned from the veteran receivers on the roster. By the end of the season, I led the entire team in receiving yards and average yards per catch, and I finished second behind only Jamaar Taylor with 36 receptions. Even though I dealt with a number of injuries and missed the season-opener in 2002, my sophomore season was even better from an individual standpoint. My overall numbers were better, and in the biggest win of the year and one of the biggest in school history, I caught five passes for 128 yards and two touchdowns in our 30-26 upset victory over No. 1-ranked and previously undefeated Oklahoma. Unfortunately, after the amazing victory over the Sooners, we dropped the next two games and Coach Slocum was fired after the season. It was extremely difficult to say goodbye to him, as well as Coach Sumlin, whom I trusted tremendously.

A&M hired Dennis Franchione as the head coach for that next season and following the devastating 2003 season for our team— it was actually my best year statistically to that point—I did plenty of praying, soul-searching and deliberating. I received plenty of calls about leaving Texas A&M early for the NFL Draft, but I could not leave my beloved university in the state that the program was headed going into my senior season. I decided to return for my senior season and I resolved to carry Texas A&M's football program and its proud history on my back. On one hand, it wasn't my job to pull the team back together. But the reality is that my senior year was on the horizon. I believed that if I didn't take the lead—with my actions and my words—the dysfunction, doubt and disgust would continue to increase while the team chemistry would continue to disintegrate. In essence, I decided I was going to do everything I could to unify the team, with or without any input from the coaching staff.

My solution was to work even harder than ever before. Not just in practices or mandatory workouts, either. When other guys would go hang out, I would go out to the practice fields to work on my quickness, conditioning and commitment in the dead of night. It didn't matter if it was 10 p.m., midnight or 12:30 a.m. I was going to put in the work to lead by actions. It didn't take long for guys—especially younger players— to begin trying to emulate my efforts. And whenever the opportunity presented itself, I used my words to encourage my teammates to push themselves beyond their comfort zones. The turnaround in 2004 certainly was not a result of only my efforts. Many other guys contributed and helped us to rally the troops, generating the unity we needed. Despite a tough start at Utah, we rolled to six straight wins and finished the regular season at 7-4 overall. It wasn't a championship season, but we did earn an invitation to the 2005 Cotton Bowl.

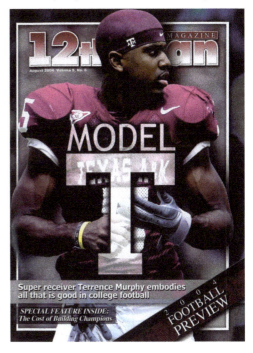

My senior season was the best of my career, as I caught 56 passes and earned first-team All-Big 12 honors. I departed A&M as the leading receiver in school history in receptions and receiving yards, and I was a three-time member of the Big 12 All-Academic team and a two-time All-Big 12 first-team selection. Most of all, I was proud of how I was leaving the football program. Practically every senior class wants to leave a legacy, and I believe the senior class of 2004-05 restored some of the luster that was completely lost during the humbling 2002 and 2003 seasons. I was proud to have played a prominent role in turning things around and placing the Aggies back in a New Year's Day bowl game for the first time since 1998. I hadn't enjoyed playing for Franchione, but I had made the most of my senior season and placed myself in position to fulfill my childhood dreams of playing in the NFL. As I looked toward the 2005 NFL Draft, my football future seemed bright. I had positioned myself as a lock for being selected in the first two rounds of the NFL Draft.

MURPHY'S MOST DIFFICULT CHALLENGE

As long as I live, I'll never forget the night of February 6, 2011. I wanted to be happy, but I couldn't even fake a grin because, at the core of my being, I was miserable. Across the country and around the world, millions of people had spent the day celebrating with friends, family and fellow football fans at Super Bowl parties. Now that the game was over, I was holding a pity party in my bedroom. The Green Bay Packers had beaten the Pittsburgh Steelers in Super Bowl XLV before a capacity crowd at AT&T Stadium in Arlington, Texas. Not only had my former team captured the biggest prize in professional sports, but one of my best friends from my time in Green Bay—quarterback Aaron Rodgers—had just been awarded the MVP. In 2005, the Packers used their first selection in the NFL Draft to take Rodgers with the 24th pick. They chose me after Nick Collins in the second round with the 58th overall pick. The three of us came into the league together, with Rodgers and Collins both playing huge roles in leading the Packers to a championship on the biggest stage in professional sports. I was pleased for Aaron, Nick and many other guys I still knew on the team. The Packers invited me to attend the game and to stand on the sidelines. I appreciated the offer, but I declined. Instead, I watched the Super Bowl from my home in College Station.

When it was all said and done, I felt sick to my stomach. I went to bed that night with tears in my eyes and a gut-wrenching emptiness in the pit of my stomach. Again and again, the thoughts that raced through my head were: "Why God? Why not me?" It had been more than five years since I suffered a severe neck injury during my 2005 rookie season. In a game against the Carolina Panthers, I was momentarily paralyzed, and I never played another down. I later officially retired from the NFL in 2007.

The Packers' Super Bowl win in 2011 brought a swarm of emotions to the forefront of my consciousness. I went to bed that night with a heavy heart. I thank God, however, for the life-altering, eye-opening transformation he provided me when I woke up the next morning. While my football career had ended more than five years earlier, I was obviously still holding on to the pain associated with no longer playing the game. And quite frankly, I was holding on to other wounds and scars, as well. For example, I returned to A&M following my NFL retirement and began working toward a postgraduate business degree with a specialty in real estate. The problem was that my heart wasn't completely in real estate yet; my heart was still in football. I figured the only way to satisfy the desires of my football-focused dreams at that time was to go into coaching.

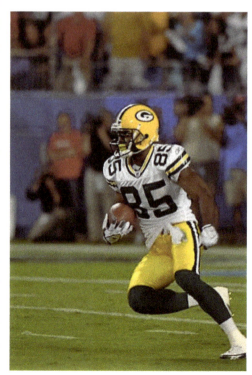

I initially interviewed with Mike Sherman, who was then the head coach at Green Bay, but he didn't offer me a job. The collegiate program that offered me a coaching position right away was Trinity Valley Community College (TVCC) in Athens, Texas. I took the offer and moved into a dorm room on campus, where I coached for a year. I eventually received job offers from Green Bay and the Seattle Seahawks and turned them down in 2008 and 2009.

Looking back now, I realize God was speaking to me, but I wasn't fully embracing the peace that transcends all understanding. At least I was focused enough on serving and honoring God that I made some good decisions that led me to where I am today. One of those decisions was to commit to pursuing a relationship with a beautiful woman—inside and out—named Erica Calabrese, whom I had first met while in college at Texas A&M. Erica, a graduate of the University of Texas, and I started off as mere acquaintances. We then developed a friendship, began communicating often and began thinking about taking things to another level. She supported me after I retired from the NFL, and our relationship developed to the point that I was first committed to dating her exclusively. Soon afterward, I asked her to marry me.

We were engaged when I was at TVCC, and we were planning a future wedding when I attended a national coaches convention in Anaheim, California. I still believed coaching was the career of my future, and I was frustrated that I didn't land a job on Mike Sherman's A&M staff after Franchione had been fired. Sherman had been at Green Bay, my former team, and he was going to A&M, my alma mater, where I was still the leading receiver in school history. When Sherman was hired in Aggieland, I had a great interview with him, but I was later told I was just too young.

Obviously, God had different plans for me, and He began revealing those plans when I attended the coaching convention on the West Coast. Late one evening I was in my hotel room, falling asleep with the TV still on, although I was not paying much attention to what was airing. I awoke to an infomercial that featured entrepreneur Robert Kiyosaki talking about financial education and generating passive income by means of business and investment opportunities, such as real estate investments. It was just background noise at first, but as I began to hear Kiyosaki, the author of the book *"Rich Dad Poor Dad,"* discuss financial education and achieving financial independence through investments rather than seeking a paycheck, I sat up in bed and began to take notes. Some people may call it coincidence, but I really took that infomercial as a sign from God. It just so happened that I had the TV on a channel that featured Robert Kiyosaki's infomercial. That infomercial was like the match that started an internal fire within me for the real estate industry. It should be noted that, while the Kiyosaki infomercial truly did serve as a spark, it did not yet light an inferno.

Erica and I were married on February 18, 2008. On our honeymoon, I told her that I felt like God was calling me back to College Station. She looked at me in stunned disbelief and said: "College Station? You didn't get the job at A&M. Why College Station?" I couldn't explain it, but I definitely felt a calling to begin a real estate career in College Station. Fortunately, my bride supported my decision. Against the stern advice of my financial advisor, I took most of my money that I had and began making my own real estate investments. One thing I learned about start-up companies or entrepreneurships is that you can read books all day long, but there's something extremely important about making the leap and going for it in the real world. It was kind of like me putting high school tapes together all over again. I didn't know exactly what I needed to do, but I knew it was time to take action.

At about that same time, the coaching job offers began pouring in from both the NFL and collegiate levels. But we had bought a house, and I really believed that entrepreneurship—not football—was my future. One of the first things I did once we returned to College Station was to visit a local bookstore. As I browsed through the real estate, finance and personal investment sections, I was drawn to a Robert Kiyosaki book called *"Who Took My Money?"* I had never been a particularly fast reader, but that book piqued my interest from the opening page, and I finished it in two days. Kiyosaki's book stoked my entrepreneurial flame. I conceived the name for my business—TM5 Properties—and eventually bought a couple of duplexes near Kyle Field that were run-down, drug-infested messes. Erica began teaching at an elementary school in College Station and I began studying the real estate market. I didn't have my real estate license, but I began calling realtors asking them to show me houses. I needed to network and make contacts; I needed to learn the market; and I needed to begin renovating the duplexes I had purchased. My original vision was merely to buy distressed properties, renovate them and sell or lease them. Eventually, I bought an entire block on Welsh Street off of George Bush Drive, tore down the dilapidated houses and built seven homes that made the street look like an entirely different neighborhood. This urban development raised plenty of eyebrows in town and catapulted me to the forefront as a serious player in the real estate market.

I generated some momentum, began producing profits and turned plenty of heads. I then shifted my attention toward possibly building custom homes, and in 2008, I decided to buy a small retail business. The goal for the retail business was to get it up and running and then turn it into passive income. I also liked the idea of income diversification. But after about a year and a half of pouring my time, energy and money into the retail business, I was miserable. I discovered that retail was a 24-hour-a-day, seven-days-a-week headache. After two years in retail and lots of discussion with Erica and my accountant, I closed the business. Our first child was born in September 2010, and I shut down the store in December. At that point, I decided I really needed to pray for God to reveal my future course of direction. I needed a true passion, and I felt like a failure in many ways, because of the way my NFL career ended and my failing in the retail business. I don't pretend to know the mind of God, but my suspicion is that, as I prayed for career direction, God must have been wondering, "How many times do I have to show you that real estate is your future?"

Fortunately, my frustration with the retail business had driven me to earn my real estate license. I initially started working at a major real estate office in the Bryan-College Station area, and I did well, but I also wasn't pouring all my efforts into it. I owned eight or nine houses that I was leasing, and I was still looking for investment homes while I was working as a realtor. In other words, I was selling homes, but I was not sold out to my career as a realtor. Looking back, I needed something to jolt me out of my half-hearted approach and my semi-depression regarding lost opportunities. That "something" I needed occurred on February 6, 2011 when the Packers beat the Steelers to win the Super Bowl.

After my morning prayers, however, I finally understood what God was trying to tell me: Real estate could be my passion, fuel my competitive drive and lead me to a business "Super Bowl" of sorts. That morning, with tears in my eyes, I told Erica that I recommitted myself to her and to lead our family. I also wrote "Real Estate is my Super Bowl" on a piece of paper and vowed to dominate the Bryan-College Station real estate market going forward. I realized my greatest achievements were not meant to be on a football field and that my best days were still ahead of me. I was meant to be an entrepreneur and to provide a service to others.

MURPHY'S PATH TO ENTREPRENEURIAL SUCCESS

Once I made the decision to truly become all that I could be in the real estate industry my ultimate success was practically predetermined. Let that statement sink in for a moment. It may initially come across as incredibly cocky or arrogant, but it's really one of the fundamental principles of success in any industry.

Success is often dependent on focus and determining exactly what you want. Perhaps there are some exceptions, but from my experience, it is virtually impossible to haphazardly enter a profession, dabble in it—as I initially had done in real estate—and become a major success in it. In that regard, life is much like a camera in that the clarity of your focus determines your overall development. Throughout history, many wise men and women have eloquently reached the same conclusion. For example:

- "There is one quality which one must possess to win, and that is definiteness of purpose, the knowledge of what one wants, and a burning desire to possess it." – Napoleon Hill
- "Once you make a decision, the universe conspires to make it happen." – Ralph Waldo Emerson
- "You can have anything you want if you want it badly enough. You can be anything you want to be, do anything you set out to accomplish if you hold to that desire with singleness of purpose. Determine that the thing can and shall be done and then… find the way." Abraham Lincoln

My favorite author, Robert Kiyosaki, agrees that focus is a critical component to achieving any goals. His memorable acronym for f-o-c-u-s is: Follow One Course Until Successful.

No matter how you say it or recall the principle, I highly recommend that you not only commit it to memory, but also put it into practice in your own life and career. So many people go through their entire careers without any real passion for their profession or focus on their goals…other than reaching the end of the day or the week. They merely put in the time and expect—perhaps magically—to rise to the top of their profession. But if making it to the end of the week is your primary goal, your end results are likely to be quite weak. And if you are merely going through the motions, don't expect to be going to any special heights in your career or to build anything of value.

Fortunately for me, I realized at a fairly young age that I was, indeed, going through the motions in my life-after-football endeavors. I had entered an entrepreneurial profession by purchasing properties, but I didn't

From left, Teryn, Terrence, Tatiana, Erica and Terrence Jr. Murphy

view myself as an entrepreneur, a realtor or anything of the sort. I still viewed myself as a football player. Furthermore, I initially figured that my name—Terrence Murphy, the football player—entitled me to entrepreneurial success, especially in College Station, where I had been a record-breaking wide receiver. But the sense of entitlement, combined with my lack of focus, passion and commitment to entrepreneurship, practically assured me of being nothing more than a mediocre entrepreneur. But once I finally made up my mind that real estate could be my passion—or my Super Bowl—I began taking some major strides in the right direction.

For one thing, I began doing the things I needed to do, even the tedious, tiresome things I didn't want to do, in order to grow and prosper as an entrepreneur. When I was a football player, nobody worked harder in the weight room or after practice than me. I practically lived in the gym, pumping iron and pouring sweat to develop a chiseled physique that helped me succeed on the field. What most of my teammates and friends never realized, however, was that I hated the weight room. I loathed lifting weights, but I did it passionately and purposefully because I knew it would give me the advantage I needed on the field.

The same goes for reading about entrepreneurship, finances, real estate, etc. When I decided to devote all my energy and efforts toward becoming a great realtor, I knew I needed to acquire a tremendous amount of knowledge. I didn't have a father, older brother or even a mentor to show me the real estate ropes or to help me avoid making multiple mistakes. In fact, I went to work for one of the larger brokerage firms in the Bryan-College Station area thinking that I would learn plenty about the industry from some of the experienced realtors in the office. You can't start your own brokerage until you earn your brokerage license, and I believed that I would receive plenty of training, advice and education from the proven and established realtors on the "team" I had joined.

I figured wrong. Most of the members of my new team viewed me more as a threat or adversary than a teammate. They didn't want to help or train me because they didn't want me to potentially cut into their sales or commissions. While that initially bothered me, it also propelled me to gain the industry knowledge I needed to succeed. With no other place to turn, I became a voracious reader, even though I hated to read as much as I once hated to lift weights. From the time I was in kindergarten until I entered Texas A&M as a student, I read one book, cover-to-cover. Just one! I would skim through a book if it was an absolute necessity, but I would go to great lengths to avoid really reading a book. Reading has never been enjoyable for me, but I realized that in the world of entrepreneurship, you are on your own unless you have partners or co-founders. I wanted the advice of great entrepreneurs who had authored books, so I committed to stepping outside my comfort zone and doing what was necessary to succeed. Leaders are readers. Period.

As an ambitious entrepreneur, I committed to reading 45 books in a span of about 18 to 24 months. And I didn't just skim through those books. I read them cover-to-cover, re-reading key chapters and making notes throughout the text. As I committed to learning and digesting as much knowledge as possible, my perspectives changed, my horizons broadened and I even began to enjoy—at least somewhat—reading on a regular basis. Reading gave me definitive strategies, techniques and game plans to take me where I wanted to go. I earned my brokerage license in 2012, but I was already hitting the ground running, which is exactly what I did, becoming, among other things, one of 50 finalists in the country for the National Association of Realtors' prestigious 30 under 30 Award.

From the time TM5 Properties was founded in 2010 until November 2016, we completed more than 2,350 transactions, and we had one of the highest transactions per agent ratios in the market. Then things really took off, as we kicked it into another gear altogether. We have been named to the exclusive Aggie 100 in 2015, 2016 and 2018. The Aggie 100 identifies, recognizes and celebrates the 100 fastest-growing Aggie-owned or Aggie-led businesses in the world. The Aggie 100 not only celebrates their success, it also provides a forum to pass lessons to the next generation of Aggie entrepreneurs.

In addition to the Aggie 100, we have also been cited as the No. 1 independent real estate brokerage in the Bryan-College Station area in 2016, 2017 and 2018. *Inc. 5,000* recognized TM5 Properties as one of the 5,000 fastest-growing privately held small companies in the U.S. in 2018 and again in 2019, and we received a Community Impact Award in 2019. The Community Impact Award program was started in 2003 to recognize Hispanic, African-American, Asian, American-Indian and Women business owners who have demonstrated a significant impact in the Bryan-College Station community.

And I am absolutely convinced that the best is yet to come. In 2021, we merged with eXp Realty, a company that is valued at $6.8 billion. In October 2009, eXp Realty International, Inc.

was launched by Glenn Sanford as the first truly cloud-based national real estate brokerage, which meant giving up the traditional brick and mortar environment and moving to a fully-immersive 3D virtual office environment where agents, brokers and staff collaborate across borders while learning and transacting business from anywhere in the world. That is the direction we are heading, which allows us to expand into all 50 states and 14 different countries. Because it is a cloud-based brokerage, we are able to do everything online. Instead of me going out and hiring to get 60 to 70 agents in each state, I only need five to 10 in each location.

Along with the success and growth of TM5, we now have 20 companies under the Terrence Murphy Companies umbrella. Murphy Signature Homes has been particularly fun for me. Way back when I was building and selling rental houses, I grew tired of seeing the same traditional look, and I knew I wanted to do something different. We are doing that, as we are building and designing luxury, modern and contemporary houses. Our main developments are in Traditions, but we are also in Miramont, Greens Prairie Reserve and Indian Lakes. No one else locally builds these designs, and it was something that I have been passionate about bringing to Bryan-College Station. We build some significant-sized homes, as I am working on a 9,000 square-foot home as I write this chapter.

One thing I have learned about myself in recent years is that I love being creative and generating growth. That's why one of the main focuses at the Terrence Murphy Companies is creating a consistent consumer experience. I learned so much from Starbucks after my wife and I bought a Starbucks and Buffalo Wild Wings in Asheville, North Carolina. We wanted to interact with them and focus on producing a similar consumer experience at the Terrence Murphy Companies. Virtually everybody knows what to expect when he or she walks into a Starbucks. We also want to give our customers a specific consumer experience, and that is what we are trying to do to take it to that next level. We want to create a wow moment with our clients each time they work with us.

Another thing that absolutely drives me is to create leaders within my organization. We have 200 to 300 people working for us directly and indirectly, and I am always looking for people who can elevate and become great leaders. You look at current Texas A&M coach Jimbo Fisher, former A&M coach R.C. Slocum or legendary Alabama coach Nick Saban, and one thing they all have in common is that they are able to grow really great leaders. You look at those coaches and you can see how many coordinators and assistants went on to become head coaches. I take those examples and relate them to my own story and figure out how many leaders I can create who can grow and lead other parts of an organization or parts in my expanding company operations.

Likewise, I am always looking for ways for my children to grow as leaders. Our oldest child, daughter Teryn, was born in September 2010, and her younger sister, Tatiana, was born in March 2014. Meanwhile, our youngest child and son, Junior, was born in June 2016. That makes all of them quite young as I write this today, but we still push our children to be the best that they can be. They attend private school at Brazos Christian, and we have them in tutoring and in accelerated learning. They are all involved in sports, and we are trying to prepare them for life. We remind them all the time that both of their parents came from single moms, and we remind them to be grateful for a home with both parents. Thanks to God and some of our achievements, they are experiencing a world that Erica and I never envisioned as children. They have been to Disney World, Hawaii, the Caribbean and different countries that many children their ages have not experienced. With that, comes responsibility, and we push them hard to understand how important it is to be grounded and grateful. We don't want them taking any of the blessings God has provided for us for granted.

People who do not know me well or do not know my story have often complimented me or commented about me being on the fast track to success. Many others have asked me about my secret to success, hoping that I might provide them with some shortcut to success. But the keys to success aren't so secretive, and they don't involve taking any shortcuts. Start by determining exactly what you want, sharpen your focus and begin working toward your dreams by taking action even if you aren't exactly sure how to begin. Take matters into your own hands. Move forward. You cannot generate any momentum without movement. I was always told God cannot steer a parked car. You've got to pull the car out the garage and start moving.

MURPHY'S ADVICE TO YOUNG ENTREPRENEURS

Humility is especially important in this day and age because it is so rare. From a young entrepreneurial/young professional standpoint, the lack of humility and the abundance of self-importance have created unrealistic expectations for so many young people who are just entering the marketplace or who are just opening their own business. As I have documented, I was not immune to those feelings despite my extremely humble, East Texas roots.

When I first left football, I believed I was entitled to a big-time job in football because, well, I deserved it. That was my mindset because of what I had done on the field at Texas A&M and the NFL. When I first entered real estate I figured that my name alone would deliver me business and a long list of clients. In any endeavor, however, you must start at the bottom and earn your right to be heard or for people to give you an opportunity. I always encourage young people to find their passion, study, learn their craft, become an industry leader in your field and then success will follow. So many times we start this process backward. What's the first thing graduates ask? How much am I going to make? Who cares? Find out if it's your passion. I know some people who are highly successful who initially worked for free just to get a foot in the door.

It wasn't until I humbled myself and began taking responsibility for my past and present that I began progressing toward reaching my dreams. So, I think my first piece of advice to any young entrepreneur is to humble yourself and to understand that entrepreneurial success, prosperity and financial independence are not your birthright and are not likely to be gained right away. When I hire young people—especially young college graduates—one of the first things I do is to give them grunt work. If they are huffing, puffing and complaining about menial paper work, they obviously aren't willing to humble themselves. I know plenty of aspiring, young entrepreneurs, particularly realtors in training, who want to see a picture of themselves on business cards, for-sale signs and billboards. Those are some of the high-profile components of the industry, but none of those things will generate an ounce of business—in the real estate industry or practically any other—unless you are first willing to be a servant to others. It's extremely difficult to be any kind of a servant without humility.

God has blessed me with a really good memory, which keeps me humble. I know where God has brought me from and how far he has brought me. I know without a shadow of a doubt that God has afforded me with this opportunity, and I must make sure that I am doing my part. If I place God first, everything works out. If I start believing that it was me who did all these things, then I will lose my humility, my calling and so much more.

Another thing is I knew I had so much in the tank from my football career. I was playing with Brett Favre and I was catching touchdowns. Honestly, playing in the NFL was easier than college and high school. Following my football retirement, I fully realized that at any day and any point your entire life can change dramatically. That makes me keep working, grinding and being grateful since I know that at any point it can change.

Secondly, you need to find an industry or profession that truly ignites your passions. I think that is the foundation of success at any level. Much wiser and more successful men than me have said the same thing. For example, Steve Jobs said, "Your work is going to fill a large part of your life, and the only way to be truly satisfied is to do what you believe is great work. And the only way to do great work is to love what you do." Similarly, Warren Buffet said, "There comes a time when you ought to start doing what you want. Take a job that you love. You will jump out of bed in the morning. I think you are out of your mind if you keep taking jobs that you don't like because you think it will look good on your résumé. Isn't that a little like saving up sex for your old age?"

That does not mean, however, that you cannot develop a great passion for what you might not initially consider your dream job. I am living proof of that. When the football door was closed, I placed all my energies into helping others through real estate. I became absolutely passionate about my profession. I think you need to put all your energy on blooming where God has planted you. If you still don't enjoy it after a couple years of genuine effort and pouring yourself into a career field, then it might be time to move on and move forward. But there is something about making the best of every situation that builds character. Positive thinking generates positive results.

Next, embrace who you are and try to understand that not everyone sees through your perspectives. I take my role as an African-American business professional seriously, and I am proud of my culture and my heritage. My ancestors are from Africa and I am proud of that. As 2020 reminded us all, there is still plenty of social unrest in this country, and there have been times when my children have come home and asked me if everything was going to be OK. As much as I would love to shield them from some of the things going on in this world and the things being broadcast on television, I must teach them about embracing who they are and living in a world that may not always see them as equals. It creates a little more stress in the home because there are a lot of people who look like me who are being killed. At the same time, I know God has a plan and I try to not put myself in those situations but sometimes those situations find you.

My focus is: "How do we educate all parties? How do we all understand people with different perspectives?" The best scenario that I have used is asking others to comprehend the difference between sympathy and empathy. Sympathy just means that a person is feeling sorry for another person who is going through something. But "empathy" is the word that I have been challenging others to understand, encouraging those who I know love me and I love them to have empathy for all people. That means really stepping into the shoes of someone else and trying to see it from that person's point of view and understanding his pain. Empathy forces you to think differently, as opposed to being quick to judge or to dismiss someone's feeling. Empathy challenges you to say, no matter if a person is perceived to be wrong or right, "let me try and see it from his perspective." That is when you understand empathy. When you lose people to violence or racial unrest, you begin to realize that some of the things that you once thought were unimportant actually do not matter. I have been trying to lead with love and patience, and I encourage you to build your network with love, patience and empathy.

Speaking of "network," as a product of Texas A&M, I believe you must understand the "Aggie network." Going through school, all I heard was: "Aggies take care of Aggies." That set me up with some false expectations because I didn't realize I had to work the network. I didn't realize how to integrate myself into the network. I just figured I would flash my ring and send out a résumé or two and I would magically be taken care of by Aggies who wanted to hire me. But it takes more than that. It takes genuine relationships

When I returned to College Station, I took on the challenge of going to every event I could where I might network. I wanted to trade business cards with anyone I could meet. There was nothing going on locally involving networking among Aggies that I didn't attend. On one hand, that taught me how to have a conversation and how to interact with people, but after a couple of months, all I had to show for my networking focus was a stack of business cards in my room. I wasn't doing anything with them, but I had them. I thought that was what networking was all about, and I couldn't understand why it wasn't working for me.

It took me a while to realize that if I didn't follow up to build an actual relationship with these people, they were just going to say, "Hey, I met Terrence Murphy. He is a nice guy and a good Aggie." But there is no relationship-building in that scenario. I was nothing more than an acquaintance. What I learned about that experience is you must work the network, but then you must build genuine relationships with people. You need a goal in mind and you must have a purpose. There has to be a specific thing. For me—and this is the secret to many industries—my goal became to develop a relationship. It wasn't about asking them for their business; it was about genuinely connecting with that person. That made all the difference for me, because I took the focus off of myself and placed it on building a relationship with others. Personal development coach Zig Ziglar stated it this way: "If people like you, they will listen to you. But if they trust you, they will do business with you."

As a result, the Aggie network began working for me, because there is no stronger network in America among college graduates than the Aggie network. I truly see that now. I didn't see that at 22 or 25, but I see it now because I know that Aggies want to work for Aggies and with Aggies. Also, I am not just reciting clichés. At the time of this writing, most of our employees at TM5 Properties in the Bryan-College Station area are Texas A&M graduates. But the key to working the network is that there first must be a relationship. My advice now is to go to the networking opportunities and to focus on making a couple of great new friends, not collecting business cards. Make friends, develop bonds and see how God blesses your focus on being a friend instead of just trying to generate business.

Finally, never lose your faith, your hope or your belief. Adversities will come your way. Trials will stop you in your tracks. Road blocks and detours will blindside you. But as you encounter difficulties remember my story and others in this book. Remember that a muscle grows stronger when it encounters resistance; diamonds are formed because of high temperatures and pressure; trees grow deep roots and develop the stress wood they need to remain upright in response to battering winds; and people develop strength, character and courage when encountering and overcoming challenges. You may not want to hear that in the midst of your struggles. But persevere. God is just strengthening you for the road ahead to make an impact in the lives of others and not just to be successful. Let me leave you with this quote by Zig Ziglar:

"Don't be distracted by criticism. Remember the only taste of success some people have is when they take a bite out of you."

Keep Pushing. Keep Dreaming. Keep Living. Keep Loving. Define Yourself. Let no one put you in a social box. We only get one shot at this life, so we must live like it is our last week on earth.

CHAPTER 6
Jeff Schiefelbein

Founder of CARPOOL
Co-Founder and Chief Culture Officer of 5
Texas A&M Class of 2000

SCHIEFELBEIN'S PATH TO TEXAS A&M

Best-selling author and public speaker Andy Andrews once wrote that "perspective is the only thing consistently more valuable than the answer itself." Regarding that same subject, he also wrote that "a grateful perspective brings happiness and abundance into a person's life." Andrews is somewhat of an authority on this particular subject, as he once spent a year homeless and sleeping under a pier along the Alabama coast following the sudden deaths of his parents. As tragic as that may seem upon first reading it, Andrews says it was that time period that forever changed his perspective in remarkably positive ways.

Unfortunately, sometimes it takes hitting rock bottom in order to develop a life-altering and powerfully positive perspective change. I am somewhat of an expert on that because my outlook changed forever after being arrested and spending the night in a Brazos County jail for driving under the influence of alcohol. I was a sophomore at Texas A&M University at the time, and I was probably at the worst part of my life in terms of drinking, partying and living as if I was bullet-proof. When the police officer pulled me over slightly after 2 a.m. on October 23, 1997, I knew I was drunk; I knew I had no business driving at that point; and I knew I was going to jail. What I didn't know fully at that point was that the arrest was literally a gift from God. It was my wake-up call, and it ultimately became my call to action. But perhaps I should back up before delving completely into that awakening.

In 1982, when I was five years old, my parents moved my three older siblings and me from the "Land of 10,000 Lakes" (Minnesota) to the Lone Star State because my father's employer, Burlington

| 89

Northern, had relocated its headquarters to Fort Worth. Prior to our arrival, none of us really knew anything about Texas or the Dallas-Fort Worth area other than it was the home of the fictional Ewing family from America's favorite prime-time television drama, "*Dallas*. Incidentally, 1982 was also the same year Texas A&M made national headlines for hiring Jackie Sherrill away from Pittsburgh to serve as the Aggies' new head coach. At the time, Sherrill signed a six-year contract valued at $1.7 million, making him the highest-paid university employee in the nation.

Sherrill's eventual success in Aggieland, however, is not what attracted me to Texas A&M. My oldest sister, Jenny, was high school-aged when we moved to Texas, enrolling at Boswell High School near Eagle Mountain Lake, roughly 15 miles northwest of downtown Fort Worth. As she began contemplating potential collegiate destinations, my family went on several college visits together. First, we went to the University of Texas at Austin. Next, we ventured down to Aggieland to experience Texas A&M. And finally, my parents and Jenny drove to the South Plains, the world's largest cotton-producing region, to visit Texas Tech. I didn't go with them to Lubbock, but there was no comparison in my mind between what I had experienced at A&M and Texas.

In Austin, I was treated like an annoying little kid (probably not too far from the truth, but I was somewhat offended) by virtually everyone. I simply didn't feel comfortable on the UT campus or practically anywhere else in the city. At Texas A&M, on the other hand, it was a completely different experience. I couldn't believe that the A&M students—actual college students—would say "howdy" to me and ask me how I was doing. I felt the warmth of Aggieland, and I instantly hoped my sister would choose to attend Texas A&M. To my delight, she did just that after her visit to Lubbock.

My sister enrolled at Texas A&M in the late-1980s, unofficially beginning the magnificent family tradition of the Schiefelbein children being consumed and captivated by virtually everything associated with Aggieland. Once my oldest sister was a student at A&M, we visited from time to time as a family, and I recall asking a member of the Corps of Cadets for his "Corps Brass," a piece of metal that cadets wear on their left collars. The brass signifies the Corps of Cadets' primary goal of producing exceptional military officers and statesmen, while the insignia of a sword crossed with a fasces symbolizes the military history of the Corps of Cadets. After asking for it, the cadet gave me his Corps Brass, which proudly sat on the table by my bed throughout my elementary school years. I polished it often, as I studied the cartoon map of campus that I purchased from Loupot's Bookstore, which closed in 2012 after more than 80 years of service to Aggieland. Thanks to that map, I knew the name of every street and every significant building and landmark on the campus long before my oldest sister graduated in 1991.

Once Jenny became immersed in the culture and traditions of Texas A&M, the rest of the Schiefelbeins followed in her footsteps. Erica enrolled one year after Jenny, and then my brother, Rick, was next in line. Finally, following my graduation from Boswell High School in the spring of 1996, I enrolled at Texas A&M in the fall of that year. I went to Fish Camp that summer, although I probably could have been one of the camp counselors because I had memorized almost every tradition, every yell and every inch of the campus map. For that matter, I had been wearing a Fish Camp T-shirt—the one Jenny brought home in the late-1980s—since I was a fifth-grader.

Once I arrived at A&M, I knew that Aggieland was, indeed, the perfect place for me. I became involved with Fish Camp, as well as the United Way Division of Student Government. In fact, I helped to organize a karaoke fundraiser night to benefit United Way, convincing former A&M (then current) and Kansas City Chiefs superstar running back Dante Hall, student body president Carl Baggett and an Aggie student who hiked across Alaska to serve as celebrity judges. A week later, I saw Carl Baggett on campus and he said hello to me, identifying me by name. That made a big impression on me. Prior to that, I had been quite intimidated by student leaders, thinking they must possess training, skills and experience that were beyond me. Simply getting to know Carl made me realize I could be a student leader, as well. It dawned on me that we were really all equal…even a lowly freshman like me.

From that moment forward, I made it a point to connect with others. I ended up becoming part of a group called TAMC (Texas Aggies Making Changes), and I formed a committee to write a freshman pocket handbook, informing incoming new students about where to study, how to contact local churches, the best places to eat and so forth. I assigned another person to work on the logistical side of the handbook, while I began seeking approvals and funding. I first met with Dr. J. Malon Southerland, then the Vice President of Student Affairs. Then I began meeting with local business owners. We raised $15,000, received approval from the university and managed to convince local artist Benjamin Knox to allow us to use one of his prints on the cover of the handbook. Three months later, I helped to pass out 8,000 pocket handbooks at the various new student orientations held on campus.

Back in high school, my nickname had been "Hustle-Bein" instead of Schiefelbein because I was never the best athlete or student, but I managed to make things happen though pure hustle. Once I started connecting with others on campus at A&M, I adopted that same "Hustle-Bein" mentality as a college student. I met so many new students and developed relationships with plenty of faculty members by producing and then passing out those new student handbooks. I loved those types of activities, and I loved promoting anything that needed to be advertised or marketed. In high school, for example, several of us formed a band that was never really good enough to perform outside our parents' garages. But many of the students at Boswell High School wore our band T-shirts because I loved bold marketing. I also took that mentality to Texas A&M. I felt like I was truly finding my niche and developing my calling in the summer and early fall of 1997. And, quite frankly, I was pretty proud of myself and my accomplishments. I was making a name for myself during the days on campus and serving as the life of the parties in the evenings, drinking and carrying on as I lived what I perceived as the crazy college way of life. Then October 23, 1997 came. I still remember the flashing lights and the siren. It was the wake-up call I desperately needed, and that moment forever changed my life.

SCHIEFELBEIN'S MOST CHALLENGING OBSTACLE

It's funny how certain things—even seemingly insignificant things—stick in your mind over time. One thing that still sticks prominently in my mind more than two decades later is seeing the reflection of my face in the paper towel dispenser at the College Station jail. I was drunk; I had been arrested; I was about to be transported to the Brazos County jail in Bryan; and most of all, I was embarrassed. Among the many thoughts that were racing through my mind, the one that seemed to return most often was the Biblical command to honor your parents. Exodus 20:12 states: "Honor your father and your mother, so that you may live long in the land the Lord your God is giving you." At that moment in my life, I realized I was not honoring my parents or my family name. My parents sacrificed and made the commitment to pay for four Schiefelbein children to attend Texas A&M. Only one of them had managed to be arrested. I was so embarrassed I didn't even call my parents that night. Instead, I called my roommate, who bailed me out the next morning.

When I did finally call my parents to inform them what had happened, they were, indeed, quite disappointed. They mentioned right away that they were going to consider taking my driver's license away from me, but I informed them that it had already happened. At the time, there was a zero-tolerance policy for minors who were arrested for an alcohol offense, and I lost my license for 60 days. I knew I could fight the stiff fines, penalties and the lost license in court by hiring a big-time lawyer, but I wanted to enter a guilty plea as fast as possible to face the consequences of my actions. I didn't want to try to hide the fact that I was guilty, and I didn't want to search for a legal loophole that would permit me to avoid any of the punishment phases. I was guilty, and I simply wanted to do what was necessary to pay for my crime and to move forward with my life.

That's essentially what happened. Part of my punishment was participating in peer groups through the Brazos Valley Correctional System, which was certainly an eye-opening experience. Suddenly, my "peers" were no longer fellow college students, but rather, heavy drug users and repeat offenders. I sat around with guys who were convicted criminals, listening to some of the gruesome stories they told. After a session or two of being in that environment, I vowed to do things the right way and to make positive changes in my life. I started with simple things, like working out, eating right and going to bed at a decent hour instead of partying into the wee hours of the morning. I also began reading in an effort to enrich my life and to improve my outlook.

I had a job at Hastings Entertainment, which was once a thriving retailer in many college towns that sold books, magazines, CDs, DVDs, software, video games, accessories, coffee and etc. One of my perks as an employee was that I could pick out a free book each week. I started by reading

James Patterson books, and I was quickly hooked by a variety of Patterson's detective stories, thrillers and science fiction novels. I would read a couple chapters, try to put the book down and find myself craving for more. Before long, I began asking my fellow employees if I could have their free book. Most of them weren't interested in a book. So I became a voracious reader, consuming the classic novels, as well as historical fiction, business books, sports biographies and practically anything else I could find. I discovered that leaders are readers, and I also developed a passion for continuing education.

I also started playing guitar, and even though I never was a great guitar player, it helped me to change my habits. Previously, I was conditioned to do something crazy or to have a drink practically every night. But by working out, reading and playing guitar, among other things, I was beginning to live as a co-creator in God's beautiful world. I began to discover the truth regarding the wise words of supermarket magnate Frank Outlaw, who once said: "Watch your thoughts, they become words; watch your words, they become actions; watch your actions, they become habits; watch your habits, they become character; watch your character, for it becomes your destiny." I found that I became a better friend, a better son and a better student at Texas A&M, where I had initially been a business marketing major, but I eventually switched to business management. Things were going well for me as I cleaned up my act and served my punishment. As I worked on becoming a better me, I was required to attend a Mother's Against Drunk Driving Victim Impact panel in Bryan on the evening of November 11, 1998. I remember that date so clearly because I literally felt led there by God and I sensed the presence of the Holy Spirit as I sat in an audience and listened to the mother of a high school student in Bryan who had been killed by a drunk driver.

I still didn't have a license at that time, so I had a friend drop me off at the location of the meeting in downtown Bryan. I walked in, took a seat and was captivated by the speaker, who passed around a picture of her daughter as she spoke. As best as I can recall, the girl was killed after she had a flat tire and was attempting to change the tire when the drunk driver hit her. My Holy Spirit moment occurred as I held the picture of the girl in my hands. She looked much like any number of my friends from high school or college. As I stared at the picture, I realized that could have been me. It could have been one of my friends. It could have been one of my siblings. She had her entire life in front of her, and in an instant—the blink of an eye or the swerve of a drunk driver's automobile—she was gone, leaving her family and friends with a hole in their hearts for the rest of their lives. God spared me from killing anyone or being killed the night I was arrested for drunk driving. But I was still guilty of the crime, and on that night in Bryan, I sensed God wanted me to do something bigger than I had ever contemplated. I didn't know exactly what I was going to do, but I felt called to do something that was going to make a difference at Texas A&M and throughout the Bryan-College Station communities. I was determined to do something that might bring the next potential drunken driver victim home safely. I was also going to do something that would allow someone like me—the drunken me who had been arrested in the fall of 1997—to make it home safely without putting myself or anyone else at risk.

Following the meeting, my friend returned to pick me up. She asked me, "How'd it go?" I was excited to share the calling that was on my heart. God was clearly inviting me to do something to honor Him, to make amends for my mistake and to make a difference. "I'm going to start the best designated driver program in the country, and I'm going to need a lot of help," I told my friend. That was November 11, and I knew that the Thanksgiving and Christmas breaks would be upon me quickly. I called my dad and told him I wanted to talk to him about starting a business when I came home for the Thanksgiving break. I then began the process of gathering the information I needed, picking up forms about how to start a student organization, how to set up a bank account, what I needed from a faculty advisor and so forth. I told my father that when I went back to A&M following the Christmas break I was determined to organize and operate a program to reduce drunk driving.

My dad had started his own business in transportation consulting. He understood the technical side of being an entrepreneur, and he was really helpful to me in shooting holes in my plans in order to help me truly construct a designated driver operation that would work. He was a major mentor for me as I designed the program. This was the late 1990s, and while the Internet existed, it wasn't helpful in my research. Nevertheless, I found some literature about a bus program that failed at A&M in the early 1990s, as well as information about a fraternity-organized program at a university that had roughly 30,000 students. Through the fraternity's initiative, 30 people had used the designated driver program in one year. My vision was much bigger than that.

I had other friends at A&M who were launching other organizations at the same time I was developing the infrastructure for what became CARPOOL. Freshman Leadership Development Retreat was started by my friend Todd Strosnider and his friend. Todd and I would switch roles and tell each other everything we were working on in order to bounce ideas off each other.

When I returned to A&M following Christmas break in January 1999, I began the exhaustive process of turning my vision for a designated driver program into CARPOOL. Quite frankly, I was overwhelmed by how much needed to be done. In fact, I ran into a good friend in January, and she asked me about how the program was progressing. "I'm starting to realize this is going to be a bigger deal then I expected," I told her in a serious I-don't-know-if-I-can-do-this tone of voice. She aggressively grabbed me by my shirt collar, as if she might slap me, and said, "You are going to make this happen because you said you were going to make it happen." To this day, I love that concept of if you speak it and you commit to it, you are creating accountability that comes back to you from people who know and love you. I borrowed the confidence my friends and family had in me and leaned on numerous people over the next nine months—easily the most difficult stretch of time in my entire life. That time frame was wonderful, terrible, scary and draining in every way imaginable.

It's important to point out that it was way too big of an operation to tackle alone. There were eight other students involved in putting everything into place, as I continued to map out a vision for what was possible. I will also say that we were lucky along the way. From the perfect timing of when we released information about the program to engaging different stakeholders in the community or in the university, there was plenty of dumb luck involved in not creating too much hype too early. We didn't want to start creating hype only to have the excitement fizzle out. We also had to start planting seeds at the right time. And so many things just seemed to fall into place. I wasn't surprised by things falling into place, because this was truly a God-inspired vision. But it always made me smile when things just magically came to fruition. For example, the name CARPOOL came into focus in February 1999 while I was sitting in the Flag Room at the Memorial Student Center waiting to attend an informational meeting about the Buck Weirus Spirit Award, which honors up to 55 students each year who demonstrate high involvement, create positive experiences throughout the Aggie community, impact student life at Texas A&M and enhance the Aggie spirit. Unlike other awards, the Buck Weirus Spirit Award recognizes students who make contributions to the university through participation in student organizations, Aggie traditions and university events.

As I was sitting in the Flag Room, I was jotting down acronyms for the designated driving program, and I didn't really like any of them. Not even the one that I finally settled on: "CARPOOL for Caring Aggies R Protecting Over Our Lives." Quite frankly, I thought the acronym was too long, but I loved the word CARPOOL, and I circled it in my planner before going to listen to Dr. Ben Welch, then the Director of Student Activities, speak about the Buck Weirus Spirit Award. After listening to the information, I approached Dr. Welch and said, "You don't know me, but I have been planning on meeting with you to present a business plan for this idea that would help students who didn't want to drink and drive to get a safe ride home. First of all, should I apply for this award even if the program doesn't actually exist yet?" Dr. Welch encouraged me to apply for the award and then told me that he couldn't wait to see my business plan.

My problem was I didn't have a business plan. Nor did I have a clear idea of what a business plan looked like. But I began researching it, and the first time I met with Dr. Welch, my business plan contained about 23 pages. From that point, Dr. Welch shared his vision for what he believed I needed to address and also pointed me to people within the community and the university who helped me solidify the plan. When it was all said and done, the business plan contained more than 100 pages. My father owned a binding machine, so I would bind the plan to make it look official. I would meet with people, and I couldn't even explain why I was seeking them out in some cases. I met with the district attorney just so that somebody at his level knew that this thing was coming. I met with all three police departments (College Station, Bryan and Texas A&M), and I wasn't asking them to do anything, but I said I want you to know this is what we are working on so that when we get closer and we come back to talk to you about it, it is not the first time you have heard about it. I did the same thing with the TAMU Department of Multicultural Services and the local Chambers of Commerce. I was trickling out information so that we gained ground on all fronts. Along the way, I received the chance to visit with the College Station police department just over a year after they had arrested me. They don't see many people trying to turn the mistake they made into something positive.

During the summer of 1999, the pace continued to pick up. My team met with legal counsels, found a place to house operations and we acquired vehicles. But even when issues seemed to be resolved, there was always something else. The apartment CARPOOL obtained needed furniture, Internet access, food supplies and phone connections. We brokered a successful contract with Enterprise Rent-a-Car, which was huge because Enterprise agreed to donate about one-third of the vehicle cost for us to use on Thursday, Friday and Saturday nights. But we had to pay for the remaining rental costs and find ways to fuel up the vehicles each weekend. Summer flew by, and during the first week of school, we recorded public service announcements, hung fliers at every bar and started doing daily PR on campus. I told my story a thousand times, and I asked for support at least a thousand more. During that week leading up to the launch of CARPOOL, I wore a suit and tie every day. I was jogging from meeting to meeting, and people on my team were kind enough to have fast food waiting for me and to be at my apartment to answer the phone.

Ultimately, my team and I created a program that satisfied the needs of all stakeholders and, quite honestly, it all just made sense. We managed to make being responsible a cool thing to do, which applied to both the members of CARPOOL and to the students using the service. As an organization, we at CARPOOL immediately vowed to never preach to students about drinking, but to accept everyone, letting them know that CARPOOL was here to help.

After almost one year of research and promotions, CARPOOL began operations on September 16, 1999 at 10 p.m. I vividly recall sitting in the apartment with my team, all watching the phone, and it finally rang. The first ride ever was called in from the Texas Hall of Fame, and the drivers for the first call were Suzy Trainer and Evan Campbell (we believed it was important to always have a male and a female student in the vehicle to prevent any accusations or uncomfortable situations). The first night went well and soon everyone was busy. Student Body President Will Hurd answered the first call and then stayed to help us perfect our first night of operations. When the night was over, 36 rides were given, an amazing success for a new program.

Of course, the night wasn't actually over. We had paperwork to do, and I had to finalize our plans for the wrecked car demonstration we were organizing for the A&M football game against Tulsa on September 18. I think I had a grand total of two hours of sleep on that first night, and I did it all over again on Friday night. Once again, I managed only a couple of hours of sleep. Sleep-deprived and exhausted, I started feeling bad on Saturday, as my throat began swelling. I couldn't eat at first, and then I couldn't drink anything. On Sunday, I went to the emergency room at the College Station Med Center, and I was admitted into the hospital later than evening. The long hours and non-stop activities had finally taken a serious toll on my body. When I was admitted into the hospital, I had gone 24 hours without food or water, and I was starting to hallucinate. I don't remember much about the next five days (the extent of my hospital stay), but a variety of people visited me.

I received flowers from the police department that arrested me two years earlier. I met the president of the local chapter of Mothers Against Drunk Driving while I was groggy in the hospital. I woke up and this woman was pinning an angel on my hospital gown. I looked at her (I still couldn't talk) and she introduced herself. She said she'd been looking for me everywhere on campus. She was told she could find me here. I eventually tracked her down and we became friends. Another time I woke up Dr. Welch was sitting in my room. I tried to speak, and I couldn't. He said God just wants you to take a rest. He kissed me on the forehead and he just calmed me down. Dr. J. Malon Southerland also visited me when my parents were in the room with me. Dr. Southerland asked my parents if the university could pay for their hotel. "What can we do to help your family in this time?" he asked my parents.

The embrace of the community and university were beautiful, and it was in that hospital room that God gave me every nod that we had done the right thing and that CARPOOL was going to outlast me. I was still in the hospital on Thursday, September 23, the first night CARPOOL hit our first 100-ride milestone. In fact, the entire second weekend of CARPOOL had to happen without me. I learned quickly the importance of creating an organization that doesn't need a founder and doesn't rely on one person. I had set this process in motion, but it was so much bigger than me. The world knew we existed, and we were making a difference.

Flash forward two decades, and it is mindboggling and inspiring to see just how far the organization has come. In the fall of 2019, CARPOOL celebrated 20 years in operation with over 286,000 rides provided. CARPOOL runs an average of 10 cars per night, taking home an average of 300 people per weekend. The organization manages an annual budget of $180,000, and in 2018, CARPOOL and another student organization, The Aggie Wranglers, broke ground on a 6,250-square-foot commercial metal building in the Aggieland Business Park, located just off of Highway 60 toward Snook. Most meaningful to me, however, is to see how CARPOOL is saving lives and keeping the Bryan and College Station communities safe. According to the College Station Police Department, statistics showed that in 2017, there were 314 DWI charges, compared to 478 in 2013. Statistically, it may be difficult to prove just how much credit CARPOOL should receive for such positive trends, but I know the organization we started in 1999 is saving lives. As I look back on my DWI and being called by God to start CARPOOL, I am inspired by God's grace and uplifted by Romans 8:28, which states, "And we know that in all things God works for the good of those who love him, who have been called according to his purpose."

I believe CARPOOL was my collegiate purpose, and I once figured that my role in starting the safe-ride program might lead me to being highly pursued by corporations and entrepreneurs upon my graduation from Texas A&M. I figured wrong. Following my graduation in May 2001, numerous CEOs of major companies invited me to apply for jobs, but I was told—over and over again—that I was overqualified for entry-level positions. It was extremely frustrating, to say the least. I had gone from being on top of the world (at least after I left the hospital), and I had received quite a bit of positive publicity for starting CARPOOL. I had graduated from a great university; I had plenty of leadership experience on my résumé; I had sensational references; and I still couldn't land a great job. I wasn't sure what was next.

Ultimately, Frito-Lay called me after seeing my résumé. I didn't apply for a position with Frito-Lay, but one of their recruiters found my résumé at the A&M Career Center. Without any other options, I accepted an offer from Frito-Lay and went to work at a factory in Rosenberg in Fort Bend County on the south side of the Brazos River. At the time, the 400,000-square-foot Frito Lay facility in Rosenberg produced more than 84 million pounds of Lay's Potato Chips, Ruffles Potato Chips, Fritos Corn Chips, Doritos Tortilla Chips and Tostitos Tortilla Chips. My title was Corn Resource, and being in the factory was definitely not the right fit for me. The factory is run by engineers, and there are not many entrepreneurial opportunities in that setting. I was appreciative for the job, but I was not happy because I wasn't using my God-given skills. Instead, I was overseeing 55 employees who handled everything from receiving the raw products all the way to packaging the snack foods. Most of my staff had worked there longer than I had been alive, and I told my parents I was going to hang with it for a year in order to ensure that I wouldn't have to return my small sign-on bonus. But after that, I was going to move to New York City to see what I could make of myself.

My parents were not pleased with that line-of-thinking because they viewed Frito-Lay as a stable job. So, before moving to the Big Apple to make a name for myself, I went on a five-day vacation to NYC to do the tourist things—shopping, sightseeing and attending Broadway shows. My friend from A&M, Austin Knight, had told me that the last show I should attend on Saturday night was an off-Broadway disco version of Shakespeare's A Midsummer Night's Dream. It was called, *"The Donkey Show: A Midsummer Night's Disco."* What made the show so memorable, we were told, was that once it ended the entire club turned into a disco party that was like a scene out of Studio 54, the former New York nightclub and fabled disco that attracted the biggest collection of stars during the 33 months it was open. It sounded like fun, and I dressed for the show, donning my cool 1970s attire and breaking out my best disco moves when the show ended. Apparently, my moves were somewhat memorable, as I was pulled up on stage by one of the cast members. Before the night was over, a woman introduced herself to me as the general manager of the show. "Would you like to audition for a part?" she asked. It didn't take me long to say "yes," as the idea of being in a show in New York City seemed "slightly" more exhilarating than keeping the "corn resource" title on my business card.

I returned home to Sugarland and emailed the general manager, who emailed me back and scheduled me for a private audition. I didn't tell my parents or practically anyone else because the idea of me being in a show in New York City seemed too outlandish to even acknowledge. To make a long story short, I returned to New York, performed in a private audition at 4 p.m. and performed as part of the cast later that night in front of about 500 people. It was probably the most nerve-racking day of my life, but it went well. After the show, I was told I had beat the other 300 applicants who auditioned earlier that day and was asked when I could start. Two weeks later, I quit my job at Frito-Lay, sold my car, packed my belongings in storage and moved to New York to be a cast member in "The Donkey Show: A Midsummer Night's Disco."

I lost about 15 pounds the first two weeks because I was dancing 40 hours a week. But I had a blast. I danced in front of stars like Cuba Gooding Jr., Brooke Shields, Gene Simmons and the original cast of *American Idol*. I performed in the Hamptons on the East End of Long Island for a party thrown by *The Hamptons Magazine*, I was part of parades on 5th Avenue, I went into major debt and I learned how to navigate the city. It was a non-equity show, so I was paid next to nothing. But it was an adventure I enjoyed for a little less than a year. I liked the show, but I couldn't handle the lifestyle. I missed everything that was true about my life while I was running CARPOOL, where I had tremendous responsibility and decision-making authority. I longed to return to that world, so I came back to Texas to launch the program that would take CARPOOL to other campuses. I called it Closing Time Incorporated, which was a non-profit I set up with two other guys. I did that for about a year, and I would guess that there are now several dozen safe-ride programs based on the CARPOOL model. There is STRIPES at University of Missouri, Ram Rides at Colorado State, Watch Dogs at the University of Georgia and various other programs. In helping to take those programs to other campuses, I learned plenty about how to run a business. Ultimately, I moved to Dallas and landed a job in a sales organization for a telecom company. It was a chop shop, and it was not a good fit. After three months, I quit, and I was rather discouraged about how my post-collegiate career was progressing...or not progressing. I needed to find something where I could make a difference while making a living. That's about the same time when an Aggie connection helped to put me on the right track.

SCHIEFELBEIN'S PATH TO ENTREPRENEURIAL SUCCESS

One of the greatest things you can do as a college student at Texas A&M to ensure yourself a bright future is to make real connections with new friends. Doing so will certainly enhance your overall enjoyment during your college years, but building a network of friends in college will likely also help you into the future. Looking back on my career, a college connection opened one of the most important doors for me as I found my professional niche. Texas Senate Bill 7 was approved on January 1, 2002, calling for electricity deregulation in Texas. As a result, 85 percent of Texas power consumers (those served by a company not owned by a municipality or a utility cooperative) could choose their electricity service from a variety of retail electric providers (REPs). Almost overnight, REPs began forming, creating a new industry in the Lone Star State. My Fish Camp co-chair from 1997, Bryan Cox, started working with one of those REPs in the Fort Worth area called First Choice Power.

I didn't know a thing about deregulation, but I submitted my résumé, and I was called to interview with the vice president of sales, who happened to be an Aggie, Class of 1982. Even though I could barely understand the deregulation terms he was using during the interview, he told me that First Choice Power was starting a new sales channel, and he wanted someone with an entrepreneurial vision to run the sales channel. I was offered an opportunity to create a sales channel that didn't exist, and I could barely contain my excitement. I wanted to holler out, "Now you are speaking my language!" It wasn't a particularly lucrative starting salary, but I leapt at the opportunity and immediately spoke with as many people as I could, asking them everything they knew about deregulation. I arrived at work before anyone else and read energy tariffs (not exactly captivating material). I discovered that with a little bit of an effort, I could become an expert in the field. After all, it's been said that if you read four books about something you know more than 95 percent of the population about that topic.

I started interviewing and hiring people, along with managing two sales groups. Our commercial business that I was running grew tremendously, and we began building a great culture within our groups. We built an environment where people looked forward to coming to work each day, and we made sure everyone understood their purpose and value to the team. Six years after starting with First Choice Power, I was promoted to Vice President of Sales. While I was not yet in position to be a true entrepreneur, I was definitely what is labeled an intrapreneur, promoting innovative product development and marketing. Whereas an entrepreneur starts a company as a means of providing a good or service, intrapreneurs seek policies, technologies and applications that will help increase an existing company's productivity. We did just that because we focused much more on culture than our prices, our products or anything else. I have always believed that if you start with culture and empower your people, the rest takes care of itself.

I came up with my own set of rules with human relations, implementing new vacation and sick leave policies without corporate's permission. We placed our people first and then we created a game-breaking technology for deregulated energy that allowed us to experience exponential growth while securing more and more commercial accounts. By 2011, we had been so successful and grown so much that Direct Energy, North America's largest competitive energy and energy-related services company at the time, reached an agreement to acquire First Choice Power for $270 million in cash plus additional working capital. I certainly could have stayed with Direct Energy, as I was asked numerous times what role or title I would like in the new company. But the idea of working with a mega electric supplier did not appeal to me. I knew all about restructuring operations, and I certainly didn't want to watch Direct Energy make changes to everything we had put into place. I offered to help them in crafting transition roles for the remaining First Choice Power team and then I began focusing on my next calling.

It was late September in 2011 when it was officially released that Direct Energy had acquired First Choice Power. In the ensuing days and weeks, I sensed there was a calling for me to apply my knowledge of the deregulated energy industry, along with my experience in generating a dynamic culture within an organization, to create a vibrant and unique company. In November of 2011, I met colleagues Brian Hayduk and Eric Plateis for dinner in Dallas. We discussed our visions for transforming an industry by combining our diverse energy backgrounds and our desire to help others. Ultimately, Brian, Eric and I, along with our other two partners, Josh Coleman and Jon Moore, wrote 10 names on a board of people we had worked with previously in the deregulated energy industry. It was our "dream team" list, so to speak, and we pondered the possibilities of recruiting as many of them as possible to join our new company, which we called "5."

In many of the books we had read over the years (for example, *Tribal Leadership* and *Good to Great*), the number 5 is recognized as the pinnacle of achievement. Level five is something that a company or team can reach but cannot sustain because, at this level, you have achieved something greater than you imagined while competing with what is possible, not any competitors. Level five means you are experiencing unprecedented levels of success and generating breakthrough results for your clients and all other stakeholders alike. Level five businesses are supposed to be pushing the envelopes, debating vigorously and striving for the absolute best conclusion. Level five companies are not satisfied because something is working; instead, they are constantly reinventing what is possible. We named the company "5" as a simple reminder of what we wanted to strive for in all aspects of our business. Besides, a business named "5" turned out to be a great conversation starter. We even managed to trademark the number 5 in the energy industry, which we were told would be impossible. When you walk into our headquarters in Irving, the trademark for the digit 5 with the stamp and the seal are on display to remind us and our clients that you are not walking into a normal place where we are merely supposed to do our jobs at satisfactory levels. But I am jumping ahead of myself. Let me go back to the "dream team" list.

My partners and I had built a reputation over the years for treating people with dignity and respect. In all our energy industry endeavors, we had placed an emphasis on our people, allowing them the opportunity to make mistakes, learn and grow. We didn't have a company bank account or even a single customer as the end of 2011 approached. But we had a crazy name, and we had a strong reputation. We also had a vision for a niche operation. Energy deregulation created a crowded industry with countless brokers, limited regulation and uninformed customers. We recognized the need for a professional organization with real skills to provide higher-order energy solutions. Our vision was to form a team of energy innovators, commodity traders, analysts, engineers and former energy supplier executives who could collaborate with clients and suppliers to provide a full-spectrum of advisory services. We believed that for too long, clients were approaching procurement, engineering, sustainability and resiliency as separate decisions from one another when, in fact, a synchronous approach was necessary to minimize the undue risks and maximize the benefits that come with deregulation. We envisioned serving as an extension of our client's energy team, helping each client implement a customized and comprehensive "Whole Health Energy Plan."

Within six weeks of meeting for the first time to talk about the company we were starting, the 10 people on our dream team list had all committed to be a part of the creation of 5. Yes, all 10 said "yes." We told them from the start that this company was going to be about creating a culture that allowed them to grow and do something meaningful. We were going to rally around a common cause (our culture and purpose) and it just so happened that we had built a team of experts in deregulated energy. My partners helped pioneer deregulated electricity first in New York and then expanded into other states. Among our dream team, we had traders, engineers, operational specialists and lawyers who had written some of the original contracts in the industry and a former president of two energy companies. There wasn't a part of the deregulated world that was outside of the realm of our expertise. But electricity and natural gas were never going to be our only focus. Our focus first and foremost was going to be treating our clients and our team the way they wanted to be treated.

We officially incorporated 5 in December 2011. We started in Texas by helping hospitals, restaurants, municipalities, schools, manufacturers and a variety of individuals who knew us before and who appreciated our reputation. We understood that most of our clients and potential clients had been receiving their energy information primarily through sales people and energy brokers. We also understood that most people didn't have the time, tools or expertise to create, execute and manage a proactive energy strategy for electricity and natural gas procurement. Without exposure to the many facets of the industry, most people and businesses were blind to the inherent risks and opportunities embedded in their procurement process as well. That's where 5 steps in to create meaningful impact. We quickly established ourselves as the best in the business in energy procurement and demand-side management. With all of our clients, we started by performing a review of their business and composing a detailed examination of their energy usage. Then we customized a set of solutions using the client's information in conjunction with our technical and fundamental analysis of the market. Our work involves engineering, trading knowledge, operations and legal expertise, but our biggest strength is the ability to explain the strategy and execution steps at whatever level the client feels comfortable.

Today, we have expanded to more than 20 states, and we also have clients throughout Mexico. Our services include energy procurement and risk management; demand side management; construction services; benchmarking and budgeting; energy efficiency and rebate programs; bill consolidation and tariff analysis; resiliency and distributed generation; and sustainability. We have many success stories in each of the aforementioned endeavors. For example, the City of Mansfield selected 5 after a thorough evaluation of energy advisors and brokers. We quickly gathered the necessary data to secure a long-term supply agreement during a significant market dip, reducing the city's electricity costs by over $500,000 per year. We also identified and addressed several demand-side opportunities. First, we helped the city to identify a power factor penalty issue, resulting in a potential savings of $12,000 per year. Then we analyzed consumption patterns at the water treatment plant and recommended some simple operational changes that ultimately reduced the city's utility delivery charges by about $13,000 per year.

Jeff (far right) and his partners at 5

Another success story involves the iconic Empire State Building and the entire Empire State Realty Trust (ESRT) portfolio. Our team crafted a custom rate structure for ESRT's properties that leveraged favorable market conditions for both energy and capacity costs, ultimately leading to more than $800,000 of savings in the first year of a multi-year contract. Thanks to the quality of our work and the impact felt by ESRT, our team was asked to play a crucial role in a collaborative project dubbed ESB 2.0 that consists of a coalition of landlords, engineers and advisors tasked with developing a financially robust and actionable plan to support the carbon reduction goals of the City of New York. This blue-sky effort is setting the stage for the future of energy in New York and beyond with scalable strategies and technologies that take into consideration the needs of all stakeholders, including the environment.

I could fill the rest of this chapter with numerous other stories of how we have won the rave reviews of our clients, and I am certainly proud of those achievements. But I am most proud of the team we have assembled at 5 and the culture we have created. We have attracted people at the top of 5 who believe in their hearts that what they are attempting to do is worthwhile. I believe human beings are God's amazing creation who are capable of doing amazing work if you inspire them with a purpose. I don't exist to make money. I exist to glorify God, to take care of my family and to build a community at 5 that is making a difference while making a living. That's my "why" I do what I do. I draw inspiration to be the best me I can be in the work setting from Colossians 3:23, which states, "Whatever you do, work at it with all your heart, as working for the Lord, not for human masters." If I work to honor God, to support my family and to build a team with great purpose, every day is exciting. Every day is an opportunity to place our best foot forward for our clients. If you have purpose that you believe in and are passionate about helping others, you are likely going to be better at your craft and produce better results.

At 5, we like to say that we treat our people like they are fully formed adults. I think that is awesome because a fully formed adult doesn't need me or any other CEO/manager to baby him/her while looking over his/her shoulder.

From the first day of operations at 5, we told our staff members there would be no vacation policy. Nor would there be an expense policy, sick-time policies or anything of the sort. The first and only policy we put in place for our employees was this: "You are a grown woman/man. Own that responsibility." We may treat each other like family in the workplace, but we make it known to our people that their real family comes first. Everyone has a job to do, and if you are not able to do it, make sure somebody else is there to cover for you. As fully formed adults, we expect you to recharge and refuel. You should go and enjoy the people and the things you are working so hard to support. We are supportive of our people taking as much vacation time as they need to be at their best when they are at work. And we don't have our own company handbook with rules and regulations. Instead, we hand out a book called, Cowboy Ethics – What Wall Street Can Learn from the Code of the West. The author, Jim Owen, makes a heartfelt case for a new approach to business ethics, one that goes back to simple, timeless principles like those of the cowboy code. Owen's code of the West involves the following 10 principles: Live each day with courage; take pride in your work; always finish what you start; do what has to be done; be tough, but fair; when you make a promise, keep it; ride for the brand; talk less and say more; remember that some things aren't for sale; and know where to draw the line. If our team embraces those principles, everything else will fall into place.

As a leader, I need to create a vision for where 5 is going and why it exists. It's not simply about making money. Nobody can consistently rally around that. But if you give your team a purpose and prove to each individual that he/she is incredibly valuable in fulfilling that purpose, you will likely have a motivated and magnificent team that is making a major difference in whatever industry you happen to have chosen. That's what I am most proud of regarding 5; we have constructed a motivated team full of stunning colleagues who are doing great things. And I believe the best is yet to come.

SCHIEFELBEIN'S ADVICE TO YOUNG ENTREPRENEURS

Looking back to the CARPOOL days, I think that the hardest thing I ever went through was exhaustion. If you are an entrepreneur (or are filled with the entrepreneurial energy), you are probably intensely driven and you probably know how to go without stopping. But you can only do so much and go so long without refueling. You must schedule time for your faith, family, friends and rest. I would recommend that you be intentional about putting something on a calendar every day and making it mandatory. For example, schedule a workout each morning or consistent time with your family each week and treat these appointments as seriously as you would any work meeting. Being with your family, spending quiet time in prayer and committing to maintain your health is just as important as seeing the person who could be your next big investor.

It is also important to be clear about why you exist and why your business exists. As I noted previously, I don't exist to make money. I exist to glorify God, to take care of my wife, Amanda, to raise our five children in a Christian, loving home and to build a community at 5 that is making a difference while making a living. It's important to clarify your personal why and your business purpose. Clarifying those two things solves many of the headaches that you run into later. You must decide which parts of your business will be the focal points of your time and energy. Are you going to bring on a certain partner or not? Are you going to take on a certain activity or not? If you don't have a purpose—if all you are doing is chasing money and trying to generate wealth—you are not going to possess a strong guide for whether or not you should begin certain activities or engage with certain partners. It is much easier if you know who you are and your purposes.

Fittingly, Jeff and Amanda Schiefelbein have five children

It's vital to make sure you surround yourself with great people and you continually empower those people. I tell entrepreneurs and CEOs all the time that one of the best things you can do for your company is to make sure that you are replaceable. If your company can't function without you, you will have problems. When I am in the office, I want to be a value-add to my team. But I must build a team that can take charge and make important decisions when I am not in the office. Think about how many companies fail because the founder dies, sells the business or retires. This a difficult lesson to learn because it requires checking your ego at the door each day when you step into the office.

Sometimes, I look back to the CARPOOL days as an example of how not to do things. I was physically depleted at the time because CARPOOL was my singular focus and I poured every ounce of my energy into it. One of the biggest mistakes I ever made was trying to be the smartest guy in the room as I was starting CARPOOL. Thanks be to God it started and survived the second week when I was in the hospital, but I think it could have kicked off better and stronger if I had not believed I was so important to every aspect of the operation. I should have taught other people along the way and brought them up to speed sooner so that there was an army of us. Don't get me wrong. We had plenty of people helping, but nobody knew what I knew because I had not shared everything; I had not empowered my people; and I had not created a team-first culture. I became a liability to the organization because I thought I was so important. I learned a valuable lesson as I spent five days in a hospital bed. The more you can embrace that uncomfortable feeling of giving away responsibility, trusting people and believing in people, the more you are going to have those moments of exponential growth. I am reminded of this all the time, especially when the next big project or problem arises, and I see myself wanting to figure it all out and tackle it instead of just playing a key role and orchestrating the team to go tackle it.

Build a team of unselfish people with a purpose. We have that at 5, but I am also constantly studying other organizations, like Zappos and many of the organizations involved in Conscious Capitalism. Commit to studying other entrepreneurs and companies and learning how you can better yourself. I look back to my days as an employee at Hastings when I became a voracious reader, consuming the classic novels, as well as historical fiction, business books, sports biographies and practically anything else I could find. As I noted previously, if you want to be a great leader, start with being a reader. And develop a never-ending passion for continuing education.

Finally, I'd strongly recommend that you use your talents to be a blessing to others, whether that's people who work for you, people you work for or simply people in need. My work with CARPOOL, First Choice Power and 5 have all given me tremendous satisfaction. But perhaps the most rewarding work I have done is in helping to establish nonprofit organizations such as In My Shoes in South Dallas. In My Shoes provides community living within a safe environment, focusing on assisting women who are pregnant and homeless or at risk of homelessness. In My Shoes is the only community living program in Dallas that provides support specifically toward pregnant, homeless women, while offering life, parenting and job skills. All women who are struggling with homelessness, faced with the decision of bringing a child into this world and are in need of a strong support system from peers and professional counselors are welcome. We opened the doors in September 2017, and we can serve up to 19 women and their babies. They reside in this safe environment during their pregnancy and the first year of their baby's life. They are being restored and repaired to be whoever God created them to be. I can't express how much it means to be able to contribute to a Christ-centered organization that is really making a difference in the lives of these young women and their babies.

I know I am called to serve, and I know I exist for a purpose much greater than working at an energy company or even starting an energy company. It is just an energy company. If it all went away, I am still Jeff Schiefelbein, son of Christ who is raising a family and trying to carve a pathway to heaven. God gave me certain gifts in the workplace that I can use to influence and impact other people's lives outside of work. Public speaking is one of those gifts, and I do plenty of it. I enjoy using my communication and motivational skills for the various ministries that honor God and help people. For example, I host a live radio show on the Guadalupe Radio Network called Undivided Intention. It provides a practical look at how you keep your faith at the forefront of everything you do. If you keep faith at the forefront of everything—not just a bucket item for a few times a week or certain times of the year—everything else falls into place. If your faith is the most important thing in your life, not only do I think you will have more success, but you will also be able to weather the storms better and bring peace and joy to others.

Jesus was once asked, "Teacher, what is the most important commandment in the Law?" He responded by saying, "Love the Lord your God with all your heart, soul and mind. This is the first and most important commandment. The second most important commandment is like this one. And it is, 'Love others as much as you love yourself.'"

If anyone asked me what the most important lesson is in entrepreneurship, I would paraphrase those words of Jesus, because the key to any business success I have obtained is certainly similar to Jesus' words. Honor God with your work and your walk. And commit to loving, helping and empowering people. Do those two things and you'll likely be blessed beyond your wildest dreams.

CHAPTER 7

Mike Shaw

Owner of Multiple Automotive Dealerships
Texas A&M Class of 1968

SHAW'S PATH TO TEXAS A&M

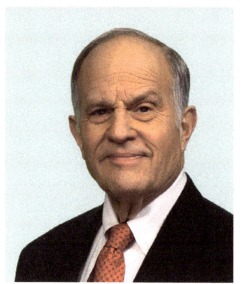

Growing up along the Texas-Mexican border—first in Brownsville and later in Weslaco—I possessed a passion that kept me busy and out of trouble: Athletics. My parents literally didn't have a dime to spare, and I really didn't have a clue regarding what I eventually wanted to do when I grew up or what college I needed to attend. I just loved the foundation that being involved in athletics provided me. My family moved from Brownsville, which is a couple football fields north of Matamoros, Mexico, to Weslaco, which is about halfway between McAllen and Harlingen, when I was in the eighth grade in late 1950s. I played football, basketball, baseball and ran track for the Weslaco High School Panthers, but I especially loved baseball.

I was a hard-nosed, solid second baseman, and there was a coach from nearby Mercedes who assembled a summer baseball team that was comprised of the best players throughout the Valley. We had a tremendous squad, and we advanced to compete against top-flight competition on a national level. Nine guys from that team eventually played Division I college baseball, including Richard L. "Ricky" Schwartz, who lettered at Texas A&M from 1966-68. I was a particularly slick-fielding defensive second baseman, as I only made two errors in four years of high school baseball. I was also a decent hitter, and there's no doubt in my mind that I could have played collegiate baseball at smaller schools like nearby Pan American or Texas A&I (now Texas A&M-Kingsville). But I was also quite the patriotic young man, and I had an aunt who worked for the Navy in Washington D.C. for about 30 years. Because of her connections, I once received the opportunity to spend a couple weeks at the Naval Academy in Annapolis, Maryland when Roger Staubach was making national headlines for the Midshipmen and won the Heisman Trophy in 1963.

I once considered pursuing entrance into the Naval Academy, but I was not crazy about the six-year military commitment that would be required following graduation. While I wanted to serve my country, six years sounded like an awfully long time. That trip to Annapolis made me realize that Texas A&M, with its military history and ties, would likely be a better fit for me. Besides, I thought I might be able to join Ricky Schwartz in trying out for the Aggie baseball team.

I really didn't know too much about Texas A&M when I graduated from Weslaco High School in 1964, as many of my friends who were college bound were headed to Austin and the University of Texas. Several of those friends talked about joining a fraternity at Texas, and I knew I absolutely couldn't afford that. My aunt gave my parents a loan to cover my first semester at A&M in the fall of '64, and I think my expenses amounted to about $600. Additionally, my parents sent me $7 week, which didn't go far…even back in the mid-1960s. Working while going to school wasn't just an option for me; it was an absolute necessity, although I didn't work much during my freshman year as I adjusted to college life. I also joined the Corps of Cadets, and I was determined to at least try out for the Aggie baseball team. In hindsight, I probably had no business trying out for the team because my first year in the Corps of Cadets was like having a full-time job of sorts. It had been a lifelong dream of mine, however, to play big-time college baseball so I literally gave it the ol' college try. If I had been a few steps quicker down the first-base line, I may have made it.

Reality and my medium-sized stature caught up with me on the old Kyle Field baseball diamond (this was long before the building of Olsen Field). I played well defensively and hit enough to be considered for the team, but college baseball requires much more speed than I could deliver. I was quick enough out of the batter's box, but I just didn't have long enough strides to make it at Texas A&M. As a result, I was one of just two players from that star-studded Valley team who did not play Division I college baseball. Instead I started focusing on the things I could control: making my grades, making enough money to stay in school and making an impact in the Corps of Cadets.

As far back as high school, I was driven to make a buck by performing whatever work was necessary. On the weekends in Weslaco, I mowed about 20 lawns. I initially charged $2 to mow and trim, but I later doubled that price. I could go down the sidewalk with an edger faster than anyone I'd ever seen, which allowed me to handle 20 lawns in a weekend. I also worked my butt off in the summers after my freshman and sophomore years at A&M, toiling seven days a week at a cotton gin. During the summer after my sophomore year, I also attended summer classes at Pan American University. I worked the night shift at the cotton gin from 6 p.m. to 6 a.m. and then went to summer school. That was a tough summer, to say the least.

As I adjusted to college life at Texas A&M, I discovered that there were better ways to make a buck than by the sweat of your brow. Working hard was fine, but working smart was even better. Living in the corps dorms on campus, I saw a need for food service delivery, and it just so happened that Shipley Do-Nuts had just opened a location on Villa Maria Drive in Bryan.

I decided to start knocking on doors in three dorms, offering to deliver hot, fresh donuts each evening at about 10:30, which is about the time most cadets finished studying. I didn't own a vehicle, but my friend, King Moss, volunteered to take me for a cut of the profits. I bought the donuts for a nickel apiece and sold them for a quarter. Things went so well for me right away that I started requiring a minimum order of a half-dozen donuts, which would net me $1.20 per order. This was a great money-maker for me until I received a call one morning from a university official who asked me if I was selling donuts in the dorms. "Yes," I said, "what's wrong with that?"

Apparently, the issue was that my door-to-door donut delivery business was dramatically cutting into the vending machine sales at the dorms. "You must have a permit to sell food in the dorms," I was told. When I asked about what I needed to do to gain a permit I was told, "Mr. Shaw, you will not be given a permit. You just need to cease the donut sales." I was disappointed that I'd lost my sales job, but those door-to-door sales had certainly awakened my entrepreneurial spirit. I learned plenty of valuable disciplines and skills while being in the Corps of Cadets, but I also gained some great hands-on experiences in trying to figure out how to make enough money to survive.

One of my next money-making endeavors was selling newspaper subscriptions. Another one of my friends had access to newspapers from both the Dallas-Fort Worth area and Houston, so I went door to door once again in the dorms, telling everyone I encountered, "This is how you are going to receive your news every day. Do you want the Dallas paper or the Houston paper?" I made a little money on those subscriptions, did a little construction work, as well, and suffered through a couple of weeks of washings pots and pans in a restaurant, which is probably still the worst job in my life.

During my junior year, a guy from New York named Tom Kitchens was in danger of flunking out of school because he was working so many hours at the Pizza Inn on Highway 6. He was a part of our corps outfit, so I told my roommate, King Moss, that we should go fill in for him at the Pizza Inn so he could study and pull his grade-point average back into the passing range. That's just what Aggies do.

King and I basically took over the Pizza Inn because the owner of the restaurant was diagnosed with brain cancer. We'd done a good job for the owner, and his wife came to us pleading for us to run the Pizza Inn. We didn't make a ton of money running the restaurant, but that experience did pay major dividends for me down the road. We also struck a deal with the owner's wife, allowing us to keep and combine the pitchers of beer that customers didn't finish. At the end of the night, we'd have four or five pitchers in the cooler. We also were permitted to make a couple of cheese pizzas at the end of the night, and we were allowed to invite our buddies to the restaurant for pizza and beer after the Pizza Inn closed.

One of my so-called claims to fame as a college student at Texas A&M also occurred during that time frame. My close childhood friend, Gene Powell, had gone to the University of Texas on a full football scholarship, where he was a backup linebacker to two-time All-American Tommy Nobis.

Gene probably would have started anywhere else in the country, but things worked out for him and he later served as the Chairman of the University of Texas System Board of Regents from February 8, 2011 through August 22, 2013. We stayed in close contact throughout college, and he invited me to Austin numerous times to double date with his future wife, the former Marlee Gilmore, and one of her good friends and sorority sisters. That friend was none other than Farrah Fawcett, one of the most iconic sex symbols in America in the 1970s. Long before she hit it big in Hollywood, she was an art major at Texas, where she was named one of the "10 most beautiful coeds on campus" during her freshman year. Gene's girlfriend also made the list. Farrah never finished school because she left for Hollywood following her junior year. She was a nice young woman, but quite frankly, she wasn't for me.

The woman who piqued my interest the most was also a student at Texas, the former Nancy James, who was originally from Houston and moved to Weslaco for her senior year in high school. Nancy's grandmother owned a bank in Weslaco, and we started dating after I attended summer camp following my junior year at A&M. We hit it off right away, and Nancy eventually helped me with my biggest money-making project while I was in college. One of the guys in my outfit from Winnie, Texas was good friends with a young woman who won the Miss Teenage America pageant. Her talent was singing, and my friend was trying to help her produce a record in Houston, where five-time Grammy Award winner B.J. Thomas was making headlines. Thomas' definitive hits included "I'm So Lonesome I Could Cry," "Hooked on a Feeling" and "Raindrops Keep Fallin' on My Head." We connected with B.J. Thomas' manager in Houston, and I came back to College Station trying to sell stock in the record.

The record business never led me to fame or fortune, but it did open my eyes to other possibilities regarding the music industry. My friend from my outfit was a great musician, who'd booked bands to perform at various events when he was in high school. He eventually flunked out of A&M, but he encouraged me to book some bands and to put together some shows. Keep in mind that this is 1967, and there just wasn't much to do for students and former students following a football game in Aggieland.

I came up with the idea of renting the Knights of Columbus Hall on a Saturday night following an Aggie football game and booking some bands who played soul music, which was really big at the time. My name was on the lease, and I was a nervous wreck before that first Saturday night show. I had gone door-to-door once again—by that time people practically knew it was me when they heard the knock on the door—selling tickets in the dorms, and Nancy came over from Austin to help me run that first show.

Fortunately, it was a big hit. Once I had paid all the expenses, I netted $2,700 for the first show. I thought I had died and gone to heaven, so I decided to do it again following the next home game. Word traveled around campus that we had produced a helluva good party on a Saturday night, and the Aggie football team also helped out in '67 by winning the first conference championship for A&M since 1956. The shows grew bigger and better as the season progressed. Looking back on my college days, there's no doubt in my mind that the entrepreneurial seeds I planted through my various work experiences while at A&M grew my confidence and my desire to succeed as an entrepreneur/businessman.

As I neared graduation day, I had accumulated a decent amount of money from booking bands in College Station and later in Austin. I'd also done well in school, keeping my grades up as I pursued a degree in business management, and I was particularly pleased that I would be honored as a distinguished military student and graduate.

That was important because the United States' military involvement in the Vietnam conflict had continued to escalate throughout the 1960s. American involvement probably peaked in 1968, the year I graduated and the same year that the communist side launched the Tet Offensive, which failed in its goal of overthrowing the South Vietnamese government. The scary thing from my perspective was that the number of U.S. deaths in Vietnam peaked in '68 at 16,899 casualties, which was roughly 5,500 more than any previous year. Richard Nixon had campaigned in the 1968 presidential election under the slogan that he would end the war in Vietnam and bring "peace with honor." But most of us knew there was no easy way out of Vietnam, which was proven by the fact that the American commitment continued for another five years.

Because I had been honored as a distinguished military student and graduate, I was able to attend graduate school instead of going directly into the military. I was also able to choose the military branch where I would eventually serve my commitment. I selected the AG Corps (the Adjutant General's Corps, which was first established as a branch of the U.S. Army in 1775). Once I graduated from A&M, I went to see my cousin, David Taylor, who had a Buick dealership in Beaumont and later owned a Cadillac dealership in Houston. I bought my first car from David, and I vividly remember making payments of $67.12 per month.

SHAW'S PATH TO ENTREPRENEURIAL SUCCESS

Following my graduation from Texas A&M, I enrolled in the MBA program at the University of Houston. I also took a job as a management trainer for a Canadian company called MacMillan Bloedel Limited, which became one of the world's largest newsprint plants and has been credited with introducing the first self-dumping log barge to British Columbia. The company agreed to pay for my schooling, but I hated the job. I did well in my role, but the person I reported to directly was a New Yorker living in Chicago who didn't possess many people skills.

Quite frankly, it was a grind, and I actually enjoyed my part-time job at that point in my life more than my role with MacMillan Bloedel Limited. In my "spare time," I sold pots, pans and other cookware. All my door-to-door training in sales at A&M paid dividends for me as I went from one home to the next, meeting with homemakers and selling them kitchen necessities.

Ultimately, I decided that, even though MacMillan Bloedel was paying my way through graduate school, dealing with my direct report was more trouble than it was worth. Besides, I knew I didn't want to work for a company like that. I possessed an entrepreneurial spirit, and working in Corporate America was not for me. I left MacMillan Bloedel and briefly took a job with a friend of mine who was managing apartments on the Gulf Freeway in Houston. It didn't take me long to figure out that collecting rent from those rather shady tenants was more dangerous than going straight to Vietnam, because there was no shortage of guns in that complex.

By that time, I'd asked Nancy to marry me, and I was particularly intrigued by an offer made to me by my cousin, David Taylor. He had been encouraging me to come to work for him, selling Buicks in Beaumont. In January of 1969, I went to work for David in my first-ever role in the automotive industry. I still had to take at least nine hours of graduate coursework to maintain my standing as a full-time student (or else I would be required to report for active military duty), so I transferred into a graduate school program at Lamar University in Beaumont.

It was not an easy time in my life. I would pick up David every day at 5 a.m., we'd run five miles, I'd report to work at 7 and work until 6 p.m. Then I would attend school in the evenings from 7 to 10. That made for some long days and nights, as I also worked on the weekends. David put me to work in the service department as an advisor during the weekdays. I also ran the used car sale lot on Saturdays. Nancy and I were married that next summer, although I rarely saw her. I was working 12 hours a day, returning home from school at 11, working all day Saturday and studying as much as possible on Sunday.

Mike and Nancy Shaw were the winners of the 2012 national TIME Dealer of the Year

Nancy has always been a patient person, but she was practically the personification of patience during those days. She was working as a bank teller, and we only had one vehicle for most of the time I was working in Beaumont. We didn't have cell phones, and there were so many times when she would have to walk home from work because I could not leave the dealership and could not reach her. I finally bought her a $400 Chrysler, so she could at least avoid walking home, but those were seriously busy times. I spent almost two years working for David Taylor Buick and learning the automotive business from the ground up before going on active duty in June 1970. Because of the schedule I had maintained, going into the army was practically like going on vacation.

The best news about the timing of my active duty was that United States' involvement in the conflict in Vietnam was winding down in 1970. When I attended my officer basic training in Indianapolis, it appeared that I would need to serve only one year stateside and one year in Vietnam. In fact, once I finished officer basic training, many of us participated in a drawing. If you drew one of the short straws, you were able to go home without any service time. I am usually pretty lucky when it comes to things like that, but I did not draw a short straw and was assigned to report to Herlong, California. Herlong, which is about 70 miles north of Reno, Nevada, was developed in 1942 after the Japanese attack on Pearl Harbor during World War II to house civilian workers to support the Sierra Army Depot, one of several ammunition storage facilities located inland in order to be safe from any other Japanese attack. It was where many of the United States' nuclear warheads were stored.

I could have never anticipated my immediate future when I arrived in Herlong, but as I noted earlier, managing the Pizza Inn at Texas A&M came back to benefit me. During 1969 and '70, senate hearings on alleged improprieties and profiteering in the operation of officers' clubs and on alleged black market currency operations in Vietnam made national headlines. The hearings followed an eight-month probe by subcommittee staff investigators. The first phase of the hearings dealt with the officers' clubs across multiple branches of the military, with witnesses testifying to widespread corruption among high-ranking officers, particularly in the army. The second phase, dealing with black market operations, brought testimony of a complicated and often bizarre currency racket in Vietnam that was reported to have involved more than $150 million annually. During the course of the hearings, Secretary of Defense Melvin R. Laird ordered annual independent audits of all NCO and officers' clubs. Among other things, it was determined that men in charge of the officers' clubs at various locations across the world had profited from the "skimming" of slot machine returns and kickbacks from suppliers to the clubs they operated and from entertainment booking agents seeking appearances in the clubs for their clients. Numerous allegations were also reported involving companies which supplied food and other goods to the clubs they operated.

Shortly after I arrived in Herlong, the commanding officer called me into his office. He said he had noticed that I had an MBA and had managed a Pizza Inn in college, and he placed me in charge of the officers' club, as well as serving as the Adjutant General. I later negotiated with him, informing him I could not perform both roles, so he left me in charge of the officers' club, which was a positive and educational opportunity. Among other things, I learned how to buy wine, how to butcher a cow, how to prepare a large variety of dishes (not just pizza) and how to run a casino night. The officers' club in Herlong was losing money on a regular basis, and as I surveyed my surroundings an idea struck me. Practically everyone who worked for me had once worked for a casino in nearby Reno. I asked the commanding officer if we could host a real casino night, and he approved it. We arranged to have the blackjack, craps and roulette tables donated, and we attracted a big crowd. I was scared to death when we hosted the first casino night because my butt was on the hook if we lost money. Instead, we made a terrific profit, and I dumped all the income into the food service account. After a year of running the officers' club and hosting a few casino nights, Herlong had the highest profit numbers of any officers' club in the army material command.

After a year, however, I was sent to Vietnam in June of 1971. Looking back, the day I left Nancy behind and stepped onto the plane bound for Southeast Asia was probably one of the darkest and most difficult times of my life. I faced plenty of fears on that flight, and I still thank God to this day for Aggie connections. Before I ever left for Vietnam, I'd done my research. There were two Adjutant General's Corps (AG) battalions in Vietnam, one in Saigon and one in Cam Ranh Bay, located at an inlet of the South China Sea situated on the southeastern coast of Vietnam. The Cam Rahn Support Command was the army's logistical organization controlling the port and depot at Cam Rahn. Typically, military personnel landing in Cam Rahn from the United States would step off the plane, check in to a duty station and then receive their assignment instructions, but I didn't follow the crowd. Instead, I went straight to headquarters and asked to speak to the commanding officer. He wasn't available, but the executive officer—the No. 2 person in command—was around to speak to me. He just so happened to be a former Texas A&M student and a career officer, and we enjoyed a great conversation.

To make a long story short, he reviewed the honors I received at A&M and my first assignment at Herlong and then offered me a job at Cam Ranh Bay, processing enlisted personnel rankings E1 through E6. The enlisted rankings are broken down by private (E1 and E2), private first class (E3), specialist/corporal (E4), sergeant (E5) and staff sergeant (E6). The most important thing that meant, however, was that I would not be sent into combat. I started off processing E1-E6, and I made sure to take care of any Aggies who landed in Cam Ranh Bay. I told anyone who came across an Aggie to send them my way. I assigned a couple to the post office and a couple more to serve as lifeguards on the beach at the South China Sea, where we'd allow military personnel to go before they were sent back home. The Aggie network kept me out of combat, and I passed it forward.

When the AG left Cam Ranh Bay, I became the Adjutant General for the 22nd Replacement Battalion. It was a great situation for a variety of reasons, including the fact that I could call Nancy on a regular basis, we were in a relatively safe area and my administrative sergeant was a wonderful man who was extremely well-connected in the army, as he served nine tours in Vietnam. When I was having a problem with my Jeep, he arranged for me to receive a new one. When my living quarters were too hot, he arranged for me to receive a new air conditioner. Eventually, he and I opened a Chinese restaurant on the compound to take care of the guys and to improve the overall morale at Cam Ranh Bay. He always managed to obtain the best food—even lobster—for the troops.

It wasn't all fun and games in Cam Ranh Bay, though, as I saw some absolutely terrible things, as well. I was overseeing operations at an orphanage and drug treatment center, as marijuana and heroin use was rampant in Vietnam. I also had to write reports on war crimes, because some of our guys were carrying horrific pictures of war crimes they had either performed or witnessed. One guy, for example, had a picture of a half-dozen North Vietnamese soldiers whom they had captured, tied up and gutted alive like a deer. He said it was payback for what they had done to Americans, but it was pretty sickening to see how the war had affected so many soldiers' appreciation for life.

Fortunately, a decision was made toward the end of 1971 that the 22nd Replacement Battalion was going to be shut down, while the one in Saigon would continue. It was my job to transfer equipment to another outfit and to send our boys home. The colonel and I were two of the last Americans to leave Cam Ranh Bay in February of '72, but thankfully, I only had to serve 10 and a half months instead of a full year. I'd spent plenty of time in Vietnam contemplating what I wanted to do for a living when I returned home, and from the time I spent working for my cousin at David Taylor Buick, I concluded that the automotive industry was the right fit for me.

Naturally, I came home and utilized the Aggie network once again. While I had hoped to return to Beaumont to work for David once again, he didn't have a position for me. Instead, I interviewed with Tommie Vaughn, the owner of an iconic Houston automotive dealership and a cornerstone of the 1939 Texas A&M national champion football team. As the center and defensive captain in '39, Tommie played a huge role in limiting the Aggies' 10 regular-season opponents to a combined total of just 18 points. He earned a bachelor's degree in marketing and finance in 1941 and enlisted in the army one week after graduation, becoming a pilot in the Army Air Corps. He left the military in 1945 as a captain and opened his first Ford dealership in Granbury in 1946. In 1950, he moved it to Glendale, Calif., after traveling to see the Rose Bowl and visiting a friend, who convinced him a dealership would do well there. Six years later, he opened a dealership in Houston. His first Houston dealership was on North Main, and he later moved it to North Shepherd. Vaughn, who died in 2005, served as chairman of the Houston Automobile Dealers Association and was named one of the nation's most distinguished automobile dealers by *Time* magazine in 1975, an honor that I would receive 37 years later.

Interestingly, I didn't immediately start in automotive sales for Tommie Vaughn. He first put me to work with his independent truck leasing company outside the dealership. I started with just three trucks, but within a year I was operating the largest Ford truck leasing operation in North America, with over 100 trucks. I hired two guys to drive around Houston, looking for anyone in a rental truck. We would spot one and follow the rental truck until the driver stopped. We would find out where they worked and where they had leased the truck. I would then follow up with the owner and let him know we were leasing brand new trucks at a great rate. It wasn't exactly a scientific recipe for success, but it worked out quite well for about 18 months until I received a phone call from another

Aggie, Frank Boggus, whom I had also interviewed with upon returning from Vietnam. Frank had an opening at Boggus Motors Sales in McAllen for a general sales manager, and in 1973 I leapt at the opportunity to return to automotive sales. I put my head down and went to work, developing relationships one customer at a time and building a salesforce. I went to work at 5:30 a.m. and went home at 10 p.m., because Nancy was still living in Houston trying to sell our home, and I had never been a general sales manager. I had to learn the business from the ground up. Within a year, we had tripled the amount of sales from the previous year.

The secret to our success was simply putting in the time. That was probably when I developed my lifelong work motto: "When the sun's up, I'm up." Until I arrived at Boggus Motors Sales, there wasn't a dealership in the Valley that was open on Saturday afternoon. We were the first dealership in the Valley to stay open all day Saturday, which is now the biggest sales day of the week. I had two salesmen who didn't show up the first Saturday, and I went to one of their homes and knocked on the door. His wife opened the door, and I told my salesman to be at the dealership in an hour or he was fired. He did just that, and he became a great salesperson, improving from about eight or nine sales per month to more than 20 a month. But the first part of stepping up your sales is showing up!

We also were among the first dealers in the Valley who capitalized on television advertising in a big way. I'd like to say that it was my sparkling personality that won over TV viewers, but that would be completely misleading. I used Nancy's well-trained Irish Setter, Shane, on our television commercials; we stayed open on Saturdays and we quadrupled the volume of sales in a 12-month period. We experienced so much success in McAllen that I received a phone call from Tradewinds, which owned 44 percent of the Boggus Motors Sales dealership. The Tradewinds executives asked me if I would be interested in moving to Corpus Christi to run the Ford dealership. I was interested, but what intrigued me the most was the possibility of ownership. I went straight to the point with Tradewinds, telling them that I wanted some sweat equity. We then negotiated a deal where I would receive four percent ownership of the dealership every five years I stayed.

We then moved to Corpus Christi in October of '73, and we planted family roots. Our children—Michael, Eleanor and Rob—were born and raised in Corpus Christi, and we really embraced the community. We established an attitude of gratitude throughout the dealership, training all of our staff members in every department that quality comes first, customers are always the focus and integrity is never compromised. I've discovered through the years that perhaps the most rewarding part of my automotive career has been participating in the professional and personal development of the people within my organization. When you invest time and effort in your employees and watch them grow, mature and prosper—whether it's an entry-level salesman, a quick-lube technician or a clerical staff member—it is similar to the pride in watching your children grow up and develop into responsible adults.

Of course, sales results are extremely important to me and to the overall health of the dealership.

When I started in Corpus, the local Charlie Thomas dealership was selling twice as many Fords as Tradewinds. Three to four years later, we were almost selling twice as many automobiles as them. Because of the reputation of our staff members, we developed more and more repeat customers. Sales are obviously critical, but they are not the only criteria by which I judge employees. Right from the start, I made my standards clear to my employees, and I rewarded and promoted those who lived up to those standards. As our dealership grew in size, sales and reputation, we also made it a focal point to give back to community organizations with our time and money, further entrenching our dealership into the fabric of the community. Things went so well at our Ford dealership that I invested in Tradewinds Subaru in 1984, Tradewinds Chrysler Imports in 1985 and Tradewinds Suzuki in '87, instilling each dealership with the same values and ethical standards that made us so successful with the Ford dealership. I was a little ahead of my time with multiple franchises, and I had my name on $50 million worth of paper in Corpus Christi. If the economy would have continued its strong surge, it would have likely been smooth sailing for the foreseeable future. That's not what happened, though. Not even close.

SHAW'S MOST CHALLENGING OBSTACLES

The great entrepreneur and animator Walt Disney once said, "You may not realize it when it happens, but a kick in the teeth may be the best thing in the world for you." While nobody plans on hitting rock bottom, life has a way of humbling you—sometimes when you least expect it. And perhaps the real definition of success is how high you bounce when you hit rock bottom, because the reality of life is that most of us will be there at some point in time.

The economy in Texas was rather one-dimensional in the early 1980s, as oil and gas impacted practically every business activity in the state. In 1986, crude oil prices fell dramatically, and the domino effect was a wave of bank and savings and loans failures, especially the large portion of financial institutions that were overly extended into energy loans. As the mid-'80s became the late '80s, another wave of failures followed as real estate loans also went bad (partially caused by a tax reform initiative that reduced returns on real estate). The Federal Savings and Loan Insurance Corporation closed or otherwise resolved 296 savings and loans institutions from 1986 to 1989. When all was said and done and the 1980s came to a close, 425 Texas commercial banks had failed, including nine of the 10 largest Texas bank holding companies.

When banks fail, loans become increasingly tough to secure. When the economy turns south, people tend to avoid making any major purchases. And when those things happen in combination, automobile dealerships can be in serious trouble. When all of those things transpired in the late 1980s and early '90s, all but two dealerships in Corpus Christi folded. With multiple franchises, those were particularly difficult times for me and my entire family. I was 43 years old, and it had taken me some 15 years to establish a strong reputation and for our dealerships to become widely recognizable and respected in the region.

The economic crash, however, was completely beyond my control, and my financial situation soon spun out of control, as I owed four banks more than a quarter of a million dollars in unsecured debt. There were some months during that time frame where we had more repossessions than we sold automobiles. It was that bad…so bad that I sold the Subaru and imports dealerships; I closed the Suzuki dealership and subleased the property; and I essentially lost everything except for the equity in my house. While it was a difficult pill for me to swallow, it was an especially tough time for Nancy and our kids. Michael was a 10th grader; Eleanor was in the eighth grade; Rob was in the first; and it certainly was not my desire to uproot my family from the comfortable environment we had enjoyed in Corpus Christi.

I turned back to my cousin, who first introduced me to the automotive sales industry in the late 1960s. In January of 1989, I left Corpus Christi and went to work at David Taylor Cadillac-Buick in Houston as a Vice President and General Manager. I was extremely grateful for the opportunity to work with David, and I was absolutely determined to pay back all the money I owed to every one of my creditors. Throughout history, many entrepreneurs have lost everything because of circumstances beyond their control. But the truly courageous entrepreneurs are the ones who keep their integrity intact despite losing big sums of money. Financial situations can quickly change, but character is much easier kept than recovered. On one hand, I felt like I had suffered a great defeat for the first time in my business career. But I knew that it was absolutely useless to waste any time feeling sorry for myself or asking, "why me?" As the late writer and newspaper publisher Harry Golden once said, "The only thing that overcomes hard luck is hard work."

David gave me an opportunity, and I absolutely committed to making the most of it. I didn't take off one day for five years. Not a single day. I worked six days a week for five years (excluding holidays), and I developed a strong reputation with General Motors. With plenty of hard work and extensive training of our staff, we became the No. 1 Cadillac and Buick dealership in Houston. It should be noted that this was a total team effort, not just at the dealership, but also at home.

My wonderful wife, Nancy, went back to school, spending three years to

From left, Mike Shaw, Fred Heldenfels, Kay Cox, Jerry Cox, Fred Caldwell and former Dean of Mays Business School Eli Jones

earn a degree from Houston Baptist University's School of Nursing and Allied Health. Once she received that degree, she took the overnight shift, working in the hospital from 11 p.m. to 7 a.m. so she could be home with our children, especially our youngest (Rob), during the day. Meanwhile, I helped Rob get ready for school and drove him to school on my way to work each day Nancy and I were literally like two ships passing in the night (and the morning), as we vigorously and relentlessly worked to pay off our debts. We had to do whatever was necessary to pay all the bills, especially the bank notes. From 1989-94, Nancy and I barely saw each other, as we grinded our way slowly out of debt.

The endless hours, exhausting schedules and sacrifices are not often noticed by friends, neighbors and associates. When things were going well in Corpus Christi, I made the time to coach Michael's Little League teams. But in Houston, I couldn't even dream of coaching Rob's youth teams. It was all I could do to make it to his games and the other important events in my kids' lives. As Nancy would attest, I usually made it to those games, functions, performances and conferences, but I was usually late. And instead of heading home with the family afterward, I was usually heading back to work.

All the sacrifices, six-day work weeks and late nights paid off as time progressed. In the early 1990s, the economy began to bounce back, and I began to build a strong reputation with General Motors. In fact, GM began calling me with some regularity, asking me if I would be interested in taking advantage of a General Motors financing incentive that would enable me to return as the owner of a dealership. I was absolutely interested…as long as it represented the right opportunity. From the time we arrived in Houston, I wrote myself notes with the "No. 48" written down. I placed the notes in my wallet, on my bathroom mirror, on my computer screen and on the rearview mirror of my car. The "48" represented my goal and desire to somehow buy another dealership by my 48th birthday. The power of writing your goals on paper is amazing.

According to goal-setting guru and best-selling author Brian Tracy: "When you take a paper and pen and write down your goals, you activate the Laws of Expectation, Attraction, and Correspondence simultaneously… The very act of writing out your goals increases the likelihood of your achieving them by as much as 10 times—1,000 percent!" I wholeheartedly believe in that theory, and it absolutely worked in my life. At age 48—some five years after hitting rock bottom—I started over when the right opportunity opened.

An older gentleman wanted out of a Chevrolet-Buick-Saab dealership in Denver that had originally been opened in the 1960s. He was leasing the property, and General Motors agreed to finance me if I used the equity in my house—roughly $300,000—as my down payment. I spent four days in Denver ironing out the deal. Then I called Nancy and told her we were moving to the Mile High City, which wasn't exactly thrilling for her. She wasn't looking to leave Texas, but I recognized a golden opportunity. We moved to Denver in 1994, and we couldn't even afford to buy a house for three years because we had given up all the equity we had amassed previously.

I then went to work with the same strategy that made us successful in Corpus Christi before the economy went south. We established an attitude of gratitude throughout the dealership, training our staff members in every department that quality comes first, customers are always the focus and integrity is never compromised. Continual and ongoing training again became a cornerstone of our employee development program. And as always, we put in the hours, doing whatever was necessary to be successful.

To make a long story short, I set a General Motors record for paying off the financing. Then I paid off everything I owed to the four banks in Corpus Christi. The core values that were instilled in me at Texas A&M inspired me to pay off my debts as quickly as possible. It practically drove me insane to be in debt of any sort, and I went to work as driven as I had ever been in my life, including when I first arrived at Texas A&M. As the first member of my family blessed with the opportunity to attend college, I arrived in Aggieland with a sense of purpose. I knew I needed to work extremely hard to make the most of my opportunities. And my experiences in the Corps of Cadets further enhanced my self-discipline, determination and work ethic. I didn't go to college to sew wild oats or to party. I went to better myself and increase my chances for success. As I did, I began looking for opportunities to serve others, and that's how I became an entrepreneur long before I ever walked the stage at graduation. I also learned the value of providing great service, whether it was delivering donuts in the dorm or putting on parties following Aggie home games.

I took that work ethic and applied it to my experiences in graduate school, MacMillan Bloedel, Vietnam and every stop I made in the automobile industry. As I evolved as a entrepreneur, I quickly grew to realize that I had to develop the people around me, because our dealership's reputation was only going to be as good as our people. Think about it: One negative experience with an individual can often shape your opinion of an organization or corporation. That's why I have always placed such an emphasis on training people, mentoring them and coaching them. My service technicians continually receive in excess of 200 percent of training as a group, as defined by General Motor requirements. I also send my staff to time-management seminars, and we put a tremendous effort on continuing education. If you take care of your employees first, training them and demanding that they exceed the expectations of our customers, everything falls into place.

That's how we made Mike Shaw Chevrolet-Buick-Saab such a success. Since purchasing it in 1994, that one dealership has made in excess of $4 million net profit in a year twice and over $3 million numerous times. It was well capitalized, with over $4 million in cash. We did so well with Mike Shaw Chevrolet-Buick-Saab that I was able to buy a home after about three years. Then I purchased a Buick-GMC dealership in Colorado Springs in 2000 and a Subaru dealership in Thornton, Colorado in 2002. Then I returned to my Southern roots in 2003, purchasing Honda of Slidell, Louisiana in 2003, Fernandez Honda in '04, a Toyota dealership in 2008 in Corpus Christi and a Kia dealership in Corpus Christi in 2010.

In 2012, I was chosen as the *Time* Dealer of the Year, the automobile industry's most prestigious and highly coveted honor. Recipients are among the nation's most successful auto dealers who must also demonstrate a long-standing commitment to community service. A panel of faculty members from the Ross School of Business at the University of Michigan selects one finalist from each of the four NADA regions and one national Dealer of the Year. I am proud of that honor, and I am quite pleased by the impact we have made in the automobile industry for decades. More than anything else, though, I am proud of the difference we've made in the communities where we operate.

I know what a difference an education from Texas A&M made in my life. Consequently, I care deeply about kids and their education, especially kids who come from low-income backgrounds. I am convinced that the key to success is education, and thus Nancy and I have a tremendous commitment to kids and education. I also believe that what you give, you receive tenfold. I have been blessed beyond my wildest expectations, and I believe it is my duty, responsibility and privilege to give my time, energy and expertise to organizations such as Texas A&M University, Boys & Girls Club of America, Crime Stoppers, Make A Wish Foundation, Boy Scouts of America, Susan G. Komen Race for the Cure, American Cancer Society, National Night Out and so many other worthwhile causes.

Because of the numerous benefits I received as part of the Boys Scouts when I was a child, it's been particularly rewarding to work with that organization and to be presented the "Silver Beaver," the highest award in Scouts and the "Scouting Vale La Pena Award," a National Boy Scout Award given for service to Hispanic American/Latino youth. I was honored and humbled as the first recipient. It is presented to the nominee who has made a significant contribution to their community, acted as an advocate for Hispanic Americans/Latinos and encouraged outreach to improve community conditions. From an early age the Boy Scouts were instrumental in molding me and instilling my ethical and core values, and it has been tremendously gratifying to pay it forward.

For example, I was asked to lead the Boy Scouts popcorn sales fundraiser. In previous years, the annual sales had never surpassed $200,000. As chair of the campaign, however, I reworked the process. I set it up as if the fundraiser was one of my dealerships and the Scouts were salesmen. As a result the sales have topped $3 million every year, and the boys continue to learn about what it takes to be successful. The opportunity

to positively help shape the lives of youths has been a blessing from God, and it's a major priority in my life.

SHAW'S ADVICE TO YOUNG ENTREPRENEURS

Do whatever it takes to achieve your goals and dreams, and never enter any situation or work environment with a sense of entitlement. No one owes you anything; it's up to you to earn it. And if things don't go your way, resolve to do whatever is necessary to turn it around and achieve your visions.

I couldn't possibly predict the obstacles you will face on your entrepreneurial journey, but I can practically guarantee that you will face major trials and challenges that will test your faith and perseverance. Don't give up, don't give in and do whatever it takes to be successful. In my own career, the late 1980s were very tough on me and my family. I lost everything I'd been building for many years, and it was really no fault of my own. The economy tanked, and my dealerships followed suit.

Nevertheless, I didn't lose faith or confidence in myself. I knew I could sell automobiles, and I went to work with a relentless mentality. As previously noted, I didn't take off one day for five years. I did whatever was necessary to pull my family out of a negative financial situation, and so did Nancy. That brings up another key element regarding any successful entrepreneur or businessperson: Your spouse.

If you plan on pursuing entrepreneurism in any way, shape or form, you are going to be required to make sacrifices. You will sacrifice your time; you will sacrifice sleep; you will sacrifice entertainment; and you will sacrifice many other opportunities that average folks are not willing to sacrifice. You are not going to be a movie expert, and you're not going to be able to watch every new television series or baseball game that your favorite team plays. The average Joe stays at an average income level because he is not willing to give up the TV shows and he is intent of getting his eight hours of sleep each night. Entrepreneurs and great businesspeople, however, are willing to work longer, stay up later, wake up earlier, travel less, spend less and sacrifice more than most of the population. Make sure that your spouse is on board with all the sacrifices that will be necessary. When you are dating someone, make sure that he/she understands that you are driven to succeed. People see Nancy and I today, and they are sometimes envious because of the trips we are able to take, the vehicles we drive, the multiple homes we own and the lifestyle we live. What they don't realize is that, in order to make it to this point in our lives, we spent years barely seeing each other, as she worked the night shift at the hospital and I worked the day shift six days a week for 52 weeks per year.

I think it's also critical to possess a fearless mentality when it comes to failure. Thomas Edison once said, "I have not failed. I've just found 10,000 ways that won't work." Another American inventor, Charles F. Kettering, said it this way, "One fails forward toward success." No matter how you phrase it, do not be afraid to fail. Entrepreneurism involves calculated risks, and sometimes risks fail…no matter how many calculations you've made. Many people are so afraid of failure that they simply want to put their heads in the sand and reluctantly decide to work for someone else the rest of their lives. That's fine, but that's not your destiny if entrepreneurism is part of your DNA. If that is in your makeup, you must possess a fearless mentality when it comes to fear.

Mike Shaw was presented with the Business, Innovation, Science and Technology Award by the Latino Leadership Institution Hall of Fame

You must also commit to continuing education and to learning from everything that happens to you. I learned so much from losing my dealerships in Corpus Christi. I grew as a businessman and became ultra conservative, realizing that cash is key. I reinvented myself as a businessman, paying off my debts as quickly as possible and paying everything with cash. I paid off the house in Denver; I bought a place in Vail with cash and I bought a ranch with cash. Debt is dangerous. Sometimes it may be necessary to take on debt when you are starting a business or expanding it, but never carry the debt any longer than necessary.

Always treat people right. That seems like common sense, but I've noticed that common sense isn't so common anymore. No matter what industry you choose, your people skills will ultimately determine your success. It's been my focus for all of my career to take care of my employees first and my customers second. If you do those two things, you will create a tremendous sense of loyalty and you will be successful. Guaranteed. I believe the most rewarding part of my retail automotive career has been participating in the professional and personal development of the people within my organization, because when my employees grow and develop, everybody wins. Watching my employees develop really is similar to the pride in watching your children grow up and develop into responsible adults.

Finally, commit to the core values that made Texas A&M what it is today. Commit to being a person and businessperson of high character and integrity. My faith, ethical behavior, integrity, principles and education are values that have guided me to success. By being a person of high moral standards and living each day with integrity, I have earned the respect of my employees, customers and residents in the community. Those ethics as a dealer have helped me become one of the largest minority-owned car dealers in the nation. I am the No. 1 minority-owned business in Colorado and third largest in the United States, per *Hispanic Business* magazine. And if your integrity is never compromised, the sky is the limit for you, too!

CHAPTER 8
Leslie Liere
Chief Executive Officer
Liere Insurance
Texas A&M Class of 1984

LIERE'S PATH TO TEXAS A&M

Starting and building your own business—regardless of the industry, the economy or the long-range profit possibility—is extremely difficult. There are not many—if any—overnight success stories in the real business world, and if the entrepreneurial journey is truly calling you, be prepared for a long, arduous and demanding path to any level of prosperity. While numerous entrepreneurs succeed, many more fail because of the risks, challenges, stresses, hours and laborious demands associated with transitioning from a startup business to an established and successful one. Bottom line: It's hard work.

Having said all that, however, starting an insurance agency and growing it into a thriving operation was a better life than the industry I first learned during my childhood. I was born in Houston to hard-working parents who were decedents of German immigrants. I grew up on a dairy farm outside of Houston in the Cypress area. At our peak of productivity, we milked 110 to 120 cows, and we cared for about 200 animals on the farm. Additionally, we farmed rice, corn and soybean, and we grew hay, as well. These were much different times, with much different technology and transportation, than in today's society. I was born in 1960 when dairy farms were quite common, even in big cities like Houston. In the early 1950s, for example, Harris County featured roughly 700 dairy farms. But times have obviously changed. According to the National Milk Producers Federation, less than two percent of the U.S. population is involved in any type of farming today, and you would be hard-pressed to find any dairy farms in Harris County nowadays.

Back in my childhood, however, when you were raised on a farm, everyone worked the farm. From an early age, my older brother and I were working in the field and milking cows. My brother, Richard, is six years older than me, but I can remember driving a tractor by myself long before I was eligible for a state-issued driver's license. I was probably nine when I first began driving a tractor on the farm, and my responsibilities essentially became a full-time job by the time I was in eighth grade.

My parents had done well earlier in my life, but low commodity prices and poor crops certainly changed our financial situation. As a result of several factors, we became cash poor and barely had enough money to pay the bills. Out of necessity, my father was forced to let go of all his paid helpers, including my brother, who landed a job away from the farm. As a result, I became one of three full-time employees who worked the farm. Mom and Dad were the other two "staffers."

My father was one of the hardest-working people I ever met, and I never met anyone who could do the physical labor that he could perform. He was a machine, waking up at 1 a.m. to milk the cows, eating breakfast at 6 and then going back out to farm. He did that every day and never, ever took a vacation. It was just the only way of life he ever knew. My father only went to school until the eighth grade because he never had a chance to go any further in school. His dad (my grandfather) was 63 years old when my father was born on a dairy farm as the youngest of nine children. His mother (my grandmother) died when he was nine. Furthermore, my grandfather became an invalid when he was 12, so my dad dropped out of school and worked that farm. Schooling or further education was not an option for him. Through my father's sheer hard work, however, he put me in a position where I had a choice, and I took advantage of it. He gave me that and encouraged me to continue my education. That's a big gift that I still appreciate to this day. I also appreciate the work ethic both my parents instilled in me. My dad started in the dairy business in 1942, and he retired in 1985 after 43 years of working seven days a week. And my mother worked every bit as hard.

As a kid growing up on a farm, I would sometimes start my work at 1 a.m., but I was occasionally allowed to "sleep in" until 2 or 3 in the morning. We'd work until 6 a.m., when my mother would have breakfast on the table. That was our sit-down, family meal of the day, and my father was back outside by 7 to work the fields. I'd join him in the summertime, but in the school year, I would eat breakfast, dress for school and attend my classes at Cy-Fair High School. After school, I'd go home, where the cows would be waiting for me.

It was draining, hard physical work, and I didn't spend much time watching television, hanging out with friends or even sleeping. My total income for all of my

A young Leslie Liere on the cover of **The Milk Producer** *magazine in 1965*

daily duties and responsibilities was $2 per day. That's not a misprint. It was what my father could afford to pay me, and it was better than nothing. Still, it wasn't much, even back in the early and mid-1970s. I tell people today that farm work and that particular salary were the best incentives for higher education that I could have possibly received. Enduring those difficult and demanding years made me long to be an entrepreneur or at least to find some sort of work that took me far away from the farm. Even back then, I really wanted to pursue another job because it would have been so much easier and so much more profitable, but I couldn't because I had to stay there and help my father. In assessing the situation, I concluded that the only way I was going to earn any more money was by trying to do something on my own. What I knew at that point in my life was cattle. Of the 200 animals on our farm, three or four of the cows were mine, and I mentioned to my father that I wanted to seek a loan and buy some cows of my own.

My dad dealt with debt issues throughout his life, but he was not afraid to ask people for a loan. He was told "no" most of the times, which is probably why he was skeptical about my chances of receiving a loan. My dad was a wonderful person, and I loved him with all my heart, but I didn't necessarily want what he had in life, so fortunately, I decided to pursue a loan to purchase the cows. Although my father doubted that I would receive a loan, I wrote a business plan, slipped on my Future Farmers of America (FFA) jacket and drove to downtown Houston to meet with a representative from the Harris County Farmers Home Administration.

Throughout high school, I had been extremely active in FFA and Rural Youth Programs, which did a great job of teaching how to give speeches, how to perform parliamentary procedure, how to run an election and win an office, as well as other leadership skills. In high school, I was on the parliamentary procedure team and was vice president of my FFA chapter. As a senior, I was president of our FFA chapter. The highest award you can earn in FFA is the American Farmer Degree, which is the equivalent to being an Eagle Scout. The year after I graduated from high school, I applied for my American Farmer Degree, which I earned. I was actually rated as the No. 1 FFA member in Texas. I point those things out not to brag or pat myself on the back, but rather to explain why I felt at least comfortable in meeting with a representative from the Harris County Farmers Home Administration.

On one hand, I was 16 years old and completely unaware of my prospects regarding a loan. But I had been trained how to present my case in person. I was a country kid from the farm, but I felt confident in my ability to communicate with adults. I met with a gentleman at the FHA, stated my case, presented my business plan and asked for a loan. He said that the organization had a Rural Youth Loan Program that would be perfect for me, and I was ultimately given a $7,000 loan.

I was delighted, and my father was pleasantly surprised and quite pleased that I received the loan. I proceeded to purchase some more cattle. Where I made the most profit was through the Houston Livestock Show and Rodeo. Every year, kids would participate in dairy scrambles, and each student who caught a calf was awarded a certificate to purchase a dairy heifer to show at the Houston Livestock Show the following year. Returning as an exhibitor, the student would show his heifer in a special competition with other calf scramble winners. Well, a dairy animal is not like a beef animal. She must be milked and must be a part of a dairy herd. Many of the city kids who participated didn't know what to do with their calf, and I would buy the dairy heifer from those kids and bring it to our farm. I would then have a calf and put it in our herd.

Back then, I would pay $600 to $700 per head. One of the last heifers I remember purchasing cost me $750. I brought her home, cared for her and ultimately she gave birth to a calf. She was a beautiful animal, and I sold her for $1,500, but kept her calf. I raised her calf, and I eventually sold it, too. So, not only did I double my original investment, but I also inherited another asset. That is how I began my career as a young entrepreneur. My father didn't mind me bringing additional cows onto the farm, because I was working for a mere $60 per month, and my dad just kept the milk proceeds to pay for the additional expenses. I received a small portion of the milk proceeds to pay my note each month, but I quickly discovered how much I enjoyed building a business and putting my money to work for me. Through all the trading, buying and selling, I paid off my $7,000 loan, paid all of my expenses and accumulated $16,000 in the bank.

By my senior year in high school, my family had moved to a 240-acre farm near Bryan in a little community called Reliance. I finished the last half of my senior year at Bryan High in the spring of 1979 and then transferred my credits back to Cy-Fair, allowing me to graduate with the kids I had attended school with throughout my life. At that point, I was considering two college destinations: Texas A&M and Sam Houston State. In all honesty, I didn't know enough about either school to realize much of a difference between them.

The reason I chose A&M came down to two factors: It's location in what was practically our backyard and the influence of an agricultural teacher I admired tremendously at Cy-Fair named Larry Ermis. Mr. Ermis was a diehard Aggie in every sense of the word, and he ended up moving to College Station and working for the university. While he was still working at Cy-Fair, however, he would take students to the A&M campus, to football games and on tours of the College of Agriculture. He was instrumental in helping me achieve the awards I won in high school, and he was a big influence in terms of my decision to attend A&M, which happens to be one of the most outstanding decisions I've ever made.

Unlike it is now, college was not a major expense in the early 1980s, especially at a place like Texas A&M for an in-state resident whose family lived close enough to campus that paying for room and board was not an issue. If I had not pursued a loan from the Farmers Home Administration, I probably would have needed to take out a student loan to pay for my education. But because I had $16,000 in the bank, paying for school was not an issue. Believe it or not, my tuition was only about $300 per semesters, and I spent another $50 to $100 per semester on books. By living at home, I saved plenty of expenses, and my entire four years at A&M cost me only about $4,000. I graduated in 1984 with no debt, becoming the first person in my family to earn a college degree.

In so many ways, Texas A&M was a perfect fit for me. At that time, there were many students at A&M who were just like me: First-generation Aggies coming from a farm and seeking a better way of life than their parents. I majored in dairy science within the College of Agriculture because, quite frankly, that's what I knew coming into A&M. Once school started, though, I discovered that the college learning experience could be so much more than merely attending classes and learning from professors.

I immediately became quite involved with the College of Agriculture, participating on the Dairy Judging Team, working with the Dairy Science Club and holding office as Treasurer of the Student Ag Council. By the time I was in my second or third year at A&M, I was on the Board of Directors of the Brazos County Farm Bureau; I was president of the Bryan Young Farmers; and I was president of the Dairy Science Club. During my junior year in college, I belonged to 10 organizations, held office in five of those organizations and was president of two of them. And those activities were on top of taking about 19 hours of classwork that semester and continuing to help my parents by working on the farm. Looking back, one semester of my junior year was probably the busiest I had ever been in my entire life. It was a bit of a blur, but it was all worth it. With all my classes and organizations, I was really beginning to see the big picture in terms of what I could become after college.

From left, the 1983 Dairy Judging Team at Texas A&M: Dr. Jimmy Horner, Leslie Liere, Monty Teel, Ricky Traweek, Ralph Freriches and Chris Woelfel

When I first arrived at A&M, I developed some really good friendships with fellow classmates and with faculty members in the College of Agriculture. I knew that networking within the Ag Department would be important because I initially figured that I would earn a degree in dairy science and earn a job within the agricultural career field. My perspectives widened dramatically, however, when Dr. Howard Hesby invited me to attend a faculty meeting with him. Dr. Hesby was a wonderful professor in the Department of Animal Science, who joined Texas A&M University in 1971 and influenced more than 15,000 students during his 35 years at the university as a teacher, advisor and mentor. Dr. Hesby, who died in 2005, was a great friend to his students and he was a magnificent mentor to me. I didn't know what I would gain by attending this meeting with Dr. Hesby, but I am certainly glad I did because it opened my eyes to an endless array of opportunities.

At the meeting, Dr. Frank E. Vandiver, who served as president of Texas A&M from September 1, 1981 to August 31, 1988, spoke to the faculty group about some of the big issues of the time. During his speech, Dr. Vandiver said something like, "We as a university have come under a lot of public criticism because our students are not technical enough when they graduate from Texas A&M. But my question is this: Are we training someone in a skill or a trade, or are we educating one's mind? I believe we are educating a person's mind, teaching that individual how to learn." When I heard him say that, I realized I could do anything with my dairy science degree that I wanted to do. If I could do well in classes like organic chemistry and other difficult and technical courses I took to earn my degree, I could learn and adapt to my environment in practically any industry or career after my graduation. It was just one of those moments in which a light went off for me in terms of breaking any self-imposed limitations I may have once placed on myself.

I held many positions and served in many capacities throughout my college career, but one of my favorite service roles was during my senior year at A&M when I was co-chairman of what was called Professional Career Planning and Agriculture. It was a college-wide activity and the largest activity in the College of Agriculture. Essentially, the other co-chairman and I recruited companies to come to A&M to hire Aggies. We recruited somewhere around 60 companies. I worked in the office of Dr. H. O. "Harry" Kunkel, who was Dean of the College of Agriculture from 1967 to 1988. He would provide me with a university car, and I would drive around Texas, making appointments and telling employers why Texas A&M would be a great place for them to participate in a career fair in order to attract young graduates to work for their company. It was great for me because it gave me a chance to interview with executives or managers with each of those companies, while I was trying to get them to come down here and hire Aggies.

I was becoming a fairly polished young man, but I was still a country boy at heart. For example, I had no idea how far Dallas and Fort Worth were from each other. I thought they were right next to each other like Bryan and College Station, I learned that was a mistake when I made numerous appointments to meet with businesses in the D-FW area, making one appointment in Dallas followed by a meeting in Fort Worth. I became quite familiar with Interstate 30 on that trip. Fortunately, I was a quick learner, and meeting with all those businesses inspired me to set a goal to be among the highest-paid students coming out of the College of Agriculture with a job offer. And in 1984, I received a lucrative job offer from a company called Ciba-Geigy for $26,000 year, which is probably the equivalent of $60,000 to $65,000 in today's market. Furthermore, I was going to be given a company car and travel expenses, as I would be traveling across the United States for 80 percent of my time as I met with cotton farmers regarding Ciba-Geigy's pesticides. It was a great job offer, and who knows how my life would have turned out differently if I had actually taken that offer.

LIERE'S PATH TO ENTREPRENEURIAL SUCCESS

My attractive offer from the Ciba-Geigy Corporation, an international organization that is the largest chemical company in Switzerland, was not the only job I was offered coming out of college.

My other consideration was, on the surface, much less attractive. The Farm Credit System in Bryan also made me an offer for $16,000 a year. While it was $10,000 less than my offer from Ciba-Geigy, the attractiveness of staying in the community was that I could build upon all the connections I made while attending Texas A&M. I couldn't put my finger on the value of the relationships I had established in the community while serving in roles such as being the President of the Young Farmers and Farm Bureau Board. I kept wondering: What is the long-term value of the network I have built here in the community. As I weighed my options, my gut feeling was to stay closer to friends, family and connections, taking the job with Farm Credit, as opposed to going completely out on my own without a network and moving to North Carolina.

One of the most attractive aspects of the role with Farm Credit System was that I was going to be introduced to lending. I wanted to be around money and I wanted to learn about money. That job was going to give me a skill set that I didn't possess. Working for the Production Credit Association, which was part of the Farm Credit System, would give me an opportunity to provide loans to farmers and ranchers in a seven-county territory. I started as a field representative, which meant I was an analyst for the other lenders. I was conducting field inspections, where we'd identify the collateral a prospective borrower owned. In a five-year period, I went from that position to Senior Vice President and Chairman of the Loan Committee.

I climbed the ladder quickly because I worked incredibly hard. One of the things I encourage young people to do is to establish a strong work ethic and reputation right away when you start a new career or job. When you're young and ambitious, you can accomplish so much if you are willing to put in plenty of extra hours.

Early in my career, I was involved in numerous farm organizations, as well as working as many hours as possible. One of the things that gave me a tremendous sense of pride was in 1988 I entered a contest for spokesperson for agriculture. It was a high-profile competition, and I won the state of Texas title in Corpus Christi, which punched my ticket to participate in the National Young Farmer Spokesperson for Agriculture contest in Salt Lake City. More than 300 people entered the contest nationwide, and 50 advanced to the national competition. When it was all said and done, I was selected as one of the three national spokespersons for agriculture. Elanco, an animal pharmaceuticals company, sponsored the event, and a media representative took the three of us across the country as we gave speeches about agriculture to a variety of groups.

That was one highlight of 1989, and another was marrying my wife, Karen Weedon, on January 28, 1989. I first met Karen at the old country dance place, the Hall of Fame in Bryan, where plenty of the young locals would hang out. Karen was from Bryan, and her family was entrenched in this community. When our daughter, Victoria, was born in 1992, she became the seventh generation on my wife's side to be born in Brazos County. Karen had also attended Texas A&M, graduating in 1982 with a degree in management.

Not long after I married my wife, I also made another life change. In 1990, I figured I had gone as far as I could go in the local office of Farm Credit. To go any higher with Farm Credit, I would have had to move to Austin or some other place, and neither my wife nor I wanted to leave the Bryan-College Station area. Instead, I went to work for First City, which was then the ninth-largest bank in the United States. It was a Texas Bank, and I was able to work for some great people who were very good to me. I worked there for two years as a lender and primarily focused on agriculture. At that time, however, many banks in Texas were failing and were going out of business. The people I was working with were worried about losing their retirement. Our bank made good decisions, and it was a well-managed bank, but it was a part of a system that was sick. The system was losing, and I believed it might be time for me to take an entirely different career path.

I had learned of an opportunity to possibly open my own business in the insurance industry, but it was a risky move for a variety of reasons. First, my wife was eight months pregnant when I began pondering the possibility of going into business for myself. Secondly, I would be giving up a good job to risk everything—at least what little we had. My wife and I spent one entire night laboring over whether I was going to pull the trigger or not. We decided to do it together, which was very important, as we both knew it would take immense sacrifices from both of us to make it work.

LIERE'S MOST CHALLENGING OBSTACLES

Sometimes when you reflect back on your life, it is rather bizarre what sticks out in your mind many years later. When I think back on my early days as an entrepreneur in the insurance industry, for example, an image that comes to mind involves taking our infant daughter out of the house for the first time and visiting Washington on the Brazos on a Sunday afternoon. Victoria was born roughly two weeks after I had opened my agency. I had left a comfortable position in banking for the uncertainty of a new business venture, and

Leslie and Karen Liere with their daughter, Victoria

I recall walking along the banks of the Brazos River, contemplating my new role and the challenges in front of me. For whatever reason, I remember looking down into the passing water and thinking to myself: It is sink-or-swim time. I wasn't necessarily intimidated, nervous or worried. After all, I remember looking down at the river and thinking, "Everything else in my life has worked out. Why would this be any different? I'll just saddle up, give it everything I have and grind my way to success."

I had originally learned about the insurance opportunity after having a conversation with a good friend of mine from the bank, Bob Stennis. Bob and I were talking, and he was telling me that he'd heard that this particular insurance company was committed to establishing a presence in Bryan-College Station, and it was probably a good opportunity for the right person.

What I liked about the opportunity was the chance to work on my own and build my own business. Insurance was a good industry, something everyone needed…much like banking. I knew I would be competing on price and service, which was essentially the same factors that determined my success at the bank. If I had stayed in banking, I would probably never have the chance to go into business for myself. But the insurance industry offered a fairly inexpensive entry point into entrepreneurship. Additionally, I'd be in business for myself, and my success or failure would be entirely up to me. The company my agency represented sent me to attend a two-week training session, where I was given instruction on insurance manuals, computers and other business practices. I then opened a 900-square-foot office on Harvey Road next to Al's Formalwear. It was initially a two-person operation, and I was open from 9 a.m. to 9 p.m. Monday through Thursday; 9 a.m. to 5 p.m. on Friday; and 10 a.m. to 2 p.m. on Saturday. That does not include the hours I spent after work building a better business plan and dreaming or the early morning meetings I attended with various community organizations in my continual attempt to network. And in all seriousness, when you go into business for yourself, you are essentially on the clock 24 hours per day. Even today, when I am sitting in my living room, I am thinking about the next day or what transpired that day.

I'd like to say that all of those hours I spent at the office and away from my family paid major dividends right away, but that would be a brazen, bald-faced lie. I struggled mightily as I was starting my career. At the end of each week, I was barely surviving. Now, please understand that I was not merely going into my office each day, reading the newspaper and waiting on the phone to ring. I was being as proactive as I could possibly be, calling practically every potential customer in the Bryan-College Station marketplace. I could initially afford to hire one assistant to answer phone calls and to handle clerical filing, so I could make all the calls myself. This was before the "do not call" lists, and people would hang up on me on a regular basis. Still, I'd cold-call every number I could find, asking if I could provide a quote on their insurance. But trying to find a "yes" was like searching for a needle in an entire hayfield.

I was putting in so many hours that I often didn't make it home for dinner. My wonderfully supportive wife would often make a great dinner for our family, but I would call her and inform her that I would not be able to make it home. If you are going to be an entrepreneur, it's so important for your family to buy into the vision. Karen and Victoria were both so supportive and understanding. Instead of being angry about me not coming home for dinner, Karen would pack the dinner in Tupperware containers and bring dinner to the office.

In the early days, though, the sacrifices didn't produce immediate results. I remember one low point, in particular, where I attended a meeting with other agents representing the same company. I made the drive to Austin for the meeting in the morning, and all the guys were talking about all their sales and how well things were going for them. This was on a Thursday, and I had yet to sell one policy. I don't know if I have ever felt so badly in my life. I had to figure how I was going to improve. I was discouraged, but I wasn't defeated. Many times I stared at the framed picture I kept on my desk containing a paraphrase from a quote that Theodore Roosevelt delivered in 1910. It states:

"The credit belongs to those who are actually in the arena, who strives valiantly; who know the great enthusiasms, the great devotions and spend themselves in a worthy cause; who at the best know the triumph of high achievement, and who at the worst, if they fail, fail while daring greatly, so that their place shall never be with those cold and timid souls who neither know victory nor defeat."

I took pride that I was in the insurance arena, and I knew I could be successful. The key was to create a value proposition for a customer that didn't exist elsewhere. I just had to find a way to meet with customers and differentiate my product from others in the marketplace by beating others on price, providing better service and bundling products into a great value. More than anything, though, I knew that if I could meet with prospects face to face, I could build a rapport with them and develop a relationship.

One of the big things that helped me when I started in the insurance business was finding other Aggies who were starting in the insurance business. The Aggie network was very valuable to me. We worked together, as we were all starting our agencies at about the same time. We were not really competitors. For example, my agency was in College Station; David Nix's office representing the same national provider was in Temple; Warren Barhorst's was in Jersey Village; and we didn't sell many policies outside our markets at that point. So, we spent time at night visiting with each other and asking each other what they were doing successfully. When we would have meetings and conferences, the Aggies would always be in the corner trying to help each other, while people from other schools were dispersed.

Ultimately, utilizing the Aggie network, building relationships and putting in all the necessary hours were the key to my building a strong customer base. I started my insurance agency in 1992, and by March 1994, I was doing 50 sales per week. I still have this note from one of the executives with my national insurance provider:

"For sales week ending March 17, 1994, you weren't high sales agent for the week but I want you to know that your 50 sales did not go unnoticed by me. Outstanding! You certainly have come a long way since I've visited your agency.
Best wishes, Earl F. Peitz, March 17, 1994."

One of the things I often tell young people when they ask me for advice is that there's a big difference in hoping and knowing. When I first started my business, I was hoping I could make it all work.

But at some point in 1994, after I had been on my own for a couple years, I began to know I could be successful. You cannot sell 50 insurance policies in a week unless people are telling their friends and family about you. There's just no way you can do it. The only way customers will tell their friends and family about you is if they like what you've done for them. If they feel like you've provided them with better value and/or service than another agency, those referrals will come, ultimately allowing you to produce 50 or more sales a week. And once you are at that point, you have the money to begin hiring people so that you can multiply your own efforts.

When you're starting out, it's vital to be able to convince prospective customers that you're going to be the guy who is willing to work harder for them than anyone else. It's even more important to prove that after the customer gives you a chance. You must value every relationship, every customer and every interaction. You don't work for anybody, but your customers. When you are running your own business, it's important to remember this old adage: "If you take care of your customers, your customers will take care of you." That's the truth. When you fulfill the promises you have made to your initial customers and when you exceed their expectations, they will tell their friends and family about you. That's the secret to any amount of success I have achieved in this industry. But here's the key to remember: There's no magic wand or overnight formula to follow to bring instant success. We live in a microwave society, where people want instant gratification. That's not how you build a successful business, though. Even though times and technology have changed, the key to business success has not. It all comes down to exceeding expectations, developing relationships and building customer loyalty one customer at a time.

Today, we estimate Liere Insurance has in excess of 15,000 customers, and we are headquartered in a beautiful office space on Copperfield Parkway in College Station. We write insurance throughout Texas. We specialize now in what is called "personal lines," which is primarily home and auto insurance policies. We lead with homeowners insurance, but typically the home and auto policies go as a package. Several years ago we made the difficult decision to become independent, which allows us to provide more options to our customers. Today we represent more than 100 insurance companies, and very few of our competitors can match our product offerings. And, of course, our service is world class. That's where we've established our niche and competitive advantage through the years.

We no longer cold call people in search of business. But rest assured, that's how I started my business, and that's the sacrifice I was willing to make to build a customer base. By doing business with us, the customer may be assured that he/she is receiving the best policy for his/her individual needs because we have the ability to shop that person's insurance through multiple markets, which is a huge advantage to the customer. As a result, we've continued to grow in the overall size of our business, but more significantly, we've continued to build upon our strong reputation.

Liere Insurance has been recognized as a 2007, 2008, 2009 and 2015 Aggie 100 company.

The Aggie 100 identifies, recognizes and celebrates the 100 fastest-growing Aggie-owned or Aggie-led businesses in the world. The Aggie 100 not only celebrates a company's success, it also provides a forum to pass lessons to the next generation of Aggie entrepreneurs. The Aggie 100 was created by Mays Business School's Center for New Ventures and Entrepreneurship. The Center provides encouragement, education, networking and assistance to entrepreneurially-minded students, faculty and Texas businesses. I am proud of those accomplishments, and our agency's success has enabled me to be recognized individually by the Texas A&M Foundation as a member of the Legacy Society and as an Eppright Distinguished Donor by the 12th Man Foundation and Texas A&M athletics. I am a lifetime member of the Houston Livestock Show and Rodeo, and I have been able to support Gary Blair Charities. I have also been able to serve on the Board of Directors for Inspiring Possibilities, an organization dedicated to inspiring individuals with physical, developmental or emotional challenges to empower themselves to develop their full potential.

None of those accomplishment, however, would be possible without focusing on one customer at a time and meeting the needs of the individual customers. I am proud of the honors we have achieved, as well as the overall growth of our customer base and the increased size of our staff. Most of all, though, I am proud of how many loyal customers we have, and how many of those clients have referred their friends and family members to us. There is no more rewarding endorsement than to see fathers recommend Liere Insurance to their sons and daughters or for local residents to send their neighbors to us. We've built our foundation on integrity, which is why we have been able to expand and prosper year after year.

LIERE'S ADVICE TO YOUNG ENTREPRENEURS

Most everybody has heard this old adage: "It takes money to make money." I understand the premise behind the motto, but I believe the adage needs some further explanation. I am living proof that you do not need to come from money to make money. But when I was in banking, I realized you had to have two things to be successful: You had to have enough capital and you had to have the right management. You had to have the money and you had to know what you were doing. You may have all the money in the world, but if you do not know what you are doing, you are not going to make it. Likewise, if you have a sound strategy but no money, you are not going to make it.

I much rather prefer this quote from Norman Vincent Peale, an American minister and author known for his best-selling book *The Power of Positive Thinking*. Peale once said, "Empty pockets never held anyone back. Only empty heads and empty hearts can do that." That's true wisdom. Peale also said, "Believe in yourself! Have faith in your abilities! Without a humble but reasonable confidence in your own powers you cannot be successful or happy." I concur. If you believe in yourself and your abilities, you can overcome practically anything…even empty pockets.

When I've told my story in the past, some people have been stunned that when I was just 16 and completely broke—making $60 a month working for my dad milking cows—I thought outside the box and wrote a business plan that allowed me to receive a $7,000 loan. My dad did not support me in my pursuit, and I suppose that would have been discouraging enough to prevent some people from even pursuing the loan. Fortunately, I did not need my father's support to seek a better way of life than he had achieved. As I noted before, I loved and admired my father, but I think it's important to remember a couple of things. First, those closest to you may doubt you the most. That doesn't mean they don't love you, but sometimes it is difficult for someone like my father to see beyond the limitations of his own bank account. His dreams were not as big as mine, and he did not see the world in the same way I viewed it.

As I milked one cow after another, I knew that I eventually wanted to leave the farm. But I also knew that in my current environment at 16 years old living on a farm, buying dairy cows was my ticket to college. I didn't have the option of counting on my parents to pay for my college education. In fact, I knew there was no possibility of that, but I also knew that God had instilled dreams within me and had given me the confidence to believe in myself. I wasn't an expert at writing business plans, and that also was not something I could turn to my parents for advice. I simply had to figure out a way to write the plan and present the representative from the Harris County Farmers Home Administration with that plan. If I had done nothing; if I had been discouraged by my father's response; if I had waited for my ship to come in; or if I had allowed any fear of rejection to prevent me from seeking the loan, I would have never accumulated $16,000 to pay my own way through Texas A&M. Perhaps that's a long-winded way of me advising you to go for your goals now.

If you have a vision for your future, go for it. Consider all your resources. Use organizations such as Startup Aggieland to your advantage, seek mentors on the A&M campus, read entrepreneurial books, study success and—most of all—take action. Nothing creates momentum like taking action. But it's also important to realize how many resources you have at your disposal as either a student or former student at Texas A&M. Being as active as possible in numerous organizations while I was a student at Texas A&M benefitted me beyond my wildest dreams. I went from being a shy farm kid, who was most comfortable "communicating with cows" to being involved in 10 student organizations by my junior year. I held office in five of those organizations and was leading two of them while taking 19 hours that semester. My involvement in those organizations taught me so much about leadership skills and filled me with confidence to pursue my dreams.

It's also wise to continually develop connections and to network with fellow students, former students, faculty and university personnel. Looking back, I had great mentors among the faculty, including Dr. Howard Hesby and Dr. H. O. "Harry" Kunkel, and I also had met so many people in the community as a student that I didn't simply take the most lucrative job offer right out of college. Instead, I took the offer that allowed me to best utilize the contacts I had made in college. As a former student or student at Texas A&M, you are probably well aware that there is no other alumni group like the Aggie network. But that network will not work for you unless you work it. Don't expect to receive a degree from Texas A&M and to simply ride the Aggie network to fortune and fame. It doesn't work that way. Make the contacts, join the organizations, become an officer in the clubs, seek mentors, find groups with similar goals and plans and work the network.

Find something you enjoy and to pay attention to the marketplace around you. If you want to be a professional landscaper and you have a passion for landscaping, seeking a law degree may make you miserable, even though there may be great income potential in law. If you want to coach, don't be afraid to coach just because your starting salary is not going to be comparable to your fellow student at A&M who earned a degree in electrical engineering. I believe there is money to be made in practically any industry or endeavor if you are passionate about being the best in that field. Put together a business plan for a business that stirs your passions and that the plan is going to change as you evolve because there is no such thing as a business plan that stays constant. There is a term called fluidity and that means you have to adjust. Start out with an idea or concept, develop a plan and update that plan yearly, monthly and even daily. One of the biggest pitfalls for many startup entrepreneurs is being so married to your original plan that you end up failing because you don't know how to adjust as circumstances demand it.

Sometimes, life and circumstances will demand a change in direction. I left the bank because the industry changed dramatically. I didn't want to go down with the ship, so I started my own business. Once I went into my own business, it seemed like many people around me expected me to fail. I heard things from friends and relatives like: "There are so many insurance agencies. There's so much competition. You have no experience. You aren't going to make it. You are going to fail."

Fortunately, my wife and I went into entrepreneurism together. We were a team. We knew the sacrifices that needed to be made, so when I didn't show up for dinner, she brought dinner and my daughter to me. It is so important that your family is on board with your dreams. It wasn't just my wife who was on board, but also my daughter. Karen and Victoria were not only my cheerleaders, but also my motivation. Any success I have achieved is with them and because of them.

When I started my business, I think some of my friends and colleagues thought I was going to be standing in the middle of Texas Avenue with a tomato crate trying to sell people insurance as they stopped at a red light. But they didn't realize how hard I was willing to work. Again, it's amazing how many people who love you—and I mean really love you—will often attempt to discourage you from making a big mistake. Their hearts might be in the right place, as they don't want you to experience pain or failure. But please, don't allow others—even folks who sincerely want what's best for you—to persuade you from taking calculated risks and stepping out on your own. As American journalist and humorist Frederick B. Wilcox once stated, "Progress always involves risks. You can't steal second base and keep your foot on first."

Finally, be willing to persevere and never give up, no matter what industry you choose to pursue. Staying with the baseball analogy, you probably didn't hit a home run the first time you ever picked up a bat. You must practice and practice and practice. Even then, the greatest baseball players of all time typically fail seven times out of every 10 times to the plate. But the key is to continually learn from your mistakes and to never become so frustrated that you give up.

Many people, whether they are in sports or business, give up on themselves and their dreams when life is difficult. When it is tough, you have to stick with it. You have to work hard in order to make it work out. Looking back on opening my business, my wife and daughter were big inspirations to me, but the bottom line is that I knew that if it was to be, it was up to me! And no matter what, I was going to be successful, no matter how many hours it required me to work or how many people hung up on me when I was trying to make a sale. I was not going to fail under any circumstances. Failure was simply not an option.

Speaking of that, I will leave you with the incredibly wise words of former British leader Winston Churchill. On October 29, 1941, while recounting Great Britain's progress during the first 10 months of World War II, Churchill said these famous words: "Never give in, never give in, never, never, never, never—in nothing, great or small, large or petty—never give in except to convictions of honor and good sense." Those words were meant to inspire the Allied troops in the war effort. But they still ring true today in terms of the key to achieving any of your entrepreneurial dreams. Find a field. Make a plan. Pursue your passions. And NEVER give up.

CHAPTER 9

Jay Conner

President & CEO
MLAW Engineers, MLA Labs, Inc., Texas Drilling Services, Inc.
Texas A&M Class of 1982

CONNER'S PATH TO TEXAS A&M

According to an article in the *Kansas City Star*, the longest odds ever to be overcome in the history of sports was the 2016 Leicester City soccer team, which won the 2016 Premier League. Before the start of that season, United Kingdom oddsmakers thought so little of Leicester City that the odds were established at 5,000-1. When Leicester shocked the Premier League by winning the 2016 title, it cost bookmakers more than $14.6 million. Closer to home, it has been estimated that the odds of the 1980 "Miracle on Ice" U.S. Olympic hockey team winning the gold medal would have been 1,000-1.

I mention those long odds to begin this story of my life because if any bookmaker would have seen me as a child and seen the environment in which I was raised, the odds of me graduating from a place like Texas A&M and becoming the president and CEO of one of the most respected structural engineering firms in Texas would have likely been more outlandish than Leicester City and the 1980 U.S. Hockey team combined. Or even multiplied.

I was born in March 1960 in Washington D.C. to parents who were, right from the start of their union, destined for a divorce. My father, who was originally from Memphis, had been in the Marine Corps during his late teens and early 20s. He was a rugged and tough disciplinarian. When he met my mother, he was a 22-year-old Fuller Brush salesman with a chip on his shoulder because he had not earned the veteran benefits that he thought he deserved. When my parents met, my mother, whose family was from Virginia, was a lovely, 24-year-old woman with four children from a previous marriage. Within two years after they were married, I arrived as the fifth child in a family headed by a traveling brush salesman.

As you might imagine, there were times when money was so scarce that I thought my parents would require us to hang the toilet paper out to dry. As you also might envision, financial pressures and my dad's drinking strained my parents' marriage as they moved the family along the East Coast in his sales efforts, stopping for various amounts of time in Virginia, the Carolinas and Georgia. That was all within the first five years of my life. Then in 1965, my parents decided to move across the country to try their luck in California. But we never actually made it to the West Coast, as we stopped in Houston to visit my aunt and uncle and ended up planting roots in "Space City." In fact, my first vivid memory of Houston was when workers were completing the construction on the Astrodome, once dubbed the "Eighth Wonder of the World." It was quite the sight to see, as the first baseball game played at the Astrodome occurred on April 9, 1965.

We first rented in Bellaire, and then purchased a home in Missouri City. It was my mom, dad, older brother, three older sisters and me. My brother was the alpha male and superstar athlete, who possessed Hollywood good looks. The girls all loved my older brother, as he excelled in every sport and practically everything he ever tried. I was the opposite in almost every way; a little wimpy kid, who looked up to my brother but realized rather quickly that I could never be like him. My brother was my bodyguard in many ways, and he was an imposing figure. Most kids wouldn't mess with me because they knew he was my brother. My brother and I had an interesting relationship, to say the least. He'd pick on me, beat on me and so forth, but he did come to my aid against others who tried to mess with me. Later in life, he would explain his bullying was in an effort to toughen me up.

When my brother was 14, he bought himself a truck so he could start working. As a result, he never really "maximized his participation" in high school, which is a shame because he could have been quite the prep sports star. He married and divorced at a young age. My older sisters left home one at a time at relatively young ages, as well. One of my sisters dropped out of school early, married a champion surfer and moved to South Padre Island. My parents' marriage began to seriously unravel in the early 1970s.

It was a dysfunctional family in virtually every sense, and my parents created quite the scene when my mother finally decided to leave the house. My mother and father were both trying to pull me away from each other on the day she finally had enough. She was crying and told me to go to my room to pack my things. Quite frankly, I didn't really know what that meant. How long were we going to be gone? How much did I need to pack? I had a ton of questions. But I knew my mother loved me dearly, so I followed her instructions, grabbed some things and packed them into a bag. We loaded up her car and started driving away. I didn't know where we were going, and as it turns out, neither did my mother. At one point when she was driving, she obviously came to the conclusion that she had nowhere else to go. We turned around, went back into the house, and we both slept in my bedroom in the bunk beds that my brother and I once shared. Ultimately, my parents divorced when I was about 12, and my mother and I moved into a townhome in Westbury Square, a 7.5-acre site near the intersection of Chimney Rock Road and West Bellfort Avenue in the Brays Oaks district of Southwest Houston.

Westbury Square was built in the early 1960s, and in its heyday, it was considered to be the premier shopping destination in the city. The property was filled with specialty shops and had a wonderful European village feel to it. There was a candle shop, a pizza parlor and an ice cream shop—among other stores—and all the buildings were set around a fountain and piazza. After the opening of The Galleria in November 1970, however, Westbury Square slowly began to decline. That's when my mother and I moved into the neighborhood. My mother was in the real estate industry, and she worked extremely hard to support the two of us. In fact, I might not see her for several days at a time as she worked to pay our bills. This situation necessitated I learn to cook, and she would leave $5 sitting on the counter for me after I came home from school. I could walk across the street, buy a package of pork chops and a box of macaroni and cheese for a few dollars and make my own dinner. Occasionally, she would be at home in the evening to cook us dinner, which was always nice, but I learned at an early age to do things for myself. For a while, my mother would take me to Luby's Cafeteria on Sunday afternoons for a nice treat.

Meanwhile, my father ended up selling furniture in Houston. He was off on Tuesdays and on many weekends. Whenever he had time off, he'd inevitably head for the coast, where he had a small boat in Galveston. As time progressed, he purchased a bigger boat, and many of his friends would regularly ask him if he would take them fishing. That opened his eyes to the opportunity to make some money by taking people fishing. He initially went to work for an older couple, who operated a fishing boat, and the captain began training my father to run the boat. My father loved fishing, loved the coast and loved the idea of running his own party fishing boat.

On one particular Tuesday, my father encouraged me to skip school so that I could accompany him (I mentioned we were dysfunctional, right?) to the coast. Naturally, I skipped school, and we drove down to Kemah in my father's 1967 Bellaire station wagon. He pulled up to the dock, told me to wait in the car and went to speak to Captain Scott about something. When he returned, he told me that he had good news: If I was willing to work on the boat, he wouldn't need to pay for me to be on the boat.

This was the "good news," I wondered silently to myself, as my father gave me an encouraging smile. I was 12 years old, and I didn't know the first thing about working on a party fishing boat. I was scared to death, but I really didn't believe my father would accept "no" for an answer. So, my father introduced me to Captain Scott and his wife, (affectionately referred to as "Sea Hag" by the deckhands, when not within earshot). She instructed me to begin carrying supplies (cases of soft drinks, big bags of ice, frozen shrimp to be used as bait and so forth) onto the ship. Loading the ship was the easy part of the job. The ship was a 65-foot, wooden hull vessel originally built in the 1940s as a harbor fire boat. Working the boat as a deck hand could be quite dangerous in numerous ways, especially for a wimpy 12-year-old novice such as myself. My father initially moved to a seedy part of Galveston, took over Captain Scott's operation and put me to work as much as possible, especially in the summers. Being freshly divorced, Dad turned to the bottle pretty heavily, continuing to live in Galveston near The Strand. He was drinking every night, but we always seemed to make the best of the situation.

We had some good times working together in Kemah over the years. He eventually moved north to League City, which was much closer to the boat. The work was exhausting, but we would almost always have a big lunch together in between the morning and afternoon fishing trips. And practically every morning my dad would make me an egg sandwich that we would eat on the boat after we had loaded everything up and before the tourists arrived. We would stand in the wheel house and talk. It was a special time that I still think back on fondly. On the other hand, I also have some painful memories from those times working on the boats. I remember a treble hook—three prongs—going through my little finger. Instead of angering my father for my carelessness, I ripped the hook from my finger, wrapped it in a paper towel secured by duct tape, and continued my deckhand chores on the boat. I also was stuck more times than I care to remember by hardhead catfish. Hardheads are voracious feeders, but you must exercise great care when removing this fish from your hook as the slime layer covering the large barbed dorsal spine is mildly toxic. A puncture will be followed by severe pain and swelling. The spine is also barbed, which makes withdrawal an additionally painful process. My dad warned all the guests not to try to remove the hardheads and to instead let me do it. He'd yell "hardhead," and I would come running. Many of those guests literally thought my name was "hardhead." We also endured some seriously scary storms out at sea. One incident involved lashing a safety line (rope) around my waist as we plucked two survivors from the water after their small boat capsized in rough seas. Their friend, who rounded out the fishing trio earlier that morning, did not survive the event.

I worked on and off with my father for four or five summers during my teen-age years, and I saw my father at his best and his worst. He could be really fun to be around, displaying a great sense of humor, and he could also be calloused and cruel, especially when he was drinking.

Another one of those life-defining moments came when I landed a job in high school working at a place called Vetco Pipelines off of Britmoore near Beltway 8. I would drive my pickup from Southwest Houston, where I was a decent student at Westbury High School, to the northwest part of town near Jersey Village. I had the vague idea that I wanted to be an architect, and I knew that I would need to go to college to attain that goal. I had not been raised in a family where college was a priority…or even a subject for discussion. But I knew I didn't want manual labor or blue collar jobs for the rest of my life, so I figured it might benefit me to gain some sort of experience in a career field that might help in preparation for college. Vetco Pipelines was the perfect place, and I actually shared an office with one of the vice presidents of the company.

I had a great job making decent money, and I learned all about the process of "pipeline pigging." Buildup in a pipeline can cause transmittal slows or even plugging of the pipeline, but cracks or flaws in the line can be disastrous. To prevent plugging and to detect any weaknesses in the pipeline, devices known as "pigs" are used to perform various maintenance operations. This is done without stopping the flow of the product in the pipeline. Without getting too technical, my first job was to serve as a draftsman to the man who was overseeing the production for the Russian pipeline, the Mexican pipeline and the Alaskan pipeline. He would tell me what he needed me to draw, and I would sketch it out for him. It was also my responsibility to monitor the pipeline pigging, detecting any issues and trying to avoid any major issues that could stop or slow the flow of the pipelines. Usually cylindrical or spherical, pigs sweep the line by scraping the sides of the pipeline and pushing debris ahead. As they travel along the pipeline, there are a number of functions the pig can perform, from clearing the line to inspecting the interior to determine if the lines are cracked or corroded.

I was essentially given the run of the office and was allowed to work whenever I could and for as long as I wanted. I was 17, making an average of about $350 per week in 1977 and feeling quite confident about a bright future. My mother was also dating a gentleman at the time who owned an insurance agency. He was a Texas A&M graduate, and his brother was a professor at A&M. My mother's boyfriend volunteered to take me up to A&M, and he introduced me to his brother. Up until that point, I thought I wanted to go to University of Texas, Texas Tech, Texas A&M or even MIT. But that visit to Aggieland convinced me that Texas A&M was the best place for me. Fortunately, my mother hounded me enough to make sure I applied, and I was accepted at A&M and began my collegiate career in the fall of 1978. That same year my mother met and eventually married a generous, brilliant man from England that I proudly refer to as my step dad.

I would like to tell you that I was a great student at Texas A&M, but that would be a bald-faced lie. I wasn't a good student; I wasn't an interested student; and I wasn't particularly driven to do much of anything, other than play softball, party and meet coeds. I basically just went through the motions for a couple of years. I quit one semester and worked a construction job in Houston. Another semester, it was suggested by the school that I sit out a while, so I took a job, again in Houston, as a delivery boy for a wholesale florist. It wasn't until my senior year when things really kicked into gear for me. I realized I had been wasting my time and talents, and my parents' money, and I went and met with the dean of the environmental design program to figure out a way to graduate as soon as possible. I pulled plenty of all-nighters and took as many full labs as I could. As a result, I managed to graduate with a degree in environmental design in December of 1983. As noted previously, my plan was to become an architect. Of course, there is a rather famous Woody Allen quote that states, "If you want to make God laugh, tell him about your plans." He obviously had other—and better—plans for me.

CONNER'S PATH TO ENTREPRENEURIAL SUCCESS

When I graduated from Texas A&M, I was engaged to a woman whose parents were rather wealthy. Her father was in the insurance business, and he owned a ranch in Dripping Springs, which is about 20 to 25 miles west of Austin. She wanted to plant roots in Austin, and she convinced me to seek a job in Austin. I knew some fellow recent Texas A&M graduates who were making anywhere between $50,000 and $75,000 working for Exxon in the oil and gas industry, but I couldn't find anything that paid much more than $13,000 in the world of architecture. Without any immediate source of income following my graduation, I first went back to work on my father's boat in Kemah, scraping and painting to help him maintain the boat in the dead of winter. It was miserable work, and it was certainly not the reason I went to college.

As winter turned into spring, I went back to the Austin area with my fiancé to look for a job. I picked up the newspaper and began searching through the job listings. I noticed an advertisement for an engineering firm that was seeking an entry-level draftsman. The words "entry-level" are typically another way of describing "low-paying," but the job was in Austin, and I did have experience as a draftsman. I called the phone number, scheduled an interview that day and received a phone call about a week later from the engineering firm when I was back working on my father's boat. The Austin-based engineering firm was called "MLA"—named in honor of partners Kirby Meyer, Robert Lytton and Frank Allen—and it had been around in some form since 1964. In 1965, the firm designed the first post-tensioned slab-on-ground foundation in Central Texas. PT slabs eventually became the standard in residential and light commercial construction. When MLA called me, the person on the other end of the phone line said I could have the job if I showed up on Monday morning. I leapt at the opportunity before I even asked how much I would be paid. The answer to that question was rather depressing: $6 an hour. But at least it was in Austin; it was inside an office; it wasn't manual labor; and I wasn't going to be in danger of ending the day with a treble hook in my little finger. So, I packed up everything I owned in my Nissan 4x4 pickup truck and moved to Austin in the spring of 1984 to begin my "career" in the engineering industry.

I intentionally chose not to focus on my income. Instead of dwelling on the fact that I was going to be earning only $6 an hour, I viewed the job as an opportunity to get my foot in the door with an established engineering firm. Besides, I figured that at least my fiancé would be extremely supportive of me as I worked my way up the MLA ladder, considering the fact that I was relocating to Austin to continue developing our relationship. Once again, my plans obviously differed from the one God had in store for me.

I started with MLA (now known as MLAW) as a draftsman, which meant I drew pictures. Back in the old days you had a drafting board with a T-square or a parallel bar and triangles, along with pens, pencils and erasers. I was drawing foundations and structural plans for houses by hand. I didn't know what I was doing at first, and I can distinctly recall telling my boss to be patient with me, promising him that I would pick it up over time. He was not pleased with my initial work, but—just as I had promised him—I did pick it up and improve the skills I needed rather quickly and began to make a positive impression on my co-workers. And I proved right away that I didn't mind putting in the extra hours. I asked my bosses how much I could work, and I was told: "as much as you like." That was music to my financially starving ears.

I definitely liked the sound of that, because I was being paid by the hour. Once I clarified that I would, indeed, be paid for every hour that I worked, I began spending 50, 60 and sometimes over 70 hours in the office. That did wonders for my paycheck each week, but it did not do much to improve—or even maintain—the relationship I had with my fiancé at the time. As you might have guessed by my use of the words "at the time," the relationship didn't last. Not long after I accepted the position paying a whopping $6 per hour, she suggested that she stay in Houston and we "date other people." I suppose she was a bit dismayed by that pay rate and just couldn't wait around to share my vision that hard work will help you climb the corporate ladder. I didn't know any high up muckety mucks to place me into a higher-level position, so I began the climb.

Her decision hurt me and was a serious short-term blow to my ego, but it turned out to be one of the most wonderful things that ever could have happened to me. The best way to mend a broken heart, I reasoned, was to focus more and more on my work. As I spent more time focusing on my career, I grew to know and enjoy visiting with a woman who worked down the hall from me near the water cooler. And I was thirsty. Unfortunately, she was married, and consequently, dating Marsha never initially crossed my mind. But I liked her as a friend and co-worker, and I could tell that she possessed an authenticity and a genuine sense of integrity that made her extremely rare. As time passed, I also learned that, while she was married and had a 6-year-old daughter, the marriage was on the rocks. I had been at MLA for almost a year when Valentine's Day rolled around in February 1985. Most of the other women in the office were receiving flower deliveries and going on lunch dates when I noticed Marsha had not received anything. Nor was she preparing to go to lunch. I made up my mind then to go to the local florist and purchase a single rose for Marsha.

I returned to the office, presented Marsha the rose and wished her a happy Valentine's Day. I think that lone action led her to begin thinking about how miserable she was in her marriage. She eventually filed for a divorce, and I asked her to go out with me. Our first date was a romantic trip to Taco Bell, the restaurant her daughter, Rebecca, chose and approved. We ultimately moved into a condo in South Austin. We didn't have a lot of money, but more significantly, we didn't have much time together away from the office. My wife will tell you that we didn't make many memories together in that condo, because I was rarely there. I was committed to my career, and my wife was supportive of that focus. If she wanted to spend time with me, she would typically bring dinner to the office. Marsha continued to work her normal hours at MLA, which changed its name in '85 to MLAW when John Whitaker, PE became a shareholder. That was also the same year MLA Labs was formed. The company was growing, and I believed I was making a name for myself by working so hard. In hindsight, I absolutely could not have climbed the ladder at MLAW without Marsha's support and encouragement.

I was the only person in the company to receive four raises during his first year at MLAW. They weren't big raises, but I was eventually bumped up to $8 an hour. I was pleased with the raises, but I was taken aback when one of the shareholders told me I was in a dead-end job. I still remember all these decades later the way I felt when he told me that. I was shocked, and I was intent on proving him wrong. I even said to myself: "I'm going to have your job one day."

With the raises I received, I was able to buy Marsha a new car, and we also bought a house. Unfortunately, just as things were looking up for us, the economy started to die. The residential housing market dried up, especially in Austin, and the commercial construction industry wasn't much better. As a result, one of the founders of the company, Kirby T. Meyer, began cutting employees to keep the office doors open. From 1987 to 1989, he cut the staff from 125 down to nine. The phones stopped ringing, and the income opportunities stopped being generated. Because of the work ethic I had always displayed, I wasn't laid off, but I was reduced to part-time hours. With mouths to feed and bills to pay, I did whatever I could, picking up work whenever and wherever I could find it. Not only did I continue working at MLAW, but I also began selling automobiles, remodeling homes and painting houses and offices. I worked every day of the week, including weekends, and I often worked into the wee hours of the morning. It was quite common for me to have 80- to 90-hour weeks. It was miserable, but all the odd jobs at least kept food on the table.

In the late 1990s, I was experiencing one setback after another, and I just couldn't see any other option other than to work, work, work. As I wondered how long I could keep it up, Mr. Meyer called me and said one of the largest homebuilders in Austin, Milburn Homes (later acquired by D.R. Horton), was looking for a new engineering company to provide soils reports and foundation designs for their building operation. "You are the only one that I can think of who can handle this for me," he said. "This company wants to meet with us about doing all their engineering, and I would love for you to come back full-time if you'll consider it."

I met with Mr. Meyer, and then we met with Milburn Homes. They believed we were still operating with our full staff, which had enabled MLA (and later MLAW) to develop a strong reputation throughout the Austin area. In reality, the MLAW staff was essentially down to just Mr. Meyer, a draftsman who had been with the company since the early 1970s, a secretary and me at that time, although we certainly did not say anything to dispel the impression that we were still a thriving, bustling engineering firm. After our meeting with Milburn Homes, I confidently told Mr. Meyer: "Let's do this. In fact, let's do this and take this city by storm!" Smoking his pipe, he looked at me like I had lost my mind. And perhaps I was thinking outlandishly. It would take a Herculean effort on my part to perform every role in the engineering production process, but what I saw was the unlimited potential, not the enormous workload. It's like the late, great Henry Ford once stated: "Whether you think you can or you can't, you are right."

I believed we could, and Mr. Meyer really had nothing to lose, as he was already about to be forced to close his operations. He made me a deal as we began this endeavor together, offering me 45 percent of the gross on any business I brought in the door. In other words, if I brought in a $1,000 piece of business, I would earn $450 right off the top. Or if I brought in a $10,000 deal, I would make $4,500. I was 31-years-old, and I needed the money. It was now 1991, and my family had grown since Marsha and I were first married. In addition to my step-daughter, Marsha had also given birth to our first child together, daughter Christine, who was then 2. I leapt at the opportunity to basically receive a commission for my efforts, knowing that I would do whatever it took to be successful. Besides, Mr. Meyer's offer meant I could drop the auto sales and odd jobs, focusing my full attention back on MLAW.

Once we began to work with Milburn Homes, I would pick up the plans from the homebuilder's headquarters, revise and produce the plans, deliver the plans wherever they needed to go, inspect the construction location, complete any other necessary paperwork and deliver the finished product to Mr. Meyer, who would review it and provide his stamp of approval. Then I would deliver everything back to Milburn Homes. I worked my butt off to make sure we brought in plenty of business, and after about a year, I was earning about $150,000 in annual commissions. Once again, things were looking extremely bright for my future.

Once again, though, Mr. Meyer, who died at age 78 in June of 2013, was rather short-sighted in his next decision. Years earlier when the economy and construction industry in Austin had begun to crumble, Mr. Meyer had essentially told many of his employees that they were to abandon ship by laying them off. Perhaps because of my upbringing and my experiences on a boat in dangerous conditions, if I had been in his position, I would have likely chosen to ride the storm out. I fully understand why he chose to lay employees off, but by cutting the payroll he also cut his income potential. Mr. Meyer was a wonderful man who earned his B.S. in civil engineering from Texas A&M in 1957, served at A&M in the Ross Volunteers, and went on to receive his master's in civil engineering; studying at Harvard, and that little place in Austin. He taught me many great things, and I had immense respect for the man. But occasionally, I also learned what not to do as a business leader by watching him.

That was the case when he called me into his office about a year after making a deal with me to pay me 45 percent of any business I delivered to MLAW. In that meeting, he informed me that he had made the decision to place me back on the payroll at $12 an hour instead of allowing me to earn my income because of my productivity. I was dumbfounded and devastated. He told me that I was making too much money because, after he paid the other employees (including the ones he had added as business picked up) and paid all the bills and expenses, I was earning more than him. I didn't see a problem with that because I was only being paid based on the revenues I was producing. Nevertheless, he had resolved to place me back on the payroll at an hourly rate. When I asked him why he chose $12 an hour, he told me it was because his long-tenured draftsman was making $13 an hour, and he didn't think it was fair to pay me more than him.

You can probably imagine how frustrated I felt. I always believed Mr. Meyer was reluctant to promote me or to provide ownership options because I didn't have an engineering degree. I could have told him at that moment that I resented him and pointed out that my environmental design degree was serving me better than any of his other employees with engineering degrees. But in hindsight, this turned out to be another defining moment in my life and career. I was tempted to quit, and most people would have agreed that I had justifiable cause. In fact, I was tempted to tell him where he could shove my hourly job. Instead, I did the prudent thing. I simply told Mr. Meyer that, while I didn't agree with his decision, I was going to prove to be so valuable to him that he was going to need to rethink his decision and rework my pay scale.

It's probably important to make a point here. Just because I was angry didn't mean that I needed to react angrily. The reality in this life is that the bridges you burn today may be the same bridges you need to cross in the future. We all have a choice in how we respond to a situation that we deem frustrating or unfair. We can choose to be angry or we can choose to stay in control. It really is that simple. It's not necessarily easy. But it is simple. As I will point out later in this chapter, there is a time and a place to respond to a situation by raising your voice, taking a stand and demanding that your opinion is heard. But more often than not, the best choice to make is to remain calm, to not overreact and to not burn bridges. Always remember that first we make a choice and then our choice makes us.

I vowed to make Mr. Meyer pay me more. And then I promptly made enough calls and knocked on enough doors that I landed contracts with several of the top builders in Austin. By 1993, I became Vice President of MLAW Consultants & Engineers; by 1994, Mr. Meyer was so impressed with the amount of business I was generating that he offered to place me on an ownership plan in the company; and by 1995, I helped to lead an expansion into the San Antonio marketplace. By 1996 or '97, I had hired a team of draftsmen and inspectors, and our staff grew to more than 50 employees. By the end of '97, I also interviewed every employee at MLA Labs, which had become a dysfunctional company that Mr. Meyer was preparing to shut down. Instead, he allowed me to review MLA Labs' entire operating structure, to fire some of the troubled employees and to bring in new people. MLA

Labs was a drilling and geotechnical company, which was basically the blue collar arm of MLAW. To make a long story short, I took over MLA Labs in 1998, retooled the operations and by 1999, I was basically running both MLAW and MLA Labs.

I possessed a laser focus on taking care of customers, taking care of all the details of the work environment and taking care of our employees. And I stayed laser focused for years and years and years. Even though Mr. Meyer always seemed to disregard me because I didn't own an engineering degree, I was so productive and influential that he felt compelled to provide me with more and more of the company's stock. By 2003—less than 20 years since I first arrived at the company making $6 an hour—I became the President and CEO of MLAW Engineers. The following year we expanded operations into the Dallas-Fort Worth area, and we now feature operations in Austin, San Antonio, Dallas-Fort Worth, Houston, Bryan-College Station, the Killeen-Waco-Temple region and the Texas Coast.

Today, MLAW Engineers works closely with MLA Labs, which is the premier leader in Texas soils expertise. MLA Labs has drilled more than 450,000 borings in Texas, providing more than five decades of data on some of the most expansive and highest-risk soils in the nation. MLAW Engineers has daily access to all soils test results, without the delays many firms experience using outside labs. This seamless integration of soils and structural engineering ensures that each site will be properly examined, soil testing will be performed and a site-specific design will be produced on each project. This also enables MLAW Engineers to produce foundation designs quickly, providing our clients with the best lead times in the industry.

In more recent years, MLAW Energy was formed in 2011 in response to new home mandates and customer demand for more energy-efficient homes. And in 2014, MLAW Forensics was introduced as a separate entity that works closely with MLAW Engineers. I serve on the Board of Directors for MLAW Forensics. In 2019 I began Texas Drilling Services, Inc.,(TDS) headquartered right here in Aggieland. TDS offers a variety of drilling services for the residential and light commercial industry, including geotechnical borings and helical pier installation.

Unlike some of the other amazing entrepreneurs featured in this book, I didn't start MLAW from scratch. But I am proud of the fact that I have stood on every rung of the corporate ladder, even throughout the depressed market years. All my experiences have provided me with solid, hands-on understanding of every aspect of the business, from plan drafting to a driller's helper, and from field inspections to marketing, sales, contract negotiations and the overall operations of the company. We have

built an organization and a team that makes me extremely proud. Our successes have allowed me to create a lifestyle that I would have never even imagined possible when I was a kid. I mention that not to boast, but rather to inspire you to seek greatness. If a guy like me can manage to create some financial security and peace of mind, I am convinced that practically anyone else can match or surpass me. And please allow me to make one point that I will expand upon in the next section: Money is not the most important thing. But it is imperative to have money when the most important things in your life are threatened.

CONNER'S MOST CHALLENGING OBSTACLES

In fictional novels or movies, predictability is often perceived as boring. Most people don't want boring at the theater; they want exciting, uplifting or even terrifying. In real life, however, it's the unpredictability that can so often be terrifying. And who wants terrifying in real life?

Regardless, sometimes we must face the scariest of real-life situations. No matter what you do or how successful you become, take my word for this: Life occasionally will remind you not to take anything for granted. After all, in this life, there are no guarantees and no assurances. Tomorrow is promised to no one.

Looking back on what was easily the most terrifying and tumultuous times of my married life, I truly believe a movie could be made about the events from about 2012 to 2016. Ultimately, it would be an uplifting movie. But there were times—many times, in fact—that the situation appeared dire for our family as my wife was quite literally on her death bed. I am also convinced that if I had merely accepted the doomed fate that the medical professionals had predicted for my wife that she would not be here today. When we were married, our vows did not include giving up on one another in times of sickness, so even though the doctors and surgeons were ready to write her off and send her to the grave, I was not. My wife was so weak that she could not be an advocate for herself. So, I took it upon myself to be her advocate, and I refused to allow any of the medical professionals working with us to pronounce her case as a hopeless one.

This is a long story, but I will make it as concise as possible. In 2012, we were told that my wife had cirrhosis of the liver. Most people associate cirrhosis with heavy drinking, but that's not the whole story. While alcohol is the leading cause of cirrhosis in the United States, even teetotalers can develop the condition. Any scarring of the liver not caused by drinking is referred to by the broad term "nonalcoholic cirrhosis." One of the liver's jobs is clearing germs from the blood. Occasionally, however, germs take the upper hand. A chronic infection by the hepatitis C virus is the most common cause of nonalcoholic cirrhosis in the United States. Chronic infections of hepatitis B can also lead to cirrhosis. Nonalcoholic steatohepatitis (NASH), a condition in which the liver contains extra fat and becomes inflamed, is another potential starting point for cirrhosis. Nobody really knows exactly how my wife developed cirrhosis, but she did not drink heavily. Doctors labeled it Idiopathic Liver Disease.

Nevertheless, it was determined in 2012 that she had end-stage renal disease, meaning her kidneys were no longer able to work as they should to meet her body's needs. Healthy kidneys filter wastes and excess fluids from your blood, which are then excreted in your urine. When your kidneys lose their filtering capabilities, however, dangerous levels of fluid, electrolytes and wastes can build up in your body. That's what was happening to Marsha, and as a result, we were told that she would be on hemodialysis for the rest of her life. That was shocking enough, but the diagnosis was even worse when it was just the doctor and me in the hallway. I point-blank asked him what this diagnosis meant in terms of her life expectancy. "It depends," he said. "It could be a few years, or it could be just a few months. We just can't tell for sure."

After two weeks in the hospital in Austin, Marsha was sent home. Before she was released, we had to locate a chair in a dialysis facility. We also had the option to set up a clean room in our home to perform the hemodialysis treatments. Each treatment lasts about four hours and must be done at least three times per week. In addition to the four-hour treatments, it requires up to an hour of prep time and up to an hour of recovery. Essentially, it consumes your life. There are also a variety of side effects such as low blood pressure, nausea, vomiting, dry and itchy skin, restless leg syndrome, muscle cramping and many other miserable conditions. Another type of dialysis allows the patient to stay home and have the treatment for 8 hours every day! This became so all-encompassing that I asked what would happen if we discontinued dialysis. "Statistics say she would be dead within a week and a half, maybe two weeks," the doctor told us. We scratched that off the list and began researching kidney transplant options, which was the only option we had that could prevent dialysis for the rest of her life. In the meantime, we decided that home dialysis was not right for us, which meant we would be in and out of dialysis clinics every other day of the week for the "next few years until her passing". Most of the days not spent in the dialysis facilities were spent in emergency rooms or doctor's offices.

Did I mention that by this time, my dad was now facing end of life realities due to heart failure, and his wife was dealing with her rapidly advancing dementia.

In those frequent trips to medical facilities and extended stays in hospitals I learned so much about the medical field that truly alarmed, disturbed and angered me. There is not enough space in this book to document all the disheartening and troublesome incidents we experienced while I was desperately trying to save my wife, but what I learned is that you must perform your own research; you must ask questions; you must take notes about all that you or your loved one is being told; you must not assume that because your caregiver is in the medical field that he/she is an expert in your ailment; you must not make the assumption that doctors and surgeons on the same staff are communicating with each other; you must demand attention, becoming the squeakiest wheel on the planet if necessary; and you must not be lulled into the false assumption that everyone in a hospital or clinic is looking out for your best interest. The bottom line is that, unless you demand the treatment you deserve and the answers you seek, there's a good chance that you will be overlooked and underwhelmed by the lack of patient-focused, high-quality care that you are not likely to receive.

I vividly recall sitting in the hospital with my wife, who was knocked out following a dialysis treatment while the woman assisting her was finishing up. The doctor walked in, addressed my wife about her overall status, told her they were releasing her to go home for the Fourth of July holiday and then asked her if she had any questions. Keep in mind that my wife was not even aware the world was turning. She, of course, said nothing, and the doctor turned to walk away. He didn't know I was sitting in the room due to the dimmed lights. As he neared the door, I stood up and said, "Wait a minute! Did you just walk in here and have a conversation with my wife, who is not even conscious? How dare you just do this and then try to leave, knowing that she wasn't capable of answering any questions."

Only because I demanded an answer to my questions did he provide it. We discussed her condition, and the hospital staff soon began preparing her to leave for the holidays, even though she could barely move. In fact, she was so sore that she was in excruciating pain as the staff awkwardly attempted to help her into my vehicle. I was not in favor of her leaving the hospital at that moment, but we did, and it was a horrible experience. Marsha was miserable, and as she laid on the couch for three days, she kept feeling worse and retaining large amounts of fluid. After three days of agony, we took her to the emergency room in the same hospital we'd been released by three days earlier. Instead of simply retrieving Marsha's records, however, we were asked to fill out paperwork and to explain the nature of our visit. That sent me into a fit of frustrations. "You have got to be kidding me," I said. "We just left here. You sent her home, even though we requested for her to be able to stay. This is absurd. Get somebody from upstairs to retrieve her records and to begin the dialysis that she desperately needs." I was scolded by the staff and told by one nurse to settle down because I was not the only person with problems. Meanwhile, my wife is in agonizing pain that is weakening her will to live. Hours later, we finally managed to get her into a hospital room, where the dialysis began. Under normal circumstances, that should have begun to make her feel better.

These, however, were not normal circumstances. Days passed, and Marsha seemed to continue to decline. She wouldn't sit up in bed. She wouldn't communicate, and when you did say something to her when she was awake, her eyes seemed glazed and eventually began to cross. She laid in the fetal position for two days straight. She had given up. One of our daughters and I were together in that room most of the time for three days, and one of us was at her side at all times. Finally, it struck us that we had not seen her eat. She had picked at her food occasionally, but she hadn't eaten anything. They would be delivering her food to her room at the same time they were wheeling her out for four hours of dialysis. And even if she was in the room at the same time as the food, as noted previously, dialysis can make you quite nauseated. During previous treatments, Marsha had been provided Nepro nutritional shakes, which allowed her to continue receiving the calories, vitamins and nutrients she needed without actually eating. She particularly liked the butter pecan-flavored Nepro drinks, but we were told they didn't have the Nepro shakes. As a result, Marsha was practically starving to death, being poisoned by the wrong meds and being sleep deprived. I called a retired muckety muck I know to see who he might possibly know that could "rattle the cage" at the hospital so we could maybe slow things down a bit; maybe just long enough to get some attention. A doctor came in, then another, then the Hospitalist, then the head of nursing, then the nutritionist. They each came in, one after the other, to assess my wife's condition. The hospital was suddenly stocked with plenty of Nepro shakes for the rest of Marsha's stay. Her meds were changed, and they altered the schedule of checking on her in the middle of the night. Then my phone rang, asking if things were better now. Our mysterious cage rattler was following up. The moral here is you never know who the people you know, might know. Six degrees of separation sort of thing. Speak up and ask questions.

Jay and Marsha Conner at Miramont Country Club

There are so many other frustrating stories I could tell, but we eventually began to place all our efforts, hopes and prayers into the idea of receiving a transplant. That is the only way she would live longer than another several months. Once we began the long, exasperating and tedious process of filling out a wide array of forms and so forth, my wife's health had begun to further deteriorate. A lump had been detected on her breast, she had some sort of mysterious infection and she also had a collapsed lung. The biggest issue, however, was that we discovered that her kidneys were also failing her. She didn't need only a liver transplant. She needed a liver and a kidney. We bounced from one medical facility to another in Austin, San Antonio, Bryan, Temple, Houston and Dallas, finally arriving at the Dallas Transplant Institute, where we were initially told that because of my wife's overall health condition, she would not be a transplant recipient. This was devastating news to me, but I was determined not to accept any diagnosis of "terminal". I realized the chances of my wife dying a miserable and agonizing death were 100 percent without the transplants, and I was committed to proving that she could be a good transplant recipient.

We ended up back in the emergency room in Bryan, and the doctor walked into the room to begin the same series of basic, get-to-know-the-patient questions I had heard at least a million times before. I didn't even wait for him to finish his first sentence before interrupting. "Look, I need you to know one thing right away," I said. "We are going to save her life. We are going to figure out what needs to be done, and then we are going to do it. Is that your attitude, yes or no? If you say no, that is fine we are going to walk out and find someone else." He walked over and shook my hand and he looked at her and said, "We need more advocates like you."

That confirmed to me that we were finally on the right track. A biopsy was performed on her breast, and we determined the lump was benign. They also gave her something for her collapsed lung, but it didn't work. Days later, they tried something else, which still didn't work. As a result of the collapsed lung, the mysterious infection, her declining bodyweight, the stomach pain, the difficulty swallowing and other ailments, she was probably coughing three to five thousand times per day. More tests were then performed; more diagnoses were considered; and it was ultimately determined that she had myeloperoxidase deficiency (MPO), which is an enzyme in the body that plays a major role in aiding in microbial killing. In laymen's terms, that meant it *could* affect her immune system. In a study conducted in Europe, about half the patients with complete myeloperoxidase deficiency had infectious complications. What that meant to us is that once again, Marsha was not deemed to be a good transplant recipient, because there was a possibility that she could die even with the transplant because of the risk of a weakened immune system.

Once again, though, I refused to simply take my wife home to die. I had to convince some doctor—or someone in charge—to take a chance on her. We had already been told that she could be on the waiting list for a kidney for as long as six to eight years. That was discouraging enough, but now we were being told that because of the MPO, she wasn't even eligible to be on the list. At that point, we essentially began making phone calls, sending emails and visiting medical facilities on my wife's behalf as often as possible. I tried to always be polite, but I also made it clear that I was not merely going to sit back and accept her death. She was doing everything she could, but she continued to decline. I knew there was a strong possibility that, no matter what I did, my wife was going to die. But I was willing to die trying every avenue to save her.

Finally, after months of doors figuratively slamming shut on our hopes and prayers, one man gave us hope. That person was Dr. Bernard V. Fischbach, a nephrologist in the Dallas-Fort Worth area, who also happened to be the chairman of a committee that reviewed and approved the transplant lists. In a nutshell, nephrology is a subspecialty of internal medicine concerned with the diagnoses, treatment and management of kidney functions and renal (kidney) replacement therapy such as dialysis and kidney transplantation. Dr. Fischbach, who graduated with honors from Creighton University School of Medicine, told us that he appreciated our efforts, sympathized with my wife and respected our relentless pursuit of a positive answer to our prayers. Dr. Fischbach told us that he was going to vote in favor of allowing Marsha to be placed on the transplant list. But he was only one vote among the committee members, so we spent the next few weeks on pins and needles as we hoped for the best and tried not to think about the worst. In the meantime, Marsha was terribly sick, and I was extremely worried that she might die before we ever even learned whether or not she had made the list. Many times, I would wake up at night just to check on her to make sure she was still breathing. Another time, I had to perform the Heimlich maneuver on her when she nearly died chocking when her collapsed lung cleared. But she was so frail I was afraid I might break her in two by administering the abdominal thrusts.

She almost passed away four specific times, and who knows how many others. One incident was the classic, "you need to make your phone calls to your family and loved ones; she's leaving us now". That was a toughie.

At 4 p.m. on November 6, 2015—the day before the Texas A&M-Auburn game at Kyle Field—we received the call we'd been anticipating. It was great news: Marsha was being placed on the transplant wait list. We had no idea how long it might take before she would receive the liver and kidney transplant because obviously, somebody would have to die before the surgeons could begin the organ procurement. The next morning at approximately 6 a.m., we received *the* call from Dallas. A suitable donor for Marsha had died that evening. We were not given any other details, but we were told to have an ultrasound done at Scott and White in Bryan-College Station. Marsha was in the midst of that ultrasound when I received another call on my cell phone. "Mr. Conner," said the voice on the other end of the phone line, "where is your wife? We need her here as soon as possible to begin the transplant!" I momentarily questioned her about why they requested an ultrasound in the first place, but I let it go and basically had to "raise a ruckus" in the emergency room to get her out of the ultrasound immediately so that I could get Marsha, load her in the truck and get her to Dallas. Once we loaded her up, I made the three-hour drive—in the pouring rain—in record-setting time, running red lights and navigating through hazardous road conditions.

By God's grace, we made it safely to Dallas, and on November 7, 2015, my wife successfully received the double organ transplant in a seven-hour operation. The Aggies lost the game that evening, 26-10, but my family celebrated one of the most unlikely victories we could have imagined. I have thought often about the organ donor since that unforgettable day in the fall of 2015. We never received any details about the person's death or anything else, but I pray for that family's loss and I thank God for the person's sacrifice. As I write this chapter, my wife is healthy and happy. She is a walking, talking miracle and reminder to me of God's grace. The mere fact that she is still here and enjoying a high quality of life is a constant reminder to me that the most important things in life are worth fighting for, no matter how frustrating or how long the fight lasts.

CONNER'S ADVICE TO YOUNG ENTREPRENEURS

As I noted previously, there are more important things in life than money, but if anyone tells you money is not important it probably means that he/she is broke. T. Harv Ecker, author of the book

"*Secrets of the Millionaire Mind*," addressed the subject this way: "Money is extremely important in the areas in which it works, and extremely unimportant in the areas in which it doesn't. And although love may make the world go round, it sure doesn't pay for the building of any hospitals, churches or homes. It also doesn't feed anybody."

Nor does it pay for healthcare. Think about it. If I had not been in the financial position to crisscross the state for four years in search of a solution for my wife—often leaving my work behind for weeks at a time—the love of my life would not be here. Likewise, there were numerous out-of-pocket expenses that had to be paid in order to simply keep her alive. What price would you pay for your mother's life? How about your sibling or significant other? In all likelihood, the answer is: Whatever it takes. But if you do not have money, you could be in big trouble.

So, part of my advice to you is to pursue wealth. And never be ashamed to pursue it with all your might. Pour yourself into your work. Dedicate yourself to continuing education. Commit to learning and pursuing excellence. Wealthy people are typically those who are absolutely committed to being wealthy. Conversely, those who do not have financial freedom are typically only "wanting" or "hoping" to become wealthy. There's a major difference. If you are committed to achieving financial freedom and fulfilling your dreams, you will do whatever it takes. You will work as long as it takes. And you will sacrifice as much as it takes.

I didn't come from any money in my family. I absolutely salute my mother for providing me with inspiration while I was growing up and putting me through school. My father—rest his soul—didn't know much about making money, investing money, making money work for him and so forth. Some people might guess that would be a hindrance to me in my pursuit of wealth. But it may have actually been a blessing. Because of my background, I didn't think anything was below me. Even with a college degree from a prestigious place like Texas A&M, I started my career at MLA making $6 an hour. Who would have thought then that I would one day be owning and operating three engineering companies? Not many people, I assure you. But I made the most of my opportunities, and I encourage you to always make the best of your situation.

During the odyssey of fighting for my wife and also fighting for my father's life, I was working with a team of various experts developing new products and services based on what I have learned in the world of engineering. And now the patents are rolling in and new companies are being formed. These are the culmination of investments of time and money, hopefully resulting in plenty of mailbox money for my wife in her old age many years from now.

My journey was not an easy road to the top of the company, and many times I was frustrated. But I refused to quit. That's another piece of advice I would like to share. If you will simply refuse to give up, your success is practically assured. I know this because the masses will give up. And they often give up right before they were about to make a breakthrough.

History is filled with inspirational stories about the greatest movers and shakers who simply refused to let go of their dreams. For example, author J.K. Rowling was divorced and on government aid in order to feed her baby in 1994, just three years before the first *Harry Potter* book was published. When she was shopping it to publishers, she was so poor she couldn't afford a computer or even the cost of photocopying the 90,000-word novel, so she manually typed out each version to send to publishers. It was rejected (and probably trashed) dozens of times until finally Bloomsbury, a small London publisher, gave it a second chance after the CEO's eight year-old daughter fell in love with it. At last count, Rowling had sold more than 400 million copies of her books and her net worth is just less than $1 billion, which makes her the world's richest author.

Former NFL quarterback Kurt Warner was released from the Green Bay Packers in 1994 and eventually landed a job sacking groceries and stocking shelves at Hy-Vee grocery store in Cedar Falls, Iowa for $5.50 an hour. From that humble start, Warner refused to give up on his dreams and eventually became an NFL and Super Bowl MVP. And Winston Churchill, the legendary Prime Minister of Great Britain and probably the most quoted person in history on the subject of never giving up, was defeated in every single election for public office until he became Prime Minister at the age of 62. Said Churchill about the subject: "Never give in–never, never, never, never, in nothing great or small, large or petty, never give in except to convictions of honor and good sense. Never yield to force; never yield to the apparently overwhelming might of the enemy."

I never gave up in my business career, no matter how many hours I had to work or how many obstacles were placed in my path. Throughout all my growth as a businessperson, I thought the reward was simply financial freedom. In reality, though, all those hardships, tough times, frustrating disappointments and long hours were preparing me to lead my wife and family through a four-year trial that we may have given up on if I had not become so committed to never giving up in any important part of my life. Keep that in mind whenever you may be tempted to throw in the towel on your dreams.

CHAPTER 10
Scott Polk and Emily Huskinson

President of Lyles-Degrazier
President and Founder of RingWraps
Texas A&M Class of 1985
Texas A&M Class of 2012

EDITOR'S NOTE: This chapter highlights a partnership that was formed by Scott Polk and Emily Huskinson, which illustrates the power of the Aggie network and epitomizes the willingness of Aggies to help other Aggies in business endeavors.

POLK'S PATH TO TEXAS A&M

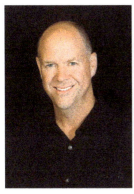

I grew up in Dallas bleeding maroon, loving Texas A&M and dreaming about one day dressing in a maroon and white uniform and playing Aggie football. My father, John, was A&M Class of 1957, the same year an Aggie running back named John David Crow won the school's first Heisman Trophy. While I did not attend many games when I was young, 1970s A&M stars like Ed Simonini, George Woodard and Bubba Bean were definitely household names in my home. I'd listen to games on the radio and dream of the possibilities of playing at Kyle Field.

My father flew helicopters in the Army and then flew commercially for American Airlines. He was a hard-working and highly motivated man, who grew up dirt poor and was determined to make something out of himself, despite coming from a broken family. I believe one of the major influences of his life was the lessons that he learned by attending Texas A&M. He is deceased, but I still have his saber and senior boots from his days in the Corps of Cadets. He was certainly a hero to me and my siblings, and he's the reason I first fell in love with Texas A&M and the idea of being an Aggie.

Coming out of W.T. White High School in Dallas, I fulfilled my childhood dream by signing with then-head coach Tom Wilson in 1980. Those were not the greatest times for A&M football, as we only went to one bowl game (the Independence Bowl in in that "dreamy" destination location of

Shreveport, Louisiana) in my five years as a letterman at A&M. Yes, I said five years as a letterman. I suppose that's a great example of Aggie math.

I tore an ACL in the the spring after my freshman year and tore my hamstring during my sophomore season, which permitted me to seek a medical hardship redshirt season. I then played the next three years (all for the legendary coach Jackie Sherrill), which technically made me a five-year letterman.

One of my favorite memories of my time in Aggieland was living as a team in Cain Hall, which is now a parking lot. As the rock band Kiss so eloquently put it many years ago, "Those were crazy, crazy nights." At Cain Hall, I learned how to play Backgammon, how to play Pente and how to hit a two-iron down the third floor hallway between pizza man robberies and trash can spills in rooms. I'm not exaggerating. It was crazy and captivating.

I had to have a knee operation as a result of my football career, and I still have "reminders" of my injuries. My wife, Stephanie, has asked me previously, "Knowing all you know now with your knee, would you do it over again?" I told her I would absolutely do it again. God provided some unbelievable relationships for me and some real growth in my life when I was at A&M. I was blessed to have been involved in a great church in Aggieland, Grace Bible Church. The friends I made and the experiences I had while I was at A&M have meant so much to my development physically, mentally and spiritually. I wouldn't change a thing if I had it to do all over again.

I certainly wouldn't change my favorite memory as a player at A&M, which is easy to pinpoint because I really only made one play that is truly worth mentioning. It occurred on Thanksgiving Night in 1984 at Austin's Memorial Stadium. We were leading the game, which was being broadcast nationally by an upstart sports cable network called ESPN. A year earlier, we had taken a 13-0 lead over Texas as Kyle Field rocked and swayed like rarely before. But then the Longhorns stormed back to score 45 unanswered points en route to a convincing 45-13 win. It was the 12th Texas victory in the last 16 meetings against the Aggies, and it was yet another painful reminder to A&M fans of the Horns' supremacy in the series.

The following year, even when we sprinted to a 20-0 halftime lead over the Longhorns in Austin, few A&M fans were breathing easily. And when Texas marched down field early in the third quarter, there was a fear among many Aggies—probably even some on our own sideline—that "here we go again." With the Longhorns at the A&M 10, Texas kicker Jeff Ward lined up for a 27-yard field goal attempt that would have cut into our lead and given the Longhorns a major momentum boost.

Instead, Domingo Bryant swooped in from the right side to block the kick. I was lined up on the left side, and I picked up the loose ball and started running. I made it 76 yards to the Texas 7. We then converted the blocked kick into an 18-yard Eric Franklin field goal and a 23-0 lead. We went on to a 37-12 win, and I instantly became a folk hero of sorts. One of the funny things is that I've seen plenty of old Ags through the years who will recall the play as a touchdown. They'll say, "I remember the game in

Austin on Thanksgiving. It was on ESPN, where you caught that block, or the fumble, or the interception and ran it back for a touchdown." More than half the guys who bring it up remember it as a touchdown. I never really bother to correct them anymore.

Quite frankly, it probably should have been a touchdown, but I tell people I was actually just trying to run out the clock. I can honestly say I recall some thoughts of what was in my head as I was running, the first of which was, "What's taking everybody so long to catch up to me?" I remember the term "lumbering" was used to describe it. That's fair. I don't think I had run that far since two-a-days. Defensive guys don't run 80 yards for sprints, we run about 40. I was good for the first 40 yards, but after that, I started to lose a little ground.

Nevertheless, that win over the Longhorns changed the series. Beginning with the '84 game, we rolled off six straight wins over Texas and won 10 of the next 11 against the Horns. Following my final season at A&M, I signed a free agent contract with the Kansas City Chiefs. If only I had possessed a little more size, a little more natural ability and much more speed, I would have been a perfect fit in the NFL.

Instead, I was with the Chiefs for only a couple of months before coming back to Dallas to become involved in the family business. My grandfather started in the diamond business in the late 1940s, and today, I run a wholesale diamond business called Lyles-DeGrazier, which manufactures fine jewelry for some of the better stores and designers.

POLK'S PATH TO ENTREPRENEURIAL SUCCESS

My maternal grandfather, Arch Lyles, was in the wholesale distributing diamond business from an early age. He was born in Dallas in 1909, and he dropped out of school at 14 to support the family because his father died of Tuberculosis. My grandfather slowly climbed the ladder within the diamond industry, and he bought Lyles-DeGrazier in 1949.

As a kid, I used to work for my grandfather, hopping on a city bus where we lived in North Dallas and riding the bus all the way into downtown Dallas to go to work for him. I would handle any odd jobs that my grandfather assigned me, stocking, shipping and performing any other duties that could easily be mastered by a 13, 14 or 15-year-old youngster.

It was certainly not my dream to ever become heir to my grandfather's business. I viewed it as a decent summer job for a teen-ager, and I really thought nothing more about it. Of course, when I first made it to the Kansas City Chiefs, I was hoping to possibly become the next Willie Lanier, a star linebacker for the Chiefs from 1967 through 1977. Lanier won postseason honors for eight consecutive years and was inducted into the Pro Football Hall of Fame in 1986. But instead of spending many great years in the NFL, I spent several forgettable months with the Chiefs. My career accomplishments in the NFL more closely resembled Willie Nelson (the musician) or Willy Wonka (the fictitious character in the 1964 novel *Charlie and the Chocolate Factory*) than the great Willie Lanier.

After my professional football career dreams were put to an end quickly, I returned to Dallas and decided to work again with my grandfather in 1986, primarily because his health was failing. I really started working for him out of sense of family obligation, and my plan was to only help him out for a few years. There is no way I went to Texas A&M thinking, "Whenever I am done with school, I am going to run the family's wholesale jewelry company."

I was a business management major at A&M, and the absolute truth is that I could care less about jewelry. To this day, I wear two rings—my wedding ring (God blessed me with a wonderful woman and a wonderful marriage) and my Aggie ring. I am not even a watch guy…or even a fan of jewelry. But my grandfather needed the help, and I decided to work for him for a "short time." That was about three decades ago, so I suppose I may be in the business for the long haul.

My grandfather was a wonderful man in so many ways, who taught me a tremendous amount about honesty and integrity in the work place. But he was not an easy person to work for, and he was reluctant to embrace any kind of change. Those were transitional times in so many businesses. For example, Federal Express was just beginning to significantly expand in the mid-1980s, changing the way companies shipped and received products. The first consumer cell phone, the Motorola DynaTAC 8000X, hit the market in 1984, while Microsoft Windows, basically an extension of MS-DOS at the time, was launched in 1985. While many of the technologies we use today were being introduced in the 1980s, my grandfather was particularly old school in his business practices. Quite frankly, he was proud to do things the old-fashioned way.

Unfortunately, being set in your ways in not typically a recipe for business success. When I started working for my grandfather following college, I heard things like this quite often: "We do it like this because that's how we've always done it." My grandfather was focused primarily on products, and his business operations relied heavily on salesmen who covered five-state areas. Our salesmen traveled across their regions, taking orders and calling my grandfather to fulfill the orders. It was an antiquated way of doing business, and the company—like many other jewelers in that timeframe—struggled to survive.

When my grandfather died in 1989, I knew I had to take the company in new directions or it would fold like so many other wholesale diamond distributors had in the mid-1980s. I did have some thoughts about selling the company, because, as I have noted, jewelry was not my passion.

Fortunately, I didn't choose to sell. God had a plan and I have been extremely blessed by that plan. In retrospect, I look back and think, "It's a good thing I didn't do what I thought was best, because it ultimately wouldn't have been." I am still not a "jewelry guy," but I am a people person. I am blessed to have some great folks on staff and to be able to influence an organization that blesses so many families. At the end of the day, I'm in the people business. On the other hand, we had to make some changes after my grandfather died to simply stay in business.

First, I moved the company from its downtown Dallas location to a more easily accessible and wholesale-focused location at the Dallas World Trade Center off of North Stemmons Freeway. When I made the move, some of the employees claimed my grandfather was probably rolling over in his grave. But the move made sense to me for a variety of reasons. The World Trade Center marketplace is closed to the public, but it is open to qualified retail buyers and interior designers, manufacturers and industry professionals. Market events throughout the year attract more than 200,000 buyers and sellers from all 50 states and more than 80 countries.

We also made the fundamental switch to go from a product-driven company to a service-driven operation. I traded rows of inventory for rows of bench jewelers. Gradually, we added lasers, 3D printers, CAD equipment and so forth. And instead of merely attempting to sell our products to jewelry stores, we became more service and repair-oriented. I concluded that there was no way we could compete with China or India in labor or production. Instead, we developed a connection with jewelry stores because of our accessibility and dependability when they needed a ring sized, a stone set or a necklace repaired. It wouldn't make financial sense for a jewelry store to ship a ring to China or India to have it sized or repaired, so we created a niche in that area. We began to do more and more work for independent jewelers in the region.

We have also continued to build relationships with some of the biggest names in merchandising. Today, we are a major supplier of fine diamonds to upscale jewelry stores such as Neiman-Marcus, Nordstrom and Saks 5th Avenue. Furthermore, professional athletes, celebrities and dignitaries have become some of our most steadfast clients due to the expert quality delivered by our bench jewelers. And, of course, we love being the diamond destination for Aggies who are in the market for any special occasion. Thanks in large part to a sensational team of employees, we've continued to grow and evolve over the years as a company.

Dallas-based *D Magazine* named Lyles-DeGrazier as "the best place to customize your bling." Using the latest in 3D-imaging software, we help individuals and large corporations design unique pieces of jewelry that will last for generations. Whether it's for an individual or a corporation, all of the work is done in-house in a shop connected to our showroom. We welcome customers to watch, as their heirlooms are being created, adjusted, cleaned or repaired.

Over the last three decades, I've also come to truly appreciate being in this industry. While I am still not personally a big jewelry fanatic, I've grown to love the industry and the opportunity it presents to add to the overall quality of life of our customers. It is enjoyable and fulfilling to work with something that is generally going to represent a meaningful time or even a lifetime commitment for couples. Jewelry is usually a symbol of someone's love for another person, and it's nice to think that what we are producing could become an heirloom and something that they are excited to receive. As I always say, it beats selling caskets.

HUSKINSON'S PATH TO TEXAS A&M

In retrospect, I believe God's plan was always for me to be an Aggie. He most certainly placed influential people in my life who loved Texas A&M and encouraged me to become passionate about all things maroon and white. Growing up in Odessa, the West Texas setting for *Friday Night Lights*, I vividly recall my third grade teacher, whom I adored, Miss Janezic. She was beautiful, young and fun, and she sported a shiny Aggie ring on her finger while speaking passionately about her love for Texas A&M. I was enamored with her Aggie ring and how she proudly wore it every day. Looking back now, that was quite the foreshadowing for what was to come for me.

My family, parents and two older brothers moved from Odessa to Flower Mound when I was nine. Once I was about halfway through high school at Flower Mound Marcus, I burned out and lost my passion for soccer, which I had played my entire life. That passion, however, was soon redirected toward my agricultural class and FFA (Future Farmers of America). FFA makes a positive difference in the lives of students by developing their potential for leadership, personal growth and career success through agricultural education. It's a great organization, and I happened to have a fabulous teacher, whom we all called "Mr. G." Mr. G and his wife were both Aggies as well.

I remember the day I came home from high school and announced to my parents that I wanted to quit soccer to devote more time to FFA. And then I casually asked, "Oh, and by the way, would you buy me a steer?" To preface, my parents are awesome and so supportive. They were a little surprised by my question, but they knew how much I enjoyed Mr. G and the people I hung out with in my agricultural classes. They also knew that if they bought me a steer, I would devote myself to caring for that animal.

They did, indeed, buy me a steer, and I was at the barn every morning between 4 and 4:30 a.m. and then back again every afternoon following school to take care of my steer, Boone, and his pen. Keeping your steer's pen clean is one of the keys to reducing the chance of disease caused by filthy conditions and contaminated feed and water. Boone was always well cared for, and I was constantly asking questions to make sure I was doing everything I could to promote his growth and development. At the end of the year, Boone looked so good and the pen had been so well maintained that my classmates gave me a John Deere shirt that stated, "I make shit look good." I sold Boone at the Houston Livestock Show. The Houston event is the largest livestock show in the country, and most first-year kids don't sell their steer at a major show. Even though I was proud of this significant accomplishment, I was absolutely devastated about losing Boone after I had grown so attached. In fact, my mom and I called every meat processing house in Texas until we found him to try to get him back.

Once I began considering collegiate destinations, I knew there was really only one choice for me: Texas A&M. My oldest brother, Matthew, attended Texas A&M and I had many

Emily, her father and two older brothers

close family friends and people I looked up to who were Aggies, as well. As a freshman at A&M in 2008, I started out in Mays Business School but switched to Agricultural Leadership and Development (ALED) after having a less than stellar experience in a senior-level engineering calculus class. "D for done" as they say.

In hindsight, knowing now my entrepreneurial career endeavors, I probably would have been better served had I stuck with my initial plans of being in the Mays Business School. But that first semester of my freshman year scared me, especially the engineering, calculus and economics classes. Those classes caused me to spend more time at a place called "TutorJohn's" than I did on campus. So, I changed to ALED, and I focused more on my overall experience at Texas A&M than earning a particular degree. I connected with people from all different backgrounds, degree programs and interests at Texas A&M, and I actually began a business in school before RingWraps ever materialized. My first business venture in college was called Rowdy Rags. It started slowly, as I began to design and produce, by hand, custom made game-day dresses that were adorned with Swarovski crystals.

My Rowdy Rags business also led me to pursue a minor in Agriculture Communications and Journalism. I was particularly interested in taking a photography class because I knew I needed to learn how to effectively operate a professional DSLR (digital single-lens reflex) camera. I also needed to master Adobe Photoshop, a photo-editing software program that would allow me to create image manipulation effects and text graphics for eye-catching advertisements. That class became particularly important to me when I started RingWraps, as I was then able to produce all of the photography and advertisements for the business myself.

I never intended to start a business with RingWraps. In fact, I was hesitant about moving forward with the business venture when Scott Polk first suggested it for several reasons, including the fact that

I was focused on Rowdy Rags. I wouldn't say that Rowdy Rags was part of my long-term plan, but it was a key element of my overall college experience. As I previously noted, I met and befriended people of diverse backgrounds while at A&M. When I would have people over to my house, it represented a broad cross-section of college life. I would have everyone over from people from the livestock judging team to sorority girls to athletes from various sports. My hodgepodge of friends was one of the reasons my overall college experience was so amazing. Building a strong network of diverse friends is endlessly important and continues to bless me to this day.

After that initial semester, when I often wondered if I could cut it in college classes, the time flew by in the blink of an eye. By April of 2011, five years after I had attended my older brother's Aggie Ring Day ceremony, it was my turn to pick up my Aggie ring. Back in '06 when my brother received his ring, I told my mother that when my time came I wanted to add diamonds around my ring to make it truly unique and eye-catching. She thought it was a great idea and said she would be on board for making it happen. I received my ring on a Friday, and I was in Dallas the next week to meet with a custom jewelry wholesaler that operated a showroom in the Dallas World Trade Center.

Now, this is exactly the point where I am absolutely sure that God opened a door for me to begin a business that has succeeded beyond my wildest initial expectations. I had a vision for what I wanted to do with my Aggie ring, and I could have easily gone to just about any jewelry designer, paid a customization fee and gone on my way. Who knows? That jeweler could have taken my vision and turned it into their own business venture. But thankfully I chose to visit with Lyles-DeGrazier, where my mother had gone for jewelry a few times over the years, as she is an interior designer who has access to the Dallas World Trade Center, where the Lyles-DeGrazier showroom is located.

I didn't know Scott Polk well at the time, but I knew he was a great jeweler, and a family-focused Aggie. Still, I was worried before going to Lyles-DeGrazier to discuss my idea. What if Scott liked my idea of producing diamond-encrusted bands to fit around my Aggie ring, and he decided to produce multiple copies? Even if he agreed not to sell my idea, there was no way I could ensure that he wouldn't make copies for his wife, daughters, nieces or other family members with A&M connections. So, upon my initial trip to Lyles-DeGrazier, I purposely met with the head jeweler and not with Scott. I asked the head jeweler if he could make me curved bands to match my Aggie ring. Then I told him, "Don't tell Scott what I'm doing. I don't want him to copy me."

I am not sure I really planned that out before it left my mouth. I realized as soon as I said it that I was placing the head jeweler in a difficult situation, especially when Scott walked into the showroom and began asking me questions about how I was doing and what brought me to the showroom. While I was still somewhat reluctant to tell him, I finally concluded it was the best thing to do. "Scott, I really didn't want to tell you about my idea because I don't want you to make anything else like this," I told him. "Please promise me that you will not produce another piece like this and that you won't tell anyone else about it."

Scott assured me that he would not do anything against my wishes. But he also began to open my eyes to a world of opportunity. He said he was thoroughly impressed with my vision, and asked me to consider turning my idea into a business. He volunteered to be the manufacturer of the diamond-encrusted bands, and he encouraged me to come up with a name for the business. Once I had the name, I began the process of filing patents and copyrights, and laying the foundation to form a business.

I was overwhelmed by a surreal, gut feeling that made me realize Scott was right. He saw a huge market for my vision, which I named RingWraps. I was a junior at Texas A&M at the time, and I looked at my own Aggie Ring and began to think about the tradition and importance of this renowned symbol of the Aggie network. Every symbol on the Aggie Ring represents the values that Texas A&M has instilled in it's students since the 1870s: excellence, integrity, leadership, loyalty, respect and selfless service. At other schools, the degree is the reward for the sacrifices made during a collegiate career, but at Texas A&M, the Aggie Ring is arguably the most coveted item. To be able to start a business that enhanced the appearance of the Aggie Ring and further added to the uniqueness of that meaningful symbol, not only began to appeal to me, it also began to captivate me.

Scott and I basically made a handshake agreement. He moved forward with manufacturing my personal set of RingWraps, and I returned to College Station with a long to-do list in order to turn this vision into a reality.

HUSKINSON'S PATH TO ENTREPRENEURIAL SUCCESS

Upon my return to College Station, I was extremely excited about the future possibilities of RingWraps, but I was also taken aback by how much needed to be done. And it needed to be done by me. It wasn't like I could seek any assistance. Prior to officially launching RingWraps, everything had to be kept extremely secretive to prevent some other jeweler or entrepreneur from stealing my idea and running with it. Remember, I was still a college student, taking a full load of classes and trying to make progress toward my graduation. In the meantime, I also had to figure out how to file copyrights and patents, locate an intellectual property lawyer, learn how to design a website and how to form a limited liability company, conceptualize the packaging for the RingWraps and where to find it, figure out how to launch the company and begin advertising, decipher how much inventory I needed, decide on a logo design and seemingly a million other details.

Fortunately, I was able to lean heavily on the trusty search engine, Google, which I used relentlessly to research every aspect of the previously mentioned details I needed to handle. I also gained some inspiration from Kendra Scott, who in 2017 was named Ernst & Young's National Entrepreneur of the Year. Kendra was born in Wisconsin and moved to Austin when she was 19. Inspired by her stepfather's battle with brain cancer, she opened her first business, the Hat Box, which specialized in comfortable hats designed for women going through chemotherapy treatment. Then in 2002, Kendra founded an LLC and designed her first collection of jewelry with $500 in the spare bedroom of her home. She started her business by walking store to store around Austin, selling to local boutiques. I think it's extremely important to find role models like that, even if you don't personally know them. I realized that if someone like Kendra Scott could begin a billion-dollar fashion brand out of a spare bedroom in Austin, I could accomplish something special roughly 100 miles away with RingWraps. After all, I already had the support and endorsement of a proven manufacturer and the president of Lyles-DeGrazier. If Scott Polk believed that RingWraps was a great idea—and he did—that was significant confirmation to me that I was on the right track.

Incidentally, Kendra Scott has more of a connection to RingWraps than merely serving as an inspiration to me. I studied her website, and particularly the history of that website, because her Internet presence really grew as her company expanded. I wanted something similar for RingWraps, and I ultimately hired the same web designer who originally built the Kendra Scott website. He was based in Austin, and allowed me to grow my web presence and the sophistication of my website.

As I began tackling all of the details in advance of the launch of the company, it was also extremely beneficial to me to have the support of so many of my professors. I had to tell one of my main professors in my agriculture communications classes what was going on because I had to miss so many classes while running around the state meeting with people to iron out specifics. All my professors were great to me, as I remember telling a few of them, "I can't make it to class today. I promise there is a good reason. I cannot tell you exactly why right now, but I will tell you in a few months. Just trust me." They all trusted and supported me, as did some of my closest friends at A&M, who also knew I was building a business.

Looking back on that time period, one of the funny things I recall is that I couldn't wear the actual set of RingWraps I had conceptualized and Scott had manufactured. I was so proud of it, but I couldn't wear it out in public as I was trying to silently launch the company. I kept having to remind myself that it was all going to be worth it once RingWraps went public.

Once I managed to position all of my ducks in a row, we officially launched RingWraps during my senior year at Texas A&M. As I mentioned previously, my mother is an interior decorator, so thanks in large part to her, my college home was really cute and nicely decorated. It wasn't a typical college house, to say the least. Because it was so nice, I was able to comfortably operate the business right out of my house. When I describe the scenario—a single girl operating a diamond business out of her house, where she is inviting people over to try on diamond-encrusted bands—people often ask me if I was ever scared. In all honesty, I never had the slightest bit of fear. Perhaps I was naïve, and maybe it was a false sense of security, but there is just something about Aggieland that made me feel remarkably safe. It should be noted that I had a pretty trustworthy clientele, and I owned an extremely protective

German Shepherd, Louis, who was constantly at my side.

God was obviously looking over me in so many ways as the RingWraps business began. Not only did He keep me safe while showing diamonds out of my house, but He also blessed my business as I did my best to honor Him with my work. When I started RingWraps, I was genuinely amazed that no one else was producing something like it. Then, when we filed the patent, it took two years for it to be approved because the United States Patent and Trademark Office (USPTO) was earnestly looking for something similar that was already in existence. Ultimately, the USTPO found nothing similar, and no one copied RingWraps during that time. Others may say that is purely coincidental, but I believe God was saving it especially for me. To this day, people ask me all the time, "Why didn't I think of RingWraps? It really is such a simple thing."

Indeed, it was, but sometimes it's the simplest ideas that can literally transform your life. I began selling RingWraps out of my home and would occasionally meet potential clients at coffee shops. In the earliest days, I really only had one example to show customers: my own set of RingWraps. Otherwise, I was passing out pictures of RingWraps on business cards. Everything grew slowly and organically at first, as I never took on any outside money, not even from my parents. In fact, my earliest models for my advertisements were just my friends, Britt McGee and Lauren Tannehill, who both happen to be models and married to Texas A&M and future NFL quarterbacks. Thankfully they were just happy to help me out, and since I was also the photographer for that shoot, I didn't have to allocate any funds for those initial advertisements.

Gradually, as I began to sell a few RingWraps and as people began to talk about some of the advertisements, I moved out of my home and began to host trunk shows. I also added many more variations to the original RingWraps, implementing graduated diamonds, larger diamonds, fancy enhancer bands, colored stones, etc.

Emily (center) and four of her RingWraps models

In those early days, every sale was a cause for celebration, especially if I sold a set of RingWraps on the website. I tried to put a personal touch on every sale I made by meeting with someone or by visiting with a customer at a trunk show. I viewed the website sales as a bonus of sorts because the piece of jewelry was selling itself. Seriously, I think I would invite half my friends over to celebrate if I made a sale on the website. The early days of the business were also adventuresome because I really had no idea how far I could go with RingWraps, and neither did my family members.

Nowadays, RingWraps is headquartered in the Dallas World Trade Center, where I first visited Scott Polk about my "secretive idea." The vision of RingWraps has been so successful since we first launched the company in 2011 that I am no longer a one-person operation, and Scott Polk sold me his portion of the ownership in the manufacturing arm of the business. We have grown into offering custom engagement rings and have an extensive collection of fine jewelry, most of which we manufacture ourselves. Furthermore, RingWraps are not exclusively designed to highlight only Aggie Rings. We now make RingWraps for more than 120 schools, including universities across the Lone Star State like TCU, SMU, Texas Tech, the University of Texas, the University of Houston, Rice, Sam Houston State, Stephen. F. Austin, Texas State, Prairie View A&M and many other schools. We also offer many colorful options, including alternating diamond and maroon sapphire RingWraps for the Aggie Ring or any other color you can think of. Texas A&M is still the heart and soul of our sales and advertising efforts, but it is exciting to see where our expansion efforts are taking us.

Speaking of advertising, I no longer rely only on my friends to serve as models. One of our more recent models, Logan Lester, came to us at a casting call and then went on to win Miss Texas USA 2018. And at our most recent casting call, more than 150 young women showed up in hopes of becoming a RingWraps model. That's visible progress because it literally took hours upon hours to photograph and interview all of the candidates. It was an extremely proud moment for me to see how many young women wanted to be associated with RingWraps.

As of 2021, we now have five full-time girls on staff, two full-time jewelers and several part-time, as well as about eight advertising and web people who work part time. We are actively hiring more people, and we now have three showrooms in the Dallas World Trade Center. It feels like each time we build a new one we outgrow it or we have to add on, which is a welcomed problem. Our Dallas showroom allows our customers to come in and view all of our jewelry and see where it is all made.

HUSKINSON'S MOST DIFFICULT CHALLENGE

Looking back over the evolution of this business, I am overwhelmed by the amount of positive feedback and touching stories I received from people who have been moved and stirred by slipping on a set of RingWraps. I'll document a couple of my favorite stories later, but first I must point out that not everyone was happy about my creation, especially during the initial launch of the business. In the early days of RingWraps, it was not uncommon for me to receive some scathing letters and social media posts about what a disservice I was doing to the Aggie Ring. "The Aggie Ring is already perfect," somebody wrote me. "Why are you trying to deface it with your gaudy diamond thing? I can't even believe you call yourself an Aggie."

People said some other mean and hurtful things, and sometimes they even said them to my face. At several trunk shows some people made spiteful and cutting comments to me about RingWraps assuming I was an employee, because I was obviously too young to be the owner of the company. Some of those things initially hurt my feelings. And at times I was tempted to respond defensively—tempted even to reply antagonistically—to derogatory and insensitive social media comments and posts. But I always reminded myself that my reputation was at stake with every post I made or advertisement I produced.

I believed it was important for me to personally respond to inflammatory social media posts, especially those claiming that I was purposely defacing the Aggie Ring or not upholding the Aggie Code of Honor. In most cases, I took a deep breath and responded as professionally as possible, explaining that I truly loved the Aggie Ring and the traditions that make Texas A&M so unique. But sometimes traditions can be enhanced by modifications. After all, if Texas A&M never modified it's traditions it would still be a small all-male, military school where membership in the Corps of Cadets was still mandatory.

I also explained that RingWraps weren't designed to permanently modify the Aggie Ring in any manner, pointing out that our two-bar cradle design makes the RingWraps non-permanent and easily removable. As I explained things like that, I realized much of the anger directed toward me and the company had been a result of misinformation. When I pointed out that RingWraps didn't physically change the Aggie Ring, people were often much more open to learning more. I also mentioned that, because of the two-bar cradle design, RingWraps actually served to protect the Aggie Ring.

People can be quite mouthy and disrespectful on social media, but the way I responded to them seemed to win over some fans, even if they didn't want a set of RingWraps. Some people were genuinely surprised when I responded directly to them, and many of them thanked me for taking the time to explain how the RingWraps worked. They wished me luck as I continued to provide an option to add some bling to the Aggie Ring.

Another challenge for me has been dealing with imitators. It is frustrating to see other jewelers copying my idea and confusing customers. I went to great lengths to make sure that RingWraps were truly original and authentic when I began the business, and the United States Patent and Trademark Office spent two years making certain that RingWraps were one of a kind before approving the patent. Yet, I have seen imposters who have produced and sold something eerily similar to RingWraps. In fact, I have been told that some of the imposters even claim that their copied products are RingWraps. I know that these imitators will never be able to produce anything even close to RingWraps' realm of quality and craftsmanship; none of them will ever get as far as us because RingWraps is and has been our specialty, and thousands of hours each year are spent on development and quality control checks. It is extremely frustrating, but I remind myself of the quote by the late Irish poet and playwright Oscar Wilde, who said, "Imitation is the sincerest form of flattery that mediocrity can pay to greatness."

The continuing challenge that I struggle with is my propensity to be a perfectionist. We never sell any

RingWraps that aren't up to par, as every set of RingWraps we produce and sell is a reflection of my commitment to the highest quality. Shortcuts could be taken, but I refuse to do so. RingWraps are meticulously handcrafted in the USA; being American-made is as important to me as being Aggie-owned. We have expert jewelers, and RingWraps undergo a rigorous quality check process. Our diamonds go through a GIA screening lab where they are confirmed as natural diamonds. We guarantee our craftsmanship and provide a one-year warranty, which includes normal wear and tear. People talk, and if someone spends that kind of money on a faulty product, word would get around quickly and vice versa. I would attribute a great deal of this company's success to the consistently high quality products we offer.

HUSKINSON'S ADVICE TO YOUNG ENTREPRENEURS

I don't know if I will ever be completely comfortable providing business advice to anyone, because I certainly don't consider myself to be an expert entrepreneur. But since advice is a component of this publication, I think it's important to remember that no matter what industry interests you, we are all ultimately in the "people business." Sure, I am in the jewelry industry, but one of the things I believe has contributed to the rapid growth of RingWraps is that we have always focused on providing a personal touch to every person who purchases one of our products. The small details matter most.

Obviously, we want every person to be happy with their purchase and to tell others about how much they love RingWraps. But we are seeking more than merely customer satisfaction. I realize that every Aggie Ring and every other class ring is an important part—if not an integral part—of that person's life story. We believe our RingWraps add flavor, personality and uniqueness to the story. With all of our customers, we care deeply about adding something to their ring's story. That's a focus in everything we do.

Take our marketing approach, for example. Our most successful marketing efforts have come from sharing our actual customers' stories. We had the Andrews family come to us years ago, and they wanted to surprise their grandmother with RingWraps on the granddaughter's Aggie Ring Day. Grandma Andrews didn't attend Texas A&M, but her late husband was an Aggie and had given her an Aggie Sweetheart Ring. The Sweetheart Rings were

Grandma Andrews reacts to receiving her RingWraps

commonly presented to the wives and/or mothers of A&M students when the school was all-male. Sweetheart Rings were phased out after women gained the opportunity for full admission to Texas A&M and the right to earn their own Aggie Rings. The Aggie Sweetheart Ring meant the world to Grandma Andrews, and we posted some moving and memorable photos of her on social media when her family presented her with her own RingWraps to highlight her Sweetheart Ring. Years later, when Grandma Andrews went to heaven to join her husband, we melted her RingWraps and sized them to fit her granddaughter's ring. We call that more than customer satisfaction; we call it adding to life stories.

Again, it's important to remember that we are in the people and memory-making business. I can say it was personally uplifting to me when my third-grade teacher purchased her RingWraps, as well as when Mr. G, my agriculture teacher from high school, purchased a set for his wife. Those are the people who first encouraged me to consider Texas A&M, and it was tremendously rewarding to add to their Aggie stories.

Another one of my favorite stories involves a different Aggie Sweetheart Ring early in my career with RingWraps. Many people mistakenly guess that only recent graduates are interested in RingWraps, but I would estimate that we sell as much as 50 percent of our product line to women who graduated before 1990. Case in point: an older woman named Bobbye, who left me a voicemail not too long after we launched the business. Fighting back tears, she explained that her husband had planned to buy her RingWraps to celebrate their 60th wedding anniversary. He was Class of '52, and her Sweetheart Ring matched his Aggie Ring. But before he could purchase the RingWraps, his health had taken a turn for the worse. He had died a few days earlier, but she wanted to fulfill her husband's desire to purchase RingWraps for her. I stayed in touch with her, and you can bet that we have used her story as a testimonial video. It's been my discovery that stories bring your business to life.

It's also been my realization that I cannot be good at all things. Beginning my business essentially as a one-person operation, I assumed that I had to do it all and be great at everything. I quickly realized that is impossible. As such, I think my biggest piece of advice would be to know your strengths and to understand your weaknesses. Furthermore, I believe it is important to understand that it is sometimes a waste of time to attempt to transform your weaknesses into strengths. Some people are always trying to improve in an area, trait or skill in which they are not wired to succeed. My advice is to focus on the things that you do really well and that help you generate income. Meanwhile, outsource or hire someone to handle those things that are your weaknesses. For example, I'm not a numbers person. Accounting, spreadsheets, tax preparations and anything else to do with numbers makes me uncomfortable. I am much better suited to instill culture and to provide direction for the business instead of tackling tasks that I am not wired to enjoy. I outsource those tasks and maximize my time and skills.

I'd also encourage aspiring entrepreneurs to research as much as possible before beginning a business and to continue researching as long as you are operating the business. It may be a wise investment to pay to have your taxes done, but it may be a total waste of money to hire lawyers to perform jobs that you can easily do for yourself. Don't misunderstand. Hiring lawyers can be important and beneficial in some cases. But if you are uncertain about how to form an LLC, how to file a patent, how to copyright something or anything else, start by researching. I learned so much by researching the Internet. Researching can also save you plenty of money when you need to find contractors or to outsource certain elements of your operation. The more bids you receive, the better it will be when determining who is best to hire or outsource to.

I believe it's also extremely important to be realistic in what you can and cannot do from an investment standpoint. With RingWraps, it was possible for me to start extremely slowly and relatively cheaply in terms of my financial resources. That's not possible with all business ideas, especially if you are still in college. I have been fortunate because I have never borrowed money. That's not always possible, either. So, make sure you have the financial resources in place before starting the business.

As you begin a business, it is also important to look at every experience as a learning moment, regardless of whether you are encountering negative criticism or making a sale. I never had a manual for success, and I had to learn things as I went along the way. I have made as many mistakes as I have made sales, but I have tried to learn from everything, both positive and negative situations. As F. Scott Fitzgerald once stated so eloquently, "Never confuse a single defeat with a final defeat." Learn from every mistake and everyone around you. And don't just celebrate the victories in life; celebrate and appreciate every step of life's journey.

Make sure you are also associating with good people. One of the reasons I believe RingWraps has been so successful right from the start is because I was partnered with a really good person in Scott Polk. Rest assured, the company you keep will most definitely impact your company's success.

I also think it is important to commit to giving back to others right from the start. This is a biblical principle: "To whom much is given, much is expected." But it is also a fact of life that those who give back are blessed many times over. Find a place or cause to serve. Give your time, talents and resources to others, and your successes will be multiplied. There may be no greater joy than positively impacting the lives of others. Where and how you choose to serve will likely change throughout your lifetime. But it's important to find a calling and to devote your time and efforts to causes or people so that you can make a positive difference in the lives of others. In a span of slightly over nine years, RingWraps has donated more than $850,000 to college scholarships, student organizations and community philanthropies. There's no better way to show how grateful you are for your blessings than to bless others with your time, talents and monetary gifts.

My greatest piece of advice though, is to keep God as your center and the rest will fall into place.

My mom always reminds me to have a grateful heart, and that everything good that has happened to me is a blessing from above. She reminds me to keep Jesus as my ultimate priority and to thank Him for every blessing. She encourages me to keep a journal (which I do) detailing what I am thankful for, as well as what I am praying for, so that I can look back on it down the road and be reminded of just how much God has done in and through me over the years.

POLK'S ADVICE TO YOUNG ENTREPRENEURS

The great American author, salesman and motivational speaker Zig Ziglar once said: "You can have everything in life you want if you just help enough other people get what they want." I think that is quite profound…and accurate. When you place the focus on the needs of others, things typically fall into place. That was my experience following college when I joined my grandfather, Arch Lyles, in the wholesale distributing diamond business. It was also my experience as it relates to this chapter in working with Emily Huskinson.

It's been quite a joy for me to see Emily transform her idea into a thriving business for many reasons. Like virtually all other Aggies, I love hearing stories of Aggies succeeding, but for obvious reasons, RingWraps is particularly special to me because I am proud to have played a role in it. When Emily first came to us, she described her idea, and I told her it was awesome. She just wanted one set of diamond-encrusted bands to highlight her Aggie Ring, and the easiest thing would have been to simply fulfill her order and to adhere to her wishes of not reproducing another piece of jewelry like it. But I think it's important for any aspiring entrepreneur or business leader to always be looking for new opportunities. It's also imperative for the leader of an organization to keep the big picture in mind, as opposed to focusing only on the details of particular tasks.

In this particular case, the details involved designing one set of RingWraps for one young woman. It would have resulted in one sale for us and, hopefully, one happy customer. But the big picture was seeing the opportunity of Emily's idea. That partly comes from experience. I had been in the jewelry business long enough to know that, sooner or later, somebody was going to see Emily's RingWrap and reproduce it without her consent, and to take claim for it. I'd also been around Texas A&M long enough to know that something that complemented a woman's Aggie Ring—dressing it up and emphasizing it with diamonds—was going to be a big hit. I had the big picture in mind when I encouraged her to consider making a business out of her concept. I thought it could be a win-win situation for her, as well as for Lyles-DeGrazier.

We basically made a handshake deal, and we eventually formed a partnership that was beneficial to both of us. I planted a seed in her mind and then I helped her to nurture that seed into a tree that has grown strong roots and is flourishing. And as her manufacturer for years, producing RingWraps were also quite beneficial to us. Throughout my lifetime, I've heard many stories of Aggies helping Aggies in so many ways. That's what made the partnership with Emily so rewarding, because it was absolutely contingent on the Aggie network and the Aggie Code of Honor. Initially, it was truly a handshake deal, where she had to trust that I wouldn't hose her. Quite frankly, I had less to lose than she did in the early stages. But it never crossed my mind to steal her idea and run with it. We were either going to make money together or I was simply going to make one set of RingWraps for Emily. Fortunately, in working together and honoring each other, we formed a great partnership. As an entrepreneur, always keep your eyes open for new opportunities. And remember that when you help others achieve their goals, things will likely fall into place for you, as well.

Scott and Stephanie Polk with their son, Cody, and daughters, Shelbi and Becca

Please understand that there is also no substitute for hard work. If you are going to start a business or take over a business, be prepared to devote plenty of time, energy, sweat equity and thought into the business. When all else fails, hard work can carry you through difficult times. You may not always be the smartest person in the room, and you may not have the connections someone else possesses, but you can always out-work others. With RingWraps, I invested a ton of time and resources to develop Emily's vision. I could've lost a lot in theory, but I look back and am thrilled that we did that, and we'd do it again. Likewise, while Emily's idea was awesome, she worked her butt off to see it through. Anyone can have a great idea, but it never comes to fruition without action and hard work.

RingWraps would not have come to fruition without our great team at Lyles-DeGrazier, which leads me to another piece of advice: Surround yourself with great people and take care of those people. At Lyles-DeGrazier, we have created a tremendous team-oriented atmosphere, and I truly believe most of our employees enjoy working for an organization that values them and their efforts. We work hard, and I expect great things from our employees, but I try to be a leader who coaches, inspires and motivates instead of merely acting as a dictator. I played for some great football coaches during my career, and I learned so much about leadership from those coaches. To this day, the greatest benefit I had from those times as a player at Texas A&M is what I learned about the importance of teamwork, discipline, leadership and so much more. My coaches inspired me to always look for ways to grow and improve.

That leads me to my next piece of advice: Be willing to adapt and change your plans when life happens. Your plans for the future may now seem perfect, and they may, indeed, lead you straight to your ultimate dreams. But from personal experience, I believe that one of the keys to success in life and entrepreneurship is being flexible enough to reexamine your goals based on the circumstances life delivers. After all, I was never going to make a living in the jewelry or diamond business. But I am now grateful that God placed me where I am, and I have chosen to bloom where I have been planted. God had a plan for my life, and even though I had other plans, I finally realized God was leading me in the best direction all along. So, the best advice I can offer any young entrepreneur is to trust in the Lord with all your heart and lean not on your own understanding (Proverbs 3:5). Whether you are a Christian or not, I believe you must have faith to be successful. One of the biggest keys to my success has been honoring God and doing things with integrity and honesty. If you are a person of integrity and honesty, doors will open and opportunities will present themselves. Stay faithful. Stay true to yourself and your values.

Lastly, if you are a student at A&M or a recent former student, you have been gifted with an incredible ticket that can open doors for you. Once you have that foot in the door, make the most of it. Do things the right way and make the most of the Aggie network. One thing I know for sure is that Aggies are willing to help Aggies, but only if they are willing to work. Be willing to work and always be open to opportunities that may arise when you are not even looking for them.

CHAPTER 11
Chris Dailey

President & Founder
Dailey Company, Inc.
Texas A&M Class of 1993

EDITOR'S NOTE: On January 8, 2022, Chris Dailey's wife, Margo Kirksey Dailey, died unexpectedly. She was only 49. May this chapter serve as a tribute to her unwavering support of her husband, daughter and friends and other family members through the years.

DAILEY'S PATH TO TEXAS A&M

Throughout the years, I've read and heard about hundreds—maybe thousands—of Aggie parents who proudly watched their children follow in their maroon and white footsteps to Aggieland. Because the university meant so much to them as students and former students, it is typically a dream come true for the parents as they watch their children drive away from home to enroll at Texas A&M.

Yet my parents were not beaming as I drove away from home. Shaking their heads in confusion is more like it. I was not just driving away from home but also driving away from a full scholarship to a local college, heading to the unknown five hours away. I was a 19 year-old boy, somewhat idealistic and sometimes guilty of impulsive decisions typical of that age, making a decision that could be a complete disaster. My father, who had always been my role model, wanted me to have all the opportunities he didn't. He wanted life to be easier for my brother and me, and that included college, but he never dreamt that might mean I would leave Wichita Falls. I was living at home for free and going to college for free. His thought was: *Why was I throwing that away to chase a dream?* As I loaded up my vehicle and prepared to leave my parents' home between Henrietta and Wichita Falls, my father looked at me and said, "You aren't going to make it. We will see you back here in a couple of months, max."

While disheartened by these words at the time, I am extremely thankful, because these words drove and inspired me to fulfill the impulsive decision by my 19 year old self. Truthfully, my father didn't have anything against Texas A&M and truly wanted to see me succeed, but he simply couldn't understand why I would want to leave a place where I was already established and where I would be able to graduate from college without incurring any significant debt. Neither of my parents had graduated from college, and they were both proud of me for earning a scholarship to Midwestern State, where my older brother was already enrolled. MSU is a small liberal arts school in Wichita Falls with a total enrollment—even today—of just 5,300 undergraduate students. It's a fine public institution, and it was quite the bargain for cost-conscious students like my brother and me at the time. I graduated high school in 1989 (two years after my brother) and earned a $1,500-per-semester scholarship, which was considered at the time to be a "full ride" at MSU.

While Midwestern State was a perfect fit for some of my high school friends and other students who grew up around the Wichita Falls area, it was not exactly my vision of the complete collegiate experience. First of all, there wasn't much atmosphere of note on campus. Students typically showed up to class, attended classes and went home. According to the school's website, only 1,500 students live on campus today, which represents more than the on-campus population in 1990. My father, who was an electrical contractor, strongly encouraged me to explore a different career option. Since my uncle was a geologist who owned an oil company, I decided to major in geology. I completed that first semester without making many new friends or generating any significant memories. It was essentially like a continuation of high school.

During the ensuing holiday break, however, I made the decision to take a trip to visit a friend who was attending Texas A&M. It was February of 1990, and I drove to Aggieland to spend a long weekend in College Station. I had never been to the campus or the community, and I really didn't know what to expect, but it just so happened to be an absolutely perfect weekend (beautiful skies and temperatures in the mid-70s), and the people I met were even warmer than the unseasonable weather. I drove back home that Sunday, but I left my heart in Aggieland. I completed the spring semester at Midwestern State, and I then began working for my father in the summer of '90—as I had done every summer from the time I was 11 or 12. Toward the end of July, however, I decided I really needed a break from the same old routine. Naturally, I gravitated toward College Station, where my friend was living and where I longed to be.

My original plan was to spend a week in Aggieland, but that plan quickly changed. Once I arrived back in College Station, I knew I needed to become an Aggie. To make a long story somewhat shorter, I told my friend about my desire to transfer to Texas A&M, and he encouraged me to go to work for his aunt, who worked within the campus registration department. Keep in mind that this was long before the registration process was handled electronically, so for a short period of time, the registration department relied heavily on temporary employees. This was my opportunity to slide my foot into the door, as I landed a temporary job and promptly met all of the full-time staff in the registration department. Those contacts didn't immediately open the door for my entrance into A&M, but they did pay off in the long run...in many ways. After working the registration for a couple of weeks, I made the decision to shift my collegiate gears. In the football vernacular, I called an audible. Well, actually I called my parents and told them that I was driving back home that afternoon, packing up my belongings that evening and driving back down to College Station the next day. I had enrolled at Blinn Junior College for the fall semester of 1990, I had lined up a job at U-Haul and I had arranged to move in with some guys I had not yet met at an off-campus apartment.

As noted previously, my parents were not jumping for joy or slipping me start-up cash as I packed my things the next day, but I had saved $2,500 to $3,000, and I was resolute about making things work...no matter how hard it might be to pay my own way through school. And rest assured, it was extremely hard. Fortunately, my father provided me all the inspiration I needed to persevere through even the most difficult circumstances when he told me I'd never make it. But more than that, he had instilled in me the work ethic to make my dream happen. When my parents came to College Station to watch me graduate, I reminded him of his words to me the day I left home. He looked at me with a puzzled face, not convinced this is what he said nor what he meant, and he assured me that he was proud of my accomplishments. Those words, however meant, were my motivation. I often wonder if I would have made it through that first year if I had not had such a strong desire to prove to my father that I would fulfill the dream outlined that day in my parents' driveway.

After all, the first year in the Bryan-College Station area was rather brutal. First of all, my new roommates lasted less than a full week. I woke up one evening from a nap and began to look for my truck keys, so I could run out and grab something to eat. To my dismay, however, one of my roommates stole my keys while I was sleeping and had taken off in my truck. He eventually returned, but I quickly moved out and into a nearby apartment complex. Ultimately, I ended up rooming with a friend I had first met while working those two weeks of registration. That's also how I met my future wife, Margo Kirksey, but I will save that story for a little later. Finding trustworthy roommates was my first obstacle, but the bigger issue was limited funds.

As I noted earlier, I landed a job at U-Haul right away on the corner of University Drive and Texas Avenue. With all the students coming and going, that was a particularly busy U-Haul, and I worked as much as possible while attending Blinn. After finally receiving my letter of acceptance to Texas A&M for the upcoming fall semester, I knew that my studying would take priority; I needed to accumulate more savings in case I was unable to work a full 40 hours per week while at Texas A&M. I took a second job toward the end of the 1991 spring semester with UPS, which required me to report to the distribution center at 3:30 a.m. daily to begin unloading 18-wheel trucks for the next four hours. It was exhausting work, especially as the temperatures and humidity levels continued to rise. I worked both jobs throughout the summer of '91, while also taking six hours of college courses each summer session at Blinn. The summer was a blur, as I was working 60 hours a week and going to school. I didn't have much weight to lose at that time in my life, but I still dropped 20 pounds that summer. I was making good money, but at the end of that summer I knew I needed to drop one of those jobs. I liked what I was doing at U-Haul, and I wasn't a big fan of the 3 a.m. alarms, so I left UPS and began truly experiencing the college life in the fall of '91. It was beyond satisfying just to be accepted into A&M because I had worked so hard to gain entrance.

Once I started classes at A&M, I stayed on the geology degree pathway until I started taking labs that involved studying and identify rocks, minerals and fossils. While I am sure that sounds captivating to most of you (please note the sarcasm), I found myself bogged down and even bored by the study of such things as igneous, sedimentary and metamorphic classifications and identifying cubic, tetragonal, hexagonal, orthorhombic and triclinic crystal form characteristics of minerals.

At that point, I began seriously contemplating what I really wanted to do with the rest of my life. Despite my father's suggestion to avoid construction-related fields as if I was allergic to them, construction was what I enjoyed. That's what interested and intrigued me. After all, I had grown up watching my mom and dad work together to build a successful electrical business. I admired their accomplishments, and they inspired me. I looked at several construction fields, but switching to those majors would have cost me to lose too many credit hours. I already was pinching pennies to make it through college on my own, so I didn't want to add more years to the degree plan. Fortunately, I'd already made plenty of friends within the registration office, and thanks to some good advice, I chose to major in Industrial Distribution in the College of Engineering. It was an excellent career choice for me because it involved taking business classes, marketing classes, engineering classes and other courses that helped me immensely when I eventually opened my own business. While the classes were limited and filled quickly, I was able to enroll in all of those classes without any issues because all of the sweet, grandmotherly ladies whom I worked with in the registration office. Working those couple of weeks before I officially made the move from Midwestern State paid off in so many ways, and not just because of my contacts who became my "registration assistants". My future bride, Margo Kirksey, didn't work in the registration office, but her roommates did, and she would join us when we all went out after work. The relationships made during that short, two week period lasted throughout my days at A&M. In fact, some of the guys I first met at the registration office from Boerne eventually became my first roommates that I really trusted, and Margo eventually became my roommate for the rest of my life!

As I switched majors in mid-stream, it took me 160 hours to actually graduate in August of 1994. By then, I was engaged to Margo, who graduated on time in May 1994. I knew she was "the one," just as I knew on that first weekend I visited Aggieland that Texas A&M was the place for me. What I didn't know at that time was what I was going to do after graduation. During spring break of my final year at A&M, I interviewed for a second time with a company called Mega Manufacturing Corporation, which sold large pieces of metal-working equipment to companies across the country. My position was going to be based out of Hutchinson, Kansas, which is about 50 miles northwest of Wichita. Some of the other sales people who were hired by Mega Manufacturing were told that they would be driving big rigs around the country year-round, but the deal I struck would require me to travel only one to two weeks a year. Since I was taking Margo some 625 miles from her parents' home in Lockhart, I had no desire to travel any more than I had to as we began our lives together. Margo and I planned to be married in December of '94, and I accepted the position with a base salary of $45,000 with potential to earn up to $30,000 bonus. I didn't bother pursuing any other potential career options. We were so sure that everything was in order that Margo applied and was accepted to begin pursuing her master's degree at Wichita State upon our arrival in the Sunflower State.

About a week before I graduated, however, I received a phone call from my future boss at Mega Manufacturing. "Circumstances have changed," he said, "and we are going to need you to travel more often than we originally discussed." I didn't like the sound of this, so I asked how much travel he had in mind. "Leaving on a Sunday night or Monday morning," he said, "and returning on Friday night or Saturday morning every week." Without hesitation, I informed him that I was no longer interested in the job. In the blink of an eye, my future career direction, which once seemed so settled, was now completely up in the air. My wedding day was on the horizon, I was in need of a good job right away and I had no leads whatsoever because I had stopped even contemplating Plan B when I accepted the role with Mega Manufacturing.

Chris Dailey and his late nephew, Spencer Squire, who died as a result of pediatric brain cancer in 2007

The next morning I did the only thing I could think of in order to land a job right away. Deep-down, I knew that I eventually wanted to start my own business. The entire experience with Mega Manufacturing only solidified that idea. I didn't want to be dependent on the whim of some other person changing my future plans with a phone call. Throughout my time at A&M, I would often discuss the possibilities of starting my own business one day with my co-workers at U-Haul. It was usually something we did to pass the time, but it was a continuing theme of conversation through the years. I would dream up various scenarios, but I always came back to what I knew: an electrical business.

My father had started his own electrical business when he was 36 and was successful because of his integrity, hard work and perseverance. Fortunately for me, he wanted to make sure that I had the same traits instilled at an early age. I can remember going in homes under construction with him starting when I was just 10 or 11 years old and climbing up into the rafters to help him run romex wire back to the electrical panel. He would also take me on residential service calls, which allowed me to see how he dealt with customers and he would always tell me "your reputation is only as good as your word." As I grew older, I was able to start working with him on some commercial projects, as well. Although he was just trying to instill some foundational traits in me to help make me a better person, by default I was also learning the electrical trade. It wasn't that I loved the electrical work back then, but I understood the process, and I enjoyed earning money. Most of all, it was time spent with my dad, and little did I know, but this was laying the foundation for my future.

After the Mega Manufacturing deal fell through, I swallowed my pride, drank a cup of humility and called my father. I told him about the change of circumstances and asked him if he would hire me. He started chuckling and said that he would, indeed, put me to work. But then he added, "The going rate for a worker with your experience is $8.50 an hour; that college degree doesn't mean anything to your value on the jobsite." I argued that I was making more than that at U-Haul, but he countered by saying, "Do you want the job or not?" At the time, I thought that this was just tough love on my dad's part and his way of trying to deter me from entering the highly-demanding construction industry. It took me a few years, but I finally realized that wasn't his intention at all. The best way to learn the electrical industry, in my dad's opinion and now mine, is to start in the field learning the installation side of the business. What he was telling me, in the only way you can tell a 23 year old kid who wants to conquer the world, is that the education you received at Texas A&M University is great and will serve you tremendously in the future, but if you truly want to learn the electrical industry, you need to grab a shovel, get in the ditch, and start from the bottom.

Quite frankly, I didn't have a ton of options. If I wanted to eventually start my own electrical business, I needed the experience and I needed to learn the ins and outs of running my own company. Margo didn't have a job, and I was about to accept my father's offer to make approximately $18,000 per year. We were not going to be living high on the hog or in the lap of luxury, but I convinced Margo it was in our best long-term interests. Besides, neither one of us were accustomed to having any disposable income at that point, so off we moved to begin our rise to riches…with one hourly job in Henrietta, Texas.

DAILEY'S PATH TO ENTREPRENEURIAL SUCCESS

The construction industry can be a cold, cut-throat work environment for a newcomer. As a beginner, you quickly realize that some of the veterans are skeptical about training. They've spent years honing their craft and are proud of their work, and they are not interested in wasting time on someone not dedicated to the profession. It can be really tough and frustrating starting off, but if the veterans discover that you are really interested in learning, even some of the most cynical and callous crew members will ultimately slow down enough to explain what they are doing and how to do it. Fortunately, my father placed me with some really good men who taught me so much as I began my journey. While my skill set didn't justify a high hourly wage, my dad was helping set me up for the future by placing me in great environments to learn.

For the first six months I was back, I was going wherever my father needed me, helping to handle smaller jobs at first and then helping to tackle much bigger jobs as my experience increased. Meanwhile, Margo picked up two part-time jobs and also enrolled at Midwestern State to pursue her master's degree in English. When I wasn't working or trying to find a moment to spare with my wife, I was studying the National Electric Code, a standard for the safe installation of electrical wiring and equipment in the United States. Eventually, I began taking on bigger roles, and I would tie up loose ends and put out fires (figuratively) wherever my father needed them. I was bouncing around, learning a ton and building my skill set. Slowly but surely, as I worked my way up, so did my wages to $13 per hour. Somehow, Margo and I even scraped up enough money to purchase a small, two-bedroom home in Henrietta. We bought our first house for $31,500, and our payments were $271.73. That may sound awfully inexpensive by today's standards, but Margo and I were both initially worried about whether we'd be able to consistently pay that mortgage.

That home became quite the happening place. Moving back to Henrietta not only meant that I was back closer to my family, but also that I was back near so many of my high school friends. The mere news that we had purchased a house traveled the Henrietta grapevine rapidly. We didn't even lock our doors in Henrietta, which was probably a mistake because friends started showing up unannounced. Then they started showing up…even when we were not home. Seriously, we'd get home from work/school and Margo and I would inevitably find friends watching our TV in the living room. Or we'd sleep in on Saturday morning only to discover friends had shown up to make themselves at home. We had a blast living in Henrietta, even though things occasionally became too close for comfort.

I also thoroughly enjoyed working for and with my father for a little over two years. He allowed me to perform a large variety of jobs, from wiring hospitals to working on projects at Sheppard Air Force Base just north of Wichita Falls. I also started helping my father with estimates in the evenings. I would take drawings home and would learn how to estimate, while also learning the National Electric Code. My dad and I worked extremely well together. We essentially have the same personality so whenever we would go estimate jobs together or were out on a job

Chris Dailey and his daughter, Sophia

working together, we didn't have to say much because we knew what each other was thinking. While I was absorbing every ounce of electrical knowledge both in the field and in the office, it could not satisfy my burning desire to one day go out on my own in the electrical industry. That was always my end goal, and even though I loved working with my father, I knew I needed to gain some experience somewhere else.

I started looking for my next career move, and Margo and I considered moving to her hometown, Lockhart, Texas, which is roughly 35 miles south of Austin. I also met and interviewed with some impressive people in Austin. But ultimately, Aggieland was again calling, and I accepted a job offer in 1996 to work for an established electrical company in the Bryan-College Station community. I actually took somewhat of a pay cut to work in the BCS area, but I wanted to learn the project management side of the business. It was an office job rather than an in-the-trenches position, and I was really fortunate to start when I did because the community and the university were undergoing dramatic growth. The company worked on major projects on the Texas A&M campus, as well as large commercial construction. It was a great move from an experience standpoint, and I learned a tremendous amount about the behind-the-scenes roles of project management, office paperwork and so much more.

Again, I wasn't being paid top dollar, and Margo was working as a teacher to help us make ends meet. After a couple of years, though, a large electrical company based out of Houston offered me a job in its San Antonio office that would pay me twice as much as I was making in BCS. It was an offer I couldn't refuse, but when I gave my resignation to my employer in Aggieland, the owner of the company said he didn't want to lose me and matched the other company's salary offer. It was a win-win situation for me in every sense, and I most certainly appreciated the owner's generosity and his loyalty to me. If things had stayed the way they were at that point, who knows how long it would have taken me to step out on my own? For better or worse, though, things did not stay the same. The founder and owner of the company in BCS sold his company to a conglomeration in Houston and things began to change. Not for the better, either.

As stresses increased and my personal job satisfaction decreased, I began seriously pondering the possibilities of starting my own company. I am extremely blessed to have had a father and a father-in-law who were both business owners and mentors to me. Margo's father, the wonderfully personable Warren "Pat" Kirksey, was a 1956 Texas A&M graduate and former Air Force Captain. He owned Kirksey Propane, and he served as the mayor of Lockhart for more than a decade. Up until his death on February 9, 2016, he was extremely active in a number of organizations such as the First Lockhart National Bank Board, the Lockhart Chamber of Commerce, Kiwanis Club, Lockhart Lodge, the 12th Man Foundation and the Association of Former Students, to name a few. He was a wise man, and when I would voice my frustration regarding the changing times within our company, he would tell me, "Chris, if you are meant to go into business, you will know when the time is right. Trust me, you will know."

He said that to me numerous times, and I often questioned him about how I would know. I certainly didn't possess a clear picture then regarding the right time, but he would just smile and assure me. I suppose that the "moment of truth" arrived for me on Christmas Eve in 2002. It was late in the afternoon on Christmas Eve, and Margo had already made the two-hour drive from College Station to Lockhart. I was supposed to meet her there in time to go to church later that evening. But the vice president of the company—my direct boss—wasn't actually completely straightforward with ownership regarding a project that I was managing that had gone south and lost money. Without going into too much detail, it was not at all surprising that the project was losing money. I had predicted it would, after all!

Much earlier, I had told my boss that there were too many employees on the project and we needed to scale back, but I was overruled because there was not another project in which to send them. But when the owner confronted us on Christmas Eve about the issue, my boss denied that I had ever mentioned the idea of scaling back. I left the office that night at 6:30, and as I drove two hours to Lockhart, I was not exactly thinking about peace on Earth, joy to the world or silent night. I was, however, thinking about a blue Christmas, since I didn't arrive in Lockhart until everybody else in the family was at church.

The next morning—Christmas Day—I was up before anyone else because I really had not managed much sleep. I was on the back porch drinking coffee, and my father-in-law joined me as the sun was rising. I told him about the current situation, he mulled it over for a few minutes and then he began to speak. "I don't know what all your job entails each day, but I know it brings stress," Pat Kirksey said. "I also know how much you are making. The amount of money you are making a year doesn't justify what you are going through. I guarantee if you quit that job tomorrow you could have another job within a week making more than what you are making now."

I was making about $62,000 annually at that point, and the stresses and hours were definitely mounting. Pat and I talked some more, and I made up my mind that Christmas morning that I needed to do something different. I didn't do anything brash, and I didn't walk in to my current employers and burn any bridges. In fact, I didn't even hint that I was planning on leaving. I simply filed the necessary paperwork to begin the process of starting my own company in January 2003. I still went to work each day, and things actually improved in the spring of '03. I began to wonder if leaving was the right thing to do because things were improving, and I was also a little worried about my financial obligations. After all, Margo and I had recently purchased 90 acres of land in Navasota, and I had also bought a tractor to take care of that land. The reality of the situation, though, was that I was just delaying the inevitable.

I liked the company; I liked the founder of the company; and I liked many aspects of my job. After the events that transpired on Christmas Eve, however, I just didn't feel the same anymore. In April 2003, after a particularly memorable and heated confrontation with my direct boss, I turned in my notice that I would be leaving in six weeks. I wanted to make sure my current projects were taken care of and to give the company plenty of time to find a replacement for me. But I had made up my mind that the Friday before Memorial Day would be my last day. The founder of the company, who had always been good to me, inquired about what it would take to change my mind. I appreciated his sincerity, but it wasn't about money; it wasn't even completely about the tension between my direct boss and me. While that contributed to the timing of my decision, I knew I wanted to do something on my own, and the longer I stayed with one company, the harder it would be to leave.

Over the course of the next six weeks, many people asked me about what I planned to do. My response was always the same: Whatever I need to do to make money. I will never forget my final day with the company. It was Friday, May 23, 2003, and I had my cell phone up to one ear and my desk phone up to the other ear. I was busy right up until I noticed it was 5:30 p.m. At that point, I took my keys and my cell phone to the office of my direct boss and walked out the door to my future. I took the next two days completely off, but on Memorial Day 2003 (May 26), I started sending out letters to any business owner I knew—even remotely—in the area, announcing that I was starting my own company. I loaded up the tools I had acquired throughout the years working with my dad into the two service trucks I purchased at a Texas A&M University auction for $4,500, and I was officially in business. It was literally a one-man operation that was headquartered in the spare bedroom of our small home on Yorkshire Drive in College Station, which is just off of Victoria Avenue near Rock Prairie Elementary School. Our garage served as my initial "warehouse," and I essentially began knocking on doors on the Tuesday after Memorial Day.

Incidentally, my wife wasn't necessarily delighted with my initial office set-up, since I started my full-fledged efforts on Memorial Day weekend, which was the beginning of her summer break from teaching. She was looking forward to sleeping in on lazy days throughout the summer, but I was up early every day, making phone calls and sending faxes in the room right next to our bedroom. But we made that office situation work for most of the summer.

The first business I personally visited in search of a customer was Frittella Italian Café on Texas Avenue in Bryan because I vaguely knew the owner, Adriano Farinola. I told him that I was opening my own company, handed him my brand new business card and told him that I was willing to do anything he needed, from rewiring to installing fixtures. As fate would have it, Mr. Farinola just so happened to need some work done. I started that day, and he kept me busy for the next couple of weeks. It turned out to be a great contact because his son-in-law at the time was running the College Station office of Vaughn Construction. From that first day, I then landed a job with Fadi Kalaouze, who was in the midst of growing and expanding Aggieland Outfitters. I also landed some jobs with an up and coming chef, Matt Bobbitt who now has Global Catering, and a local real estate investor, Michael Beckendorf, who owns residential rental homes, as well as commercial properties throughout the community. In all of those initial jobs, I handled everything myself. Just like in my college days working at UPS, I lost a few pounds after starting my own business because I spent most of the summer days in attics and was just doing whatever grunt jobs I could find to make some income. It wasn't until I landed a job at the Plaza Hotel in College Station, rewiring an entire floor, that I realized that I could not continue to do everything on my own. It was time to find some help, which created a whole new issue that was not easy to handle.

DAILEY'S MOST DIFFICULT CHALLENGE

One of the things that every entrepreneur discovers is that relationships are the key to building practically any business in any field. I've heard that many times, and the first thing that comes to mind is typically the relationships you build with customers or clients. But let me assure you that it is every bit as important to build quality relationships with the people who work with you and for you. My biggest challenge as an entrepreneur was not stepping out on my own or finding clients who were willing to take a chance on me. The biggest challenge—by far—was finding employees who were willing to take a risk to work for me.

I needed help on the Plaza Hotel project because tackling the entire floor was too daunting for me alone. Naturally, the electricians I knew in the area were the ones I had met while working with my previous employer. But when I called some of those electricians to offer them some extra money by working with me at night after they had completed their full-time job responsibilities, many of them declined because they had been told by my previous boss that they would be terminated if they were ever found to be working for me.

It was frustrating, to say the least, but it was not totally shocking. As I have also previously noted, the construction industry can be a cold, cut-throat work environment. I had to work much harder and assure complete anonymity to the handful of electricians who finally volunteered to lend a hand…for a nice hourly wage, of course. Looking back, though, it was extremely tough to find good help.

It was such a relief when Gerald Bozeman finally agreed to work with me. It also involves a memorable story. On the day I was supposed to meet with Gerald to formally offer him a position, I was working at Frittella Italian Café. After I finished that project, Adriano Farinola asked me if I could come look at something at his home. I declined because I had a dinner meeting at Outback Steakhouse with Gerald and his wife in about an hour. But Adriano was in a pinch, and it was not like I could easily say "no" to any job. So, I went to his house in the middle of summertime because he said it would only take a few minutes and that it was probably an easy fix. He was wrong. In a matter of minutes in his attic, I was absolutely drenched in sweat. I told him that I couldn't finish the job because I had to go home to clean up in order to meet my prospective employee and his wife. But Adriano was persistent, offering me an opportunity to shower at his house and wear his clean underwear if I would finish the job. I did just that, but I declined to wear another man's underwear.

Instead, drenched in sweat, I showed up to our dinner meeting with Gerald "Hoss" Bozeman and both of our wives. Apparently, Hoss appreciated my willingness to do whatever it takes to make a profit. And his wife, Tina, just wanted to know one thing: Will you keep him employed even if you don't have work for him to perform. Margo and I both answered: "Yes! If nothing else, he can mow our yard."

Fortunately, we always found work for Gerald. That turned out to be a tremendously beneficial relationship as he worked for me for several years and eventually left and started his own business. He also brought his helper, Justin Kerl, who has gone on to start his own business. Once I started hiring people, however, I knew it was time to move my office out of the house. After all, it was bad enough that I was waking my wife up each morning with phone calls and faxes. I didn't also want to start each morning with staff meetings inside my own home.

When I worked in Wichita Falls, I met a salesman named Jim Jones, class of 1989, who moved to College Station shortly after we did. We reconnected, and he told his father-in-law about my business and needing a rental space. A few days later, I received a call from Dennis Goehring, to come meet with him. When I mentioned where I was going to my father-in-law, he said "I'll go with you...I've been friends with Dennis since high school and haven't seen him in a long time." Dennis Goehring was an All-American offensive lineman for Texas A&M in 1956 when legendary head coach Bear Bryant led the Aggies to the Southwest Conference title. After his football career, Mr. Goehring became chairman and president of the Bank of A&M and later became one of the key local figures in economic development for both Bryan and College Station. Mr. Goehring had plenty of investment properties, and as a favor to Jim, my father-in-law, and Margo, he practically gave me my first office space on Finfeather, charging me just $200 a month. Later, when we outgrew that property, Mr. Goehring also made us another terrific deal on a much larger location on Ashford Hills. We stayed in that location until November 2008. As much as I hated to pay discounted rates, it was a necessity—especially in the early days because every penny was so important back then. Looking back, I realize that what was even more important was Dennis' belief in my business and the opportunity to become a fixture in the Bryan-College Station community.

The point I want to make here is that it is extremely hard to start your own business, especially if your new start-up is going to be in competition against established companies in the community. Expect roadblocks. Anticipate difficult circumstances. Be ready to work extra hard to find clients and personnel because your competition is absolutely not going to roll out the red carpet. Nor is your competition going to happily share its customers or employees. Above all, be ready to persevere, and once you land a client or employee, make sure you treat them with tremendous respect and appreciation.

One of the biggest hurdles for me initially was that even local suppliers were hesitant to work with me. I remember one of the first major bids that I was putting together almost never materialized because every local supplier said they could not give me a quote on the light fixtures, panels, and switchgear I needed to bid the job. Without a good estimate on the cost of supplies, there was no way I was going to win the job. Fortunately, from the years I worked for my dad, I still had plenty of contacts with suppliers in the Wichita Falls area, who were more than happy to sell me whatever was needed to bid the job. Once the local suppliers figured out that I was going to be in business for the long haul and that I was going to find a way to bid any project, they became much more receptive to working with me.

Slowly but surely, we began to win a job here and there. My goal was to bid on everything that I could possibly perform. I didn't win most of those early bids. Nor did I win many of them. But we won a bid here and there, and we placed 100 percent of our focus on providing outstanding quality and finishing the job when we said it would be done. There are some things in the construction industry—like weather—that cannot be controlled or anticipated. But whenever possible, we made sure to do what we said we were going to do. We knew that the key to establishing any type of a foothold in the area was satisfied customers telling their friends and fellow business owners about the quality and professionalism of our work.

With each person I hired, customer satisfaction and quality installation were hammered home as our top priorities. The other thing that benefitted us tremendously was to not worry about what we couldn't control. We were the newcomers, the start-up that wanted to prove itself. I told all of our employees not to worry about any competitors; all we could do to assure our long-term success was to handle the projects of the people who had entrusted us with their business. Nothing else mattered.

As the days, weeks, months and even years passed, we slowly developed a reputation for excellence, and we continually grew the company. We added vans, supplies and personnel whenever we could afford it. In fact, for the first three and a half years of the company, I didn't even take a salary. We lived off the salary Margo was making as a teacher in the Navasota Independent School District; we didn't ever go out to eat unless it was a really special occasion; Margo cut my hair each month because we didn't have an extra $20 to spare; and I brought a turkey sandwich in a brown paper bag every day for my lunch. We paid our suppliers and all of our invoices on the 10th of every month, if they would give us a discount for paying early. If not, we paid all of our invoices on the 15th of each month. To help our hourly staff members, we paid our employees every week, and I put everything left over at the end of each month—and I do mean everything—back into the company.

It wasn't until Margo became pregnant with our daughter, Sophia, late in the 2005-06 school year that I even began to contemplate taking a salary. Margo loved teaching, but we decided that once Sophia was born in November 2006 that it would be best for her to stay at home. That first full year of Margo staying at home (2007), I took a salary of $36,000, which felt like a significant amount after living the previous few years on Margo's teacher salary alone. The humbling thing was that I discovered an accordion box early in 2008 that contained our tax returns from the first year we were married and living in Henrietta, Texas. We were both making close to $20,000 annually, so we were actually taking home more income back in 1995 than we were in 2007. Of course, we didn't own a company in '95, and we both knew that our delayed gratification would ultimately pay big dividends.

The big payoff probably began in 2010, when our sacrifices and penny-pinching enabled us to purchase a contractor in Houston called Berger Electric Co. We'd been battling for every possible job we could land in Bryan-College Station, and primarily out of curiosity, I had begun looking for other electrical companies that might be available for purchase. I wasn't necessarily seriously looking, but I did search online often so that I would stay on top of the marketplace and know what was selling and for how much. (Margo always tells friends that I don't have many hobbies other than work. She says it jokingly, but it's pretty accurate).

After about 10 to 12 months of searching online for various companies throughout the state, one in Houston popped up that intrigued me. I wasn't sure how serious I was when I made the call inquiring about Berger Electric Co., but I was at least somewhat interested by a couple of things. First and foremost, this company had been in business for more than 30 years—since 1974—and had a strong reputation. Secondly, I knew it was time to invest and diversify. As our College Station business grew, Margo and I had purchased several rental homes in the area as investment properties. The prices were right at the time, and in the Bryan-College Station marketplace, rent homes for college students is typically a good investment, although they were certainly not my passion or area of expertise.

What I knew and what I knew I wanted to expand was the electrical business. So, when this particular company in Houston appeared, I called and asked for some financial information and detailed list of Berger Electric Co.'s assets. I analyzed the numbers, called the contact back and asked for a meeting. In the meantime, I told Margo about the opportunity. I am convinced about women's intuition—or at least Margo's sixth sense—because as soon as I told her about the company, she said: "We're about to buy a business in Houston, aren't we?" I told her we were only going to look, but she knows me too well. She often says that my willingness to take risks and to seek opportunities that require financial risks are the reason she uses hair color to hide her gray hairs.

The bottom line, though, is that she has learned to trust my business judgements. I knew it was the right time to expand into another market, and as I analyzed the numbers, I believed it was a good business deal. So, after careful consideration, we took out a business loan and bought the Houston business in 2010. In the blink of an eye, we went from 60 employees to more than 120 in two locations. Thankfully, we absolutely hit the ground running in Houston, and we did not run into any of the roadblocks that we'd encountered in our "home" marketplace. Two years into the Houston market things were going so well that I made the decision to sell all of our rent houses, which helped me completely pay off the business loan that we opened in a matter of just three years.

Without a doubt, God has blessed our persistence and our insistence to do the right thing all of the time. In fact, in March of 2017, we once again embarked on another expansion. This time, we chose Lockhart, Margo's hometown and where she currently serves on the First Lockhart National Bank Board of Directors, and the hub of the Austin-San Antonio corridor sitting on the 130 Toll Road. This office has grown quickly with the boom of the Kyle, San Marcos, San Antonio, Austin and Lockhart economies. Landing contracts to rewire the President's office and The Welcome Center at the University of Texas was not something we ever dreamt we would be doing. This has allowed for many jokes with our Longhorn friends as I tell them they needed an Aggie to do the job right, but we all agree money is green, not orange or maroon!

These opportunities in various markets also transformed discussions for our strategic plan. While we have always provided residential electrical service work in Bryan-College Station out of necessity, our primary professional focus in the three locations was on commercial construction. In 2019, we recognized the need for reliable, quality residential service work, not only in electrical, but also HVAC and plumbing. We hired an HVAC technician and began servicing air conditioning and heating, and a year later, we incorporated plumbing. This transformation meant we were going to be more than Dailey "Electric," so to reflect our electrical commercial specialty, as well as the various residential services, we changed our name to Dailey Company, Inc. Today, our corporate office in College Station is a 34,000-square-feet, state-of-the-art facility with 6,000 square feet dedicated to pre-fabrication. The facility sits on 10 acres in the Aggieland Business Park, which gives us plenty of room to expand in the future. Our Houston facility is located right outside of the Sam Houston Tollway on Brittmoore Road with convenient access to all areas of Houston, and our Houston Residential Service division located in The Woodlands offers an ideal location to span the North Houston service area. Our Lockhart location sits on the 130 toll road for quick access to surrounding cities, but the beautiful 43-acre tract filled with live oak trees offers us the peaceful reminder of our small-town roots.

Whether our employees are wearing a t-shirt with the original Dailey Electric logo or the new Dailey Company logo, the commitment to honesty, quality installation and friendly relationships remains the same. We have won numerous awards for excellence in service. At the time of this writing, we had been honored four times with the Aggie 100 Award. The Aggie 100 identifies, recognizes and celebrates the 100 fastest-growing Aggie-owned or Aggie-led businesses in the world. The Aggie 100 not only celebrates their success, it also provides a forum to pass lessons to the next generation of Aggie entrepreneurs. It was created in 2005 by Mays Business School's Center for New Ventures and Entrepreneurship (CNVE). CNVE solicits nominations from around the world through the Aggie Network. To be considered for the Aggie 100, a company must have been in operation for five years or more; must have verifiable revenues of $250,000 or more; must be owned or operated by a TAMU former student or group of former students; and must operate in a manner consistent with the Aggie Code of Honor and in keeping with the values and image of Texas A&M. It's quite humbling to receive that type of recognition, and we have also received the Business Performance Award from the Bryan Rotary Club. Those honors, along with our praise and recommendations from our customers, encourages us in our work and our dedication to service with excellence.

It's truly been an amazing journey from making $8.50 an hour working for my father and sweating about paying our $271.73 monthly mortgage to where we are today. And I am absolutely convinced that the best is yet to come because of our commitment to provide great quality at a fair price and to always deliver upon our promises. Looking back, we faced so many hurdles that they are difficult to even recall, but crossing those hurdles making all the necessary sacrifices has made reaching this part of the journey even more rewarding.

DAILEY'S ADVICE TO YOUNG ENTREPRENEURS

Looking back, I suppose I have always possessed an entrepreneurial gene. As far back as second grade in elementary school, I can recall running a business of sorts from my own desk. From an early age, I noticed that many of my fellow students didn't always come to class fully prepared, so I stocked my desk with pencils, erasers and other supplies and sold them to other students when they needed an item. I listed the prices at my desk, and I would occasionally come home with change and $1 bills falling out of my pockets. When I explained to my mother how I acquired this cash, she made me stop. I argued that my teacher was fully aware of what I was doing, and I was essentially providing a service to my fellow students. Nevertheless, she made me stop, but I never stopped enjoying the process of making an honest income.

I suppose that's a lead-in to my first piece of advice: Make sure you truly possess an entrepreneurial spirit before you ever contemplate starting a business. It's not easy, and you will not be an overnight success. I practically guarantee that, so make sure that entrepreneurism is part of your genetic DNA, and make doubly certain you are in an industry that you enjoy. Figure out what you like doing, what environment makes you comfortable, what fuels your competitive desires and so forth. When many young men and women walk across the stage to pick up their college degrees, they don't fully anticipate that their choice of career fields could determine what they will be doing for the next 30 to 40 or even 50 years. Figure out what sparks your interests, and it may be wise to shift gears if you discover that your current major or career path doesn't really interest you. Whether your passion is developing a social media platform like Mark Zuckerberg or designing athletic shoes like Phil Knight, follow what intrigues and inspires you because you will probably be doing it 80 to 120 hours per week for many years.

Sophia, Margo and Chris Dailey

Just as significantly, be wise about budgeting. Most people do not like to hear this because it involves sacrifice, but here goes: Live below your means. Not just for a year or two, either. Live below your means for the long haul. Speaking of "haul," perhaps this story will paint a clearer picture of what I mean by delayed gratification. Back when I was a student at Texas A&M and working many hours each week at U-Haul, a man offered me a couch, a loveseat and a washer and dryer for $200, because his daughter had just graduated from A&M and he had recently undergone a heart bypass surgery and did not want to move the items out of her apartment. He offered me a great deal…as long as I picked them up. Much to my wife's chagrin, we kept and used that couch, loveseat and washer and dryer until we moved into our current home—roughly 15 years after I had first acquired those possessions. By the time we actually replaced that washer and dryer, you could not even see the dials. We didn't keep those items because we were attached to them; we kept them because we were putting every penny we could back into the business. And it's not that we didn't want to eat at a place—at least occasionally—like The Republic or Christopher's, but we simply chose to live beneath our means to save as much money as we could for as long as possible. Turkey sandwiches and a bag of chips can fill you up just as much as filet mignon, even though it may be far less appealing.

I think it is also extremely important to manage your money wisely. I've always tried to keep a significant amount of money in the bank "just in case." Perhaps that's because I have so many vivid memories of my early days as a business owner. There were many days I would go to the post office, reciting this prayer as I drove, "Please God, let there be a check in there so that I can make payroll." The check wasn't always in my post office box, and there were plenty of sleepless nights I endured figuring out how to pay all my employees. It was often a close call, but fortunately, we always made payroll. As business improved, I made it a point to save as much money as I could, and not just for a "rainy day fund" or an emergency. It's imperative as an entrepreneur to maintain a long-term perspective. Personally, I always like to be thinking at least seven years in advance regarding how we might grow the company. I would not have been able to expand into the Houston and Austin/San Antonio marketplaces without big-picture thinking and a long-term perspective.

With that said, it's wise to establish good credit by borrowing some money and paying it back. That was a tough lesson for me to learn, because I initially thought that taking on any debt was a weakness. But the fact is that it is good to keep a line of credit. In our construction-related industry so much happens in the summertime that it is sometimes necessary to borrow money to pay for all the projects, supplies, labor and so forth. I once was so opposed to this that I might turn down opportunities simply to avoid accumulating any debt. But I have learned that if you are responsible in paying back any loan or debt that has been incurred, it becomes much easier and cost-effective to expand your business because you will receive prime interest rates and outstanding incentives. The key is to be responsible and to pay your loans and debts in a timely and consistent manner. Keep in mind that it is easy to lose control of credit, so be wise with it.

Finally, as I have noted previously, it is every bit as important to take care of your personnel as it is to perform for you customers and clients. No matter how visionary you are or how ingenious your business concept may be, you cannot build a great business without attracting and keeping great people. It's not enough to merely pay your employees fairly. We make every effort to treat all of our employees—no matter if he is a manager or a helper—like a member of the family. If you begin your business endeavors by treating every staff member with the same level of respect, you will create a tremendous sense of loyalty that will stand the test of time.

I encourage you to constantly work on developing your people skills and focusing on building meaningful relationships with people. I am convinced that business is 99 percent about people, and people are all looking for genuine and meaningful relationships. To quote former President Ronald Reagan, "Surround yourself with great people; delegate authority; get out of the way."

I will never forget how relieved I was when I made my first few hires, along with the sense of responsibility that comes with being an employer. If that person is willing to come to work for you, he/she trusts you to provide work, a salary, benefits and so forth so that he/she can build a better life. Keep this in mind: **Your business should never be just about you. Or just about your future. You may have started it, but once you hire one other person, the business is much bigger than yourself. It's much more than just that employee, too. It's about his/her family and future, as well.**

I am extremely proud of all that we have accomplished since Memorial Day Weekend in 2003 when I first embarked on the entrepreneurial journey. But most of all I am proud of how many lives we have touched and improved. We have plenty of satisfied customers, and we also have more than 300 employees who are grateful to be part of Dailey Company because they feel like they are part of something much bigger than themselves: They are truly part of a business family. I certainly never envisioned any of this when I made that first road trip to Aggieland in the winter of 1990, but I think even my father would acknowledge now that it was pretty wise to plant roots in Bryan-College Station. We've grown by leaps and bounds over the years, and like a tree that grows deeper roots and develops the stress wood it needs to remain upright in battering winds, we're entrenched in this community for generations to come. It hasn't been an easy journey, but it's definitely been worth it.

Here's to paving your road to entrepreneurial success, as well. Roadblocks, detours and dangerous conditions will inevitably come your way, but keep pushing forward and continue to persevere. I am living proof that with extraordinary perseverance even an ordinary person can achieve great things.

CHAPTER 12
Hendler Family: Barry, Laura, Hollie, BJ and Joe
As told by Barry Hendler
American Lumber
Texas A&M Classes of 1971, 2000 and 2004

HENDLER'S PATH TO TEXAS A&M

This chapter is not really about me. I am simply the eldest in the immediate family, which makes me the logical narrator. American Lumber's growth from a start-up business to a successful mid-sized company that employs more than 150 people has truly been a family affair right from the start, and it continues to be a family-centered and family-owned organization. It's grown to include many leaders with different last names, but we refer to them all as the American Lumber family. Hopefully, the Hendler family will continue to be part of this company for generations, long after I am no longer here. And rest assured, this family bleeds maroon and white, although not all of us actually attended Texas A&M. All the males in the family—BJ, Joe and I—graduated from A&M, while the ladies—my wife, Laura, and my daughter, Hollie—graduated from Texas Woman's University.

The two schools have a long and storied history of being tied together that dates back to the early 1900s. For many decades, only TWU students were eligible to become the official annual "Aggie Sweetheart." Selection of a new Aggie Sweetheart each year was a major event for the students at both institutions. Some Ol' Ags like me remember the well-organized Corps Trips when the Aggie football team played SMU or TCU in the old Southwest Conference days. On those trips, many Aggies ventured a bit further north to Denton and the TWU campus. In some instances, the arrangements included organized train trips from Denton, just as there were some train trips from College Station. I actually met my wife, Laura, before she enrolled at TWU. She is the proud owner of an Aggie Sweetheart Ring. That ring program, which was discontinued the year after I graduated, was designed to allow students and former students to honor their mothers or their wives for their support they provided in helping them through school. By the way, it's no coincidence that TWU's school colors are maroon and white. As I noted, those colors run deep in our family.

I was blessed with the opportunity to become the first member of my immediate family to graduate from a university. My father was an immigrant who arrived in Texas by himself from Lithuania at the age of 16. He didn't speak any English, and everything he owned fit in one small piece of luggage. He ultimately met and married my mother, and along with my Lithuanian lineage, I'm a seventh-generation Texan on my mother's side. My parents settled in Temple, where I was raised and eventually graduated from Temple High School in 1967. Two or three days after my high school graduation, I was shipped off to Junction, a small Hill Country town about 115 miles northwest of San Antonio, where Texas A&M had a 411-acre adjunct campus that is now the Texas Tech University Center at Junction. Thirteen years before I arrived in Junction, the town had been the destination where legendary head coach Paul "Bear" Bryant took his first Texas A&M football team for a memorable 10-day camp. Close to 100 players went to the camp, but only 38 stayed all 10 days and returned to College Station to start the 1954 season. After A&M had endured six losing seasons in the previous eight years prior to his arrival in Aggieland, Bear Bryant believed his team needed a tremendous amount of discipline and toughness.

I probably needed the same two qualities when I arrived at the adjunct campus in '67. I was sent to the adjunct campus—as opposed to the College Station campus—because I initially had the not-so-bright idea of studying oceanography, which required a zoology major. That major required a trigonometry credit from the high school curriculum, which I did not possess. So, I went off to Junction to check that box and received a quick education in why I did not want to be a zoologist.

The ultimate challenge was organic chemistry. It was brutal. I spent the summer in Junction, where we were not even allowed to leave the campus unless it was to go to church on Sunday mornings. It was quite a militaristic setting, which was good training for what was ahead of me in the Corps of Cadets.

In preparation for this chapter, I was asked if I enjoyed my time in the Corps of Cadets. That's a difficult question to answer because, quite frankly, it was extremely tough and demanding at times. But in hindsight, I most certainly needed the structure and discipline that it provided, as did my sons, BJ and Joe...especially BJ, who was a bit of a rebel at times during his childhood. According to its official website, the Corps of Cadets "is one of the largest uniformed bodies of students in the nation that provides hands-on leadership experience**,** enhances a world-class education from Texas A&M **and** directly involves cadets in the traditions that make Aggieland so different from all other schools... The Corps is, at its heart, a program that helps young men and women learn, practice and develop critical leadership skills that will serve them for the rest of their life." I wholeheartedly agree, and that's why I "encouraged" my boys to enter the Corps.

For a variety of reasons, BJ was not admitted to Texas A&M straight out of high school, and he ended up taking his first 31 college hours at a junior college in Uvalde, Texas. To give him some privacy, Laura and I allowed him to live in a small hunting cabin on our property in Uvalde while he went to high school and junior college. He worked hard in those freshman classes and eventually earned an acceptance letter to Texas A&M. Although he'd spent much of his life dreaming about being in the Corps of Cadets he also enjoyed his independence, living on his own even though the hunting house was just a stone's throw from our main home. As he prepared to attend A&M, he was seriously considering a college experience that did not include membership in the Corps of Cadets. When he told me that, I remained calm—something that was not always my natural personality trait—and told him, "Good luck paying for college."

The bottom line is that I knew BJ needed the structure and discipline of the Corps, and I was concerned he wouldn't make it through A&M without those qualities being instilled in him. The thought of paying his own way through A&M made him reconsider, and he would be the first to acknowledge today that his participation in the Corps at A&M was a tremendously positive and life-shaping experience. BJ entered the Corps as a fish, even though he had enough hours to join as a sophomore. Four years later, when it was time for Joe to attend A&M, he never hesitated about joining the Corps.

BJ, Joe and I all became better leaders in the Corps because we learned so many principles of success. Membership in the Corps of Cadets also made us better students during our years at Texas A&M because it required us to develop time management skills. I knew from my own experiences in the Corps that BJ and Joe would leave A&M in far better condition to lead their families, their communities and their businesses. I certainly never dreamed that any of my children—let alone all of them—would one day join the family business.

During my time at Texas A&M, I was honored to brush shoulders with some of the greatest leaders of "the Greatest Generation." The president of Texas A&M during my college days was none other than Gen. James Earl Rudder, Class of '32. Among many other things, Col. Rudder was the commander of the Ranger Company that took Pointe du Hoc, which was part of the Invasion of Normandy. Lt. Col. Rudder's U.S. Army Rangers stormed the beach at Pointe du Hoc, scaling a 100-foot vertical cliff under heavy enemy fire to reach and destroy German gun batteries. The battalion's casualty rate was greater than 50 percent, and Lt. Col. Rudder was wounded twice during the course of the fighting. Still, the Rangers dug in and fought off German counterattacks for two days until relieved. Lt. Col. Rudder and his men helped to successfully establish a beachhead for the Allied forces. That action was depicted in the 1962 epic film *"The Longest Day."*

The commandant of the Corps of Cadets during my time at A&M was Col. James H. McCoy, Class of '40. *Col.* McCoy served valiantly under Rudder's leadership during World War II, and he was part of the 109th Infantry Regiment, 28th Division during the Battle of the Bulge. The 109th was placed in a direct line of the advancing German assault into the Hurtgen Forest and the Ardennes. Rudder dug in his exposed left flank to stop the German advance into Luxembourg. Merely being in the presence of men like that greatly shaped my outlook and my pride in being part of the Corps.

I built many friendships in the Corps that are still alive today. In fact, my closest friends today are classmates. Compared to so many students today, none of us really had any money back then, and many of us were like me in being first-generation college students. Only a handful of us owned vehicles, and those inevitably became community Corps cars. It was a completely different environment that led to developing numerous lifelong bonds. I speak often of my Corps of Cadets memories, possibly because my classroom memories are not quite as vivid and nostalgic.

For the most part, I was a decent student at Texas A&M, and because of the timeframe (the late 1960s and early '70s) there was a tremendous incentive to graduate in four years. The U.S. involvement in the conflict in Vietnam was on everyone's mind at A&M, especially those of us in the Corps. We were given a four-year deferment from the draft, but after four years and a day, the deferment was gone. To make a long story short, I put off an economics class until the last semester of my senior year, and it was brutal (or maybe it was just me who was brutal in the class). Whatever the case, I bombed the final exam and was going to be three hours short of graduating with my degree in marketing. So, I went to Nagle Hall—where the entire economic department was located at that time—and pleaded with my professor. I argued that he needed to give me a "D" in the class, and he was adamant that I had earned my "F" the old-fashioned way: failing to display any mastery of the subject matter. Still, I pleaded and argued. Then I begged and disputed. This went on for quite some time, and I think he ultimately grew tired of hearing me plead my case. Finally, he said, "OK, Mr. Hendler. I will give you a D, but you have to make a promise to me. You must promise me that you will never, ever step into this building again." To this day, I have never returned to Nagle Hall.

Fortunately, I was able to walk the stage with my classmates in the spring of 1971. Even more fortunately, I was not shipped off to Vietnam. In 1969, President Richard Nixon introduced the so-called "Vietnamization" strategy, which gradually built up South Vietnamese forces so that they could defend their nation on their own. As a result, the U.S. began reducing the number of American soldiers and officers who were being sent to Southeast Asia. Almost all U.S. troops left South Vietnam by the end of 1973. Therefore, many of my buddies and I ended up serving short reserve tours after we had graduated. I have always thanked God for the timing of the end of the conflict. In 1982, the Vietnam Veterans Memorial was dedicated in Washington, D.C., inscribed with the names of 57,939 members of the U.S. armed forces who had paid the ultimate price as a result of the war. Texas A&M produced the highest number of casualties after the service academies.

I have also continued to thank God for another event during that collegiate timeframe that had a tremendously positive impact on my life. During my college days, there were very few women on the A&M campus. A handful of professors' daughters did attend classes, but there were no women's dorms. It wasn't until 1972 that campus housing opened to women for the first time. In other words, the pickings were slim when it came to seeking dates during college. That's why I made sure to find out which of my Corps buddies had sisters back at home. One of my classmates, who lived in the same dorm as me but was in a different Corps outfit, had two high school-aged sisters back in his hometown of Fort Worth. His mother loved for him to bring Aggies home for the weekend, because she loved to cook. I went to Fort Worth with him in January 1969—my sophomore year—and one of his sisters set me up with a blind date. The young lady's name was Laura Brazil, who was a senior at Carter Riverside High School.

Being quite the romantic type, I took her out on a Saturday night to a hockey game in the newly completed Tarrant County Convention Center. At the time, the Fort Worth Wings were a minor league affiliate for the NHL's Detroit Red Wings. We had a great time, and I immediately wanted to see her again. Unfortunately, her mother had a policy that she couldn't date the same boy two nights in a row. As fate would have it, though, we had a week off before the spring semester officially started at A&M, so I was able to stick around for a couple of extra days in Cowtown.

The following Monday was "rodeo day" for all the public schools in Fort Worth, and the students in the area were given the day off to attend the Fort Worth Stock Show and Rodeo. Laura had mentioned to me on our first date that she wanted to go to the rodeo, and that's all I needed to know to ask her to go with me. Since the rodeo was on a Monday—two days after our initial date—her mother permitted us to go together. That was on January 25, 1969. Fifty years later—January 25, 2019—we returned to Fort Worth with our children and grandchildren, and I presented Laura with 50 yellow roses to mark that significant anniversary. Laura and I married in August of 1971, and we have been partners in this game of life ever since that first weekend together in Fort Worth.

Following my short stint in the reserves, I landed a job with the Otis Elevator Company at a regional office in Dallas. Otis Elevator is an international company with a long history. In 1854, Elisha Otis travelled to the New York World's Fair to promote his new invention. Standing high above the crowd on a platform elevator, he ordered the only rope supporting him to be cut. The crowd cried out, fearing Elisha would fall to his death. His safety brake held. In that moment, one man changed the world's perspective on what's possible.

In the early 1970s, the Otis Elevator Company was hiring a significant number of Aggies, especially in its Texas locations. I was hired as a sales trainee, and I immediately began the training program that taught me all aspects of the company. In the middle of that training period, a union strike affected the Otis Elevator Company for seven months, which meant sales trainees like me suddenly became responsible for the maintenance of existing elevators in office buildings, hospital buildings and so forth. With my marketing degree from Texas A&M, I never anticipated installing elevators in 40-story skyscrapers in downtown Dallas, but that's exactly what I found myself doing. It was a blessing in disguise, as I learned so much about mechanics, engineering and construction in that job. In that time, drafting was not a computerized process; it was a hand-drawn process, and I spent several months drawing elevators. I discovered I was comfortable in the construction environment, and during the four years or so that I was with the Otis Elevator Company, I first learned the value of being opportunistic.

There are plenty of quotes about opportunity knocking, but my favorite one may be from Thomas Edison, who once stated: "Opportunity is missed by most people because it is dressed in overalls and looks like work." From personal experience, I can tell you that nothing may prove to be more costly to you than missed opportunities. No matter what professional field you choose, it's extremely important to seize opportunities when you see them. Tomorrow may be too late.

HENDLER'S MOST CHALLENGING OBSTACLES

Through the years, I've learned that it's not enough to dream about success. Sometimes achievement is simply a result of staying awake longer than others and continuing to work after most people have called it a day. In the midst of working for Otis Elevator, I detected an opportunity to perhaps start a business of our own in the mid-1970s. Laura's uncle owned a shop in Hurst, which is located in northeast Tarrant County about 15 miles from the Dallas-Fort Worth International Airport. Through various construction contacts I'd made, I saw an opportunity to produce some fabricated metal parts that could be used for building components. I didn't know a great deal about it, but I saw an opportunity, and I was confident that I could source the material at relatively low costs. I was also able to use Laura's uncle's equipment and shop in the evenings after the shop was closed, so it was only a matter of finding the labor to manufacture the parts.

That's where Laura and I factored into the entrepreneurial equation. While both of us were working in the daytime—Laura teaching special education at a school in Dallas and me learning the ins and outs of the elevator business—we began our metal manufacturing endeavors, cranking out fabricated metal parts throughout the evenings and occasionally into the mornings. It was truly a trial-and-error endeavor, as we didn't initially have a clue as to what we were doing. At the time, the concept of modular buildings (or portable buildings) was becoming quite popular, and with a little elbow grease and plenty of sleep-deprived nights and weekends, Laura and I were able to take large coils of steel and design the siding that could be used to construct portable buildings. Over time, we gradually evolved to produce other components, manufacturing exterior trim items that we had already sold even before we had produced them. Quite frankly, we couldn't afford to do business any other way because we had absolutely no disposable income.

Looking back, those were some awfully long days. Laura and I would wake up around 5 in the morning, and I would drive her to the school in Dallas and then go to work (we could only afford one vehicle at the time). We would work all day, and I'd pick Laura up after her classes had ended. From there, we would drive to Hurst and begin working on our sheet metal operations, grinding away on most evenings until at least 10 p.m. We did that for a couple of years, saving as much money as possible until we were able to hire some help and open our own manufacturing facility in Haltom City, which is roughly six miles northeast of downtown Fort Worth. By that point, I had made the decision to leave Otis Elevator to work full time for our startup business, while Laura was able to stop teaching once our oldest child, Hollie, was born on February 6, 1975.

Meanwhile, we grew the business slowly but steadily over the course of a decade and ultimately employed about 50 people. I have occasionally been asked if I was ever apprehensive about going out on my own. In all sincerity, I did not feel bulletproof in any way, and there were certainly some difficult and lean times. We worked horrendous hours for a couple of years, and most of the weekends were a blur because they were so busy. But I always had the confidence that we would find a way to be successful, and to a large extent, I credit my involvement with the Corps of Cadets for instilling within me a do-whatever-it-takes mentality. Laura and I have also shared that philosophy with all three of our children, who are quite confident in their abilities and determined to make great things happen.

We were rocking and rolling along at our own business for about 10 years, a span of time when all three of the kids were born (BJ was born in April of 1977 and Joe arrived in late April of '81). The mid-1980s, however, produced some extremely difficult financial times for the economy in the state of Texas, which is heavily dependent on the prices of oil and gas. Texas reported 366,200 jobs related to oil and gas extraction and oilfield equipment in the early 1980s, according to the Federal Reserve Bank of Dallas. By 1987, only a year after the great oil price collapse of '86, 175,000 of those jobs had vanished. Like the Ford Pinto or the AMC Pacer, they were everywhere one day and practically gone the next. According to a 2006 article in *The Explorer*, a publication of the American Association of Petroleum Geologists, the state of Texas lost more than $1 billion in oil and gas severance taxes in 1986. The standard oilfield joke then was that the biggest employer of petroleum engineers after 1986 collapse was Safeway grocery stores. The industry was in terrible shape, and it quickly began to affect practically every other business in Texas, including the construction trade.

Our business' fate was much the same as so many other small companies in those days, as we initially struggled to keep the business afloat but ultimately had to shut down operations. It wasn't because of anything we did or didn't do; it was simply a case of the market shrinking so much that we couldn't afford to keep our doors open because many of our customers couldn't pay their bills. In one particular case, an individual who purchased materials from us couldn't make his payments, so he offered me his wood-working equipment from his own company. I didn't really want the equipment at first, but I decided to accept it and be open-minded about making a career transition.

We couldn't continue with our business, and we couldn't really continue to operate a construction-oriented business in the state of Texas while the economy was so volatile. As I noted previously, however, I've always tried to look at every situation—even a perceived negative event—as more of an opportunity than an obstacle.

Helen Keller, the noted American educator who was born blind and deaf, once wrote: "When one door of happiness closes, another opens, but often we look so long at the closed door that we do not see the one that has been opened for us." I completely agree. Our business was a good one for over a decade, but I needed to change directions once that door closed. So, we liquidated our business and started the search for our next mountain to climb.

While my start-up was gone, I did still possess seed capital from the liquidation and some woodworking equipment. That led me to begin thinking about beginning a lumber company, but not one based in Texas. After plenty of prayer, careful consideration and research, we decided to take advantage of the Maquiladora Program, which allowed American manufacturing companies to operate in Mexico under a preferential duty-free program established and administered by the United States and Mexico governments. Materials, assembly components and production equipment used in maquiladoras are allowed to enter Mexico duty-free. Products that had added value could then be returned to the U.S. duty-free. The program was initiated in Mexico in 1964, long before the North American Free Trade Agreement (NAFTA) was approved in 1994. In essence, the Maquiladora Program was developed to foster border-region employment rates, as well as to further attract foreign investments in Mexico.

What I ultimately concluded was that our operating costs would likely be cheaper in Mexico than in Texas. So, I began doing the research and found an opportunity to open a lumber manufacturing company in Nuevo Laredo, a city in the Mexican state of Tamaulipas, which lies on the banks of the Rio Grande River across the border from Laredo, Texas. While I attempted to begin a lumber company in Nuevo Laredo, Laura and the kids stayed in the Fort Worth area to sell our home and the warehouse that had been the headquarters of our business. In the meantime, I found an apartment in Laredo and quickly determined that a border town might not be the best setting to raise a family. Laura and the kids would visit me in Laredo on occasion, and during one of their trips we drove north to

On the left, BJ, Barry and Joe; on the right, BJ and Hollie at Aggie Bonfire

Uvalde, which is about halfway between San Antonio and Del Rio and about two and one-half hours north of Laredo. We immediately fell in love with Uvalde and found some property outside the city in 1988 that was a perfect place to raise a family.

It certainly wasn't an easy commute to our manufacturing facility in Mexico, but we made it work, as I would work two-to-four days in Mexico and come back to Uvalde to see the family on the weekends. During that time period, Laura truly proved herself as "superwoman." I was in another country during most of the week, and she went back to teaching once Joe started attending school. She also raised the kids, kept the house and sacrificed her time to do all that was necessary. She is an amazing woman, wife, mother and now grandmother. I am not sure how many marriages could have survived that schedule and long-distance relationship, but I thank God that we did whatever was necessary to build the business and keep our family strong. Every Friday night, we had a sit-down family dinner. It didn't matter what else we had going on in life, we were sitting down together as a family on Friday nights. I would cook the main course on the grill, and Laura would handle all the sides, but the most important aspect of those meals was not food; it was family fellowship.

The reason Laura went back to teaching was because we needed every dime we could earn. Business in Mexico didn't immediately take off, as there were definitely some learning curves for me to experience and absorb. What I quickly discovered was that the only thing worse than dealing with one government was coping with two. The reality is there are numerous other costs that you don't see, and there is also plenty of lost time that often duplicates and multiplies. At that time, Mexico certainly had a criminal element, but it was not nearly as menacing as it is today. I never felt physically threatened there. I knew my way around, spoke the language relatively well and I could maneuver out of trouble. Nevertheless, it was a Wild, Wild West setting. In Mexico, the law is often more of a suggestion than what most Americans consider it to be. And the law keepers, well, many of them could easily be bought. Many of them also made bribery part of the daily routine. The Policía Federal—commonly known as the "Federales"—and the Portal de Servicios de Aduana could be quite difficult to work with at times. I went down to Mexico with the attitude I was not going to pay them one penny. The first time you pay them, they own you. I have many examples I could cite, but I will stick with two.

We had a truck that was dedicated to transporting finished material from our plant across the border to Texas after we had added value to the lumber in Nuevo Laredo. The truck would unload in Texas and come right back again to be reloaded. That truck was running constantly, and practically everyone on both sides knew the driver and recognized the truck. Nevertheless, I received a call one afternoon informing me that the Mexican Aduana had seized the truck and trailer. Without hesitation, I drove to the border, and they informed me that I was in violation of something that they had essentially created. They said if I paid them I could have my truck back. Bluntly and not so eloquently, I told them I wasn't paying them anything. That started the standoff. I went back there every day for about a month asking for my truck, and every day, I received the same response: pay the violation. Finally, after about a month, I walked into the office and was told I could have my truck. They gave me the keys and I walked out into the yard to discover my truck had literally been stripped of anything and everything they could remove from the vehicle. It was their message to me that you may have a truck, but we are going to be paid one way or another. We had to have everything refitted, but I never had another problem with the Mexican Aduana. It's like dealing with a bully on school playgrounds. If you allow the bully to intimidate you, he owns you. I didn't want to be owned.

My other example involves the Federales. I had driven downtown to our Mexican bank in Nuevo Laredo. The front of the bank is on the main thoroughfare, and I pulled my four-wheel drive Chevrolet Blazer onto the side street, parallel parked and went into the bank. I spoke briefly to the bank president, returned to the truck and turned the key just as someone was tapping on my window with a .45 pistol. I rolled the window down, and a Policía Federal introduced himself, said I was illegally parked and informed me that he needed to tow the vehicle. I might add that it was a really sharp-looking truck that turned heads wherever I drove it. I told him politely but firmly, "No, you are not going to tow this vehicle," and we continued to argue back and forth while his partner walked up to join the "Mexican standoff."

Finally, I stepped out of the truck, and I was informed of my lack of rights. That's when I went back into the bank and asked the bank president to join me. The argument continued when the president arrived outside. The president told them that the situation was nonsense, and they needed to leave me alone. After another four or five minutes with the president arguing on my side, they finally agreed that the towing was probably not going to happen. Those two federal policemen then returned to their patrol car...a pink, Mary Kay Cadillac Eldorado. Obviously, these "policemen" were simply attempting to steal a Blazer to upgrade their "patrol car."

Despite those difficulties and many others in Mexico, doing business in the country was good for us for a number of years. In fact, it was white hot for us for a considerable time, but like anything else that runs so hot, it burned itself out. In hindsight, that was probably one of the best things that happened to us because it really forced us to look stateside before the Mexican peso crisis of 1994. The Mexican economy experienced hyperinflation of around 52 percent and mutual funds began liquidating Mexican assets as well as emerging market assets in general. There were many reasons to move our operations back to the United States. One of the things that I learned from operating a business in Mexico was that we often take our blessings in America for granted. The reality is this is a blessed nation, and there are just so many opportunities stateside. We still do some business in Mexico today, but I am extremely grateful that we are operating our American Lumber business in the USA.

HENDLER FAMILY'S PATH TO ENTREPRENEURIAL SUCCESS

Once we relocated American Lumber's headquarters to Uvalde, we did well stateside and ultimately also began wholesaling it back into Mexico following the United States' $50 billion bailout for Mexico in January 1995. We had a considerable amount of success selling to clients throughout the northern half of Mexico. Meanwhile, much of our stateside business was initially concentrated heavily in Texas, although we were expanding into other states. For the most part, we grew slowly and steadily throughout the mid-1990s, and in the late '90s, the first of our three children, Hollie, joined the company. Hollie graduated from Texas Woman's University in just three years, proving that she received her intelligence from Laura. Hollie's degree was in elementary education, and she had a teaching job lined up with the Uvalde Independent School District. However, it didn't start for several months after she returned to Uvalde, and she came to me and said, "Dad I need something to do until I start teaching. Do you have a job for me?"

I had an entry-level position where she would be on the phone dispatching trucks. Hollie did well, and she eventually came to Laura and me and told us she could go into teaching at any time, but that she wanted to try her hand by trading lumber. It caught us off guard, but Hollie was quite serious about wanting to be a salesperson at American Lumber. I will never forget her first cold call. She just happened to call a crotchety old man with crackly voice that had been hoarsened by years—probably decades—of cigarette smoking. He picked up the phone, and she launched into her carefully rehearsed pitch, describing the greatness of American Lumber. He allowed her to ramble for 30 seconds or so before he stopped her in mid-sentence and said, "Little girl, when you actually learn something about the lumber business, call me back." Then he abruptly hung up the phone. That was her first sales call. She excused herself, marched to the ladies room and began to cry. A few moments later, she came back and started dialing again. I knew right then that she was going to be successful.

By nature, Hollie is a sweet and meek person. The word "meek" is sometimes taken in a derogatory context nowadays, but that's not Hollie. She is humble and caring for others. When she was in high school, she went through training so that she could volunteer to provide hospice care. She would actually stay with families with young children with terminal illnesses to provide support for the parents and siblings. She also learned sign language so she could communicate with a deaf couple who lived about a mile's walk upstream from us in Uvalde County. She was mature beyond her age, but what has impressed me the most is how she has also continued to grow stronger as a businesswoman. She is naturally caring, but she has learned to be tough when she needs to be.

When Hollie first joined us, we were strictly a wholesale business, but things were happening in the market that were forcing us to look seriously into opening a manufacturing facility in the Bryan-College Station area. BJ, who is a 2000 graduate of Texas A&M, had expressed his desire to run the facility upon his graduation. I am not sure if I would have initially approved of that idea if BJ had not been with me for such a long time while I was running our operations in Mexico.

About halfway through BJ's fifth-grade year, Laura called me in Laredo and said, "I'm taking your son to the airport. I'm flying him to San Antonio where you can pick him up." She did not want to discuss any other possibilities. BJ had pushed her patience to the limit, and I was the one person whom BJ truly feared because I was the firm disciplinarian in the family. We had a home-school course that I tried to teach to BJ while in Mexico, but his real education was probably earned while stacking lumber at the end of a band saw in the manufacturing facility. So many stories come to mind from those days when BJ lived with me in Laredo and went to Mexico every morning. If you asked BJ, he would probably tell you that he still has nightmares of us eating Gorton's Fish Sticks on a regular basis or having his dog, Whiskey, run over accidently by a forklift operator. But I remember plenty of humorous moments, as well.

For example, I remember him grabbing some pink "while-you-were-out" notes used for taking phone messages and walking around the plant and handing them to employees, explaining that they had just been fired because they had playfully bound him to a pole with lumber packaging wrap. Of course, the employees who were being "fired" either didn't understand him or knew to simply ignore him. I also remember taking him to baseball games on the border, as the minor league Tecolotes de los Dos Laredos (translated "the Owls of the Two Laredos") played half their home games at Parque la Junta in Mexico and half their games at Uni-Trade Stadium across the river in Laredo. More than anything else, though, I remember BJ learning the lumber business by watching me and picking things up along the way. He has always proven to be a bit of an entrepreneur, as well.

In seventh grade, for example, BJ began selling candy to school kids, making $20 to $40 a day. Laura would take him to a Sam's in San Antonio so he could buy his inventory for the month, and he would mark it up and sell it to his classmates at school. Later in life, while BJ was in the Corps of Cadets, it became quite popular to "borrow" farm-to-market road signs with a particular class years on it. Farm-to-Market Road 1971 in Harrison County was quite popular for Class of '71 graduates to "borrow," while FM 2004, a 5.4-mile stretch of roadway also in Harrison County was popular among '99 graduates.

BJ found a manufacturer in Nebraska who could match the Texas Department of Transportation reflective paint, and he was selling them as quickly as he could have them shipped to College Station. They looked so authentic that the Texas A&M Police Department required him to place a sticker on the manufactured signs so that it was not assumed that the signs had been stolen. And BJ's girlfriend at the time—now his wife, Sarah—placed flyers on vehicles across campus to help him advertise the signs. He probably made about $15 to $20 a sign for quite some time before Aggie Mom's Clubs also began selling the signs for fundraising projects. But the point is that BJ possessed an entrepreneurial spirit from an early age, and he already had a great feel for the lumber business. So it made sense to allow him to run the facility that we were going to open in the Bryan-College

Station area, even though I was initially concerned that his lack of professional experience outside the company could limit him.

In hindsight, I should not have been concerned. BJ is an incorrigible practical joker, and he is the life of the party. Laura says that the air in a room is occasionally sucked out when BJ walks into it because he has so much personality and practically demands everyone's attention. The bottom line is that he is remarkably personable. He also can adapt to any environment, which has made him a tremendous businessperson. BJ simply understands the lumber business, probably because he has been in a lumber environment for practically his entire life. Whatever the case, he seems to possess a sixth sense about the industry, and he never needed instructions on any specifics within the day-to-day operations. In many ways, BJ and Hollie are complete opposites in their personalities and approaches, but they have both been outstanding additions because they complement each other so well.

With the addition of the manufacturing plant in northwest Bryan, American Lumber began to grow considerably in terms of our production and employees. By 2004, we'd grown enough to justify adding another plant located further east to handle the increasing demands. That's also about the time that Joe graduated and expressed a desire to follow in his sister's and brother's footsteps by joining American Lumber. Even though Laura and I had never planned on building a family business,

it simply evolved. We were excited about Joe joining the business, although Laura was not happy with me for sending her "baby" to Alabama to start a manufacturing facility.

After watching BJ start and lead the Bryan facility, I had no worries about Joe being equally successful in Alabama. Like BJ, Joe attained Eagle Scout status as a youth, which is the highest achievement rank attainable from the Boy Scouts of America. Since its inception in 1911, only four percent of Scouts have earned this rank after a lengthy process. Both of the boys are extremely competitive and success-oriented. Although Joe was not with me in Mexico, sawdust was certainly part of his genetic code.

Joe spent plenty of childhood and adolescent time in the manufacturing facility, although he walked a much straighter path than his older brother. In high school, for example, Joe was class president, class favorite, prom king and a standout on the athletic fields. As an adult, Joe is an interesting mix of his brother and sister. He is quiet like his sister and a natural leader like his brother. He also possesses a heart of gold. I recall he went to work one day in Alabama, and there was a car blocking the gate. He was going to have the car towed, and he called the tow company, but just as the truck arrived, a little, elderly woman showed up and asked him not to tow her vehicle. She was out of gas. He had compassion for her and decided to pay the tow truck driver to "tow" her to a gas station. Joe also gave her enough cash to purchase gas. Joe has always made friends easily, and he is an extremely humble individual. Joe is slow to anger, and he does not want to be the center of attention. For the most part, Joe lives up to his name: he is just an ordinary guy, but he has become an extraordinary businessman. Like his siblings, he is also hard-working and continues to be a tremendous asset to our business operations.

Joe spent several years in Alabama, building up the plant and growing as a leader. He also met his wife, Gretchen, while working there. Once they started having children, we brought the family back to Central Texas, where Joe now serves as Vice President of Procurement. Hollie has also relocated to Bryan, moving from Uvalde to serve as our Vice President of Administration. She is extremely detail-oriented, which makes her a perfect fit for that position. And, at least for the time being, BJ serves as our Chief Operating Officer, while I still hold the position of President and CEO. I'm not sure how much longer I need to still be involved in the business because these three children are outstanding leaders, especially when they work together on a common cause or issue.

Individually, Hollie, BJ and Joe have been quite successful. Each of them has their own goals and strengths. I've said it many times before, and I will continue to say it: I would not want to be a competitor trying to oppose the three of them. I have watched the three of them in difficult decision-making situations. They become laser-focused on whatever issue or difficulty we are facing. It is not a fair fight for our competitors. The Hendler trio will kick your butt. I don't say that in a bad way, but they are extremely competitive. When they are out there in the marketplace, they are not out looking for a fight, but if someone starts a fight, they will finish it. I say that with complete confidence because I have seen it happen, as we have evolved as a company. I am also quite confident in the long-term prognosis for American Lumber because the three of them are such strong leaders. While BJ is the most outspoken of the siblings, our growth as a company since the late 1990s is directly related to all three of our children joining the team, which makes me exceptionally proud as a father and an entrepreneur.

Today, American Lumber has locations in Uvalde, Bryan and Birmingham, as well as Fort Worth and Jacksonville, Texas. Our American Lumber "family" has grown to well over 150 people who strive to strengthen partnerships with customers and vendors every day. In the United States, our marketplace now is basically the eastern half of the United States. If you draw a line from El Paso straight up to the Canadian border, everything east of that is our primary market. We do sell some lumber west of that line, but not significantly. We also continue to do business in Mexico, Canada and the Caribbean.

In the midst of the growth in the mid-2000s, we also realized the need for "just-in-time deliveries," and we incorporated distribution centers into the manufacturing facilities along with a new trucking company: Great American Freight. This freight company started acquiring rolling stock so that it would not be solely dependent on outside freight companies. These changes have allowed American Lumber to not only better service our current customers, but also increase sales to both commercial yards and the customers that do not buy full truckloads.

I envision American Lumber continuing to grow. Hollie, BJ and Joe balance each other out; they control their spending and continue to invest in the business. According to the Ohio-based Conway Center for Family Business, only slightly more than 30 percent of all family-owned businesses make the transition into the second generation. In many ways, I believe we have already beaten the odds with the second generation, because Laura and I have complete confidence in where BJ, Hollie and Joe will take the business.

If our grandchildren choose to follow in their parents' footsteps that would be wonderful, although we want each of them to pursue their own passions. Statistics suggest that only 12 percent of family businesses will still be viable into the third generation, with only three percent of all family businesses operating at the fourth-generation level and beyond. Perhaps our grandchildren will defy those odds. Regardless, I am extremely proud of what Laura and I started, how we've bounced back from adversities and how we have evolved as a family business that is thriving into the second generation. God has truly blessed us in so many ways.

HENDLER'S ADVICE TO YOUNG ENTREPRENEURS

Throughout my entrepreneurial endeavors, I have enjoyed such tremendous job satisfaction that I haven't really viewed my career as "work." It's been more of an adventure in that we have gone through good times and bad times, but we have always made it a point to try to enjoy the ride. I am passionate about my work, and in my book, success is not so much about reaching a particular destination or income level. Instead, it's about enjoying the journey and finding satisfaction in your life's work. So, my first piece of advice would be to find a profession that ignites your professional passion.

Although there are some people who do it effectively, be careful about going into business for yourself right out of college. For most people, it may be wise to find a job and gain work experience before starting a business. That's what I did when I took a position with the Otis Elevator Company. That position allowed me to make a living while I searched for opportunities. Training and working with Otis Elevator Company allowed me to gain a grasp of how a business operates at all levels of a company or organization. Too many young people go into the workforce and focus only on their own jobs and daily roles. But if you truly have a dream of running your own organization, study every department and talk to other employees in various departments. View your initial jobs as paid training in preparation for one day leading your own venture. Finally, never, never stop learning. You can continue to learn or you can die. I suspect that is true in your business life, as well as your personal life.

As business owners, Laura and I haven't always made the right decisions, and we have most certainly gone through difficult times. When we started our own business by working nights in her uncle's shop, we had nothing and we really had nothing to lose. Gradually, we built that business to the point where we were able to raise our children on a horse ranch and sent them all to private schools. Then, when the economy turned south at no fault of our own, we ended up living in a double-wide mobile home with our two boys sharing a room and all three kids attending public schools in Uvalde. We had lost money, but we never lost our sense of direction or the drive to succeed.

Never lose your faith, hope or belief in yourself. Adversities will come your way. Trials will stop you in your tracks. Road blocks and detours might blindside you. But as you encounter difficulties remember that a muscle only grows stronger when it encounters resistance; diamonds are formed because of high temperatures and pressure; trees grow deep roots and develop the stress wood they need to remain upright in response to battering winds; and people develop strength, character and courage when encountering and overcoming challenges.

I think it's important to realize early in life and business that everyone fails, but not everyone understands how beneficial failing can be. Learn from mistakes; evolve with changing times; never accept a single failure as a final defeat; and continue to look for opportunities. As I have already pointed out, I believe that one of the keys to any amount of success we have enjoyed, especially in the early days of American Lumber, was to take advantages of the opportunities that presented themselves. The economy in Texas was so bleak at one point in the mid-1980s that our market completely dried up, but fortunately, I saw an opportunity to shift gears and begin another operation in Mexico. Years later, it became necessary for us to move operations back to stateside, but we had seized a window of opportunity and made the most of it. I am convinced that the foundation of entrepreneurship is opportunity.

Like many other people in my generation, I am disturbed by a growing trend among young people who are protesting—sometimes violently—and speaking out against America and its leaders. No matter who the president is or what your politics may be, I encourage you to be grateful for the opportunities that this country continues to provide. I remember as a youth sitting around extended family members who were immigrants. They were all immigrants. One of the things I remember well is that they didn't refer to the country as the United States of America. They always called it the "Land of Opportunity."

They had come to America from difficult circumstances, and they recognized how good it was here. Simply being grateful for this country and its opportunities has helped me throughout my life. That appreciation and gratitude were only intensified after running a business in another country. If you are a college student at Texas A&M right now or a recent graduate, you have so much to be grateful for because your education and citizenship can open up opportunities that can take you to wherever your dreams can imagine. I still recall a wise, old man telling me when I was younger that the greatest sin of all is the lack of gratitude. If you really play that through in your mind, you will realize that we all have multiple reasons to be grateful.

I also encourage you to commit to a lifetime of learning and development. Simply earning a degree from a school like Texas A&M is a big step in the right direction, but if you are not continuing to grow, learn and evolve as a businessperson and as an individual, you will not reach your full potential. I believe we only succeed to the degree of our personal growth, thinking, action and goals. One of the great Aggie entrepreneurs of all time, Artie McFerrin, once wrote: "(Entrepreneurial success) is not due to our business schemes, intelligence, knowledge and luck like most of the naive think. That's why we need to keep working on mastering success principles and refining the way we think." My wife refers to me as a voracious reader because I usually have two or three books going at all times, which helps me to continue to grow and learn. I am so grateful for the foundation Texas A&M and the Corps of Cadets provided me, but that was many decades ago. I must evolve with the times. When we first started our first business

Barry and Laura Hendler

and later American Lumber, our office supplies basically consisted of pencils, pens and notepads. There's no way we could still be in business today if we were not utilizing advanced technology.

The world is changing constantly, and it is extremely important to continually evolve. I realize many young people today did not grow up reading like I did, but at least commit to listening to audio books, attending self-help seminars and learning throughout your life. Committing to a lifetime of continuing education can be quite enjoyable as you begin to see the world differently through the eyes and experiences of various authors and entrepreneurs. As the late author and motivational speaker Charlie "Tremendous" Jones once noted, ""You will be the same person in five years as you are today except for the people you meet and the books you read."

It's also so important to have a plan. Not just a plan for next week, next month or next year, but also develop a long-term plan that includes long-range goal setting. At American Lumber, I've often spent time developing and sharing our 100-year plan. Will American Lumber be around 100 years from now? I have no idea, and at that point, I will long be gone. But I do know that American Lumber has a much better chance of still being here many decades from now if we have a plan in place. As it has been said often, "Nobody plans to fail. They simply fail to plan."

Finally, surround yourself with great people, especially people who are strong in areas where you may be weak. We have been blessed to recruit and hire some sensational, loyal and hard-working employees who have been by our side through the ups and downs. We all have strengths. Likewise, we all have weaknesses. We can't be all things, but we can serve our customers by surrounding ourselves with employees who complement us and make up for our shortcomings. Figure out what you're really, really good at, and then as you scale up your business, hire people who are better and smarter than you in your weak areas. It's great to know your strengths, but it's even wiser to know your weaknesses and then to address them by hiring others who can handle what you find difficult.

Perhaps those great people you hire one day will refer to you as "Mom" or "Dad." I can't tell you how rewarding it has been to see my children grow and flourish as business leaders. Laura and I never intended this to be a family business, but the evolution of it has been one of God's greatest blessings in our lives.

About the Book

A book unlike any other Aggie-related publication that has ever been produced, *The Entrepreneurial Spirit of Aggieland II* details the insightful, fascinating and inspirational stories of twelve Aggies who have chased their entrepreneurial dreams, endured hardships, conquered obstacles and succeeded beyond their wildest imaginations. Their stories will serve as a roadmap to success for current and former Texas A&M students with their own entrepreneurial dreams, as each first-person narrative features advice to aspiring entrepreneurs. These innovators have walked the Texas A&M campus and achieved tremendous success, and they each believe you can, too!

Perhaps best of all, **every penny of proceeds from the sale of this book will be donated to Startup Aggieland**, a globally-recognized, award-winning and multidisciplinary business accelerator that is already helping current Aggies pursue their dreams. This is truly a one-of-a-kind book designed to propel current and former student to reach their entrepreneurial dreams!

About the Author

Rusty Burson is currently the Director of Membership and Communications at Miramont Country Club, where he started in September 2014.

From 1998-2014, Burson was the associate editor of *12th Man Magazine* and vice president with the 12th Man Foundation. Burson, a 1990 graduate of Sam Houston State, began his professional career as a newspaper sports reporter and editor with *The Galveston Daily News* in 1990. He spent three years in Galveston before moving to *The Fort Worth Star-Telegram*. After leaving the newspaper industry in 1995, Burson took a role in municipal public relations and then became an editor for numerous business publications in the Dallas-Fort Worth area. Burson joined the 12th Man Foundation, the fundraising organization for Texas A&M athletics full time, in 1998.

He has more than 20 years experience as a sportswriter, beginning with his first newspaper jobs in college, first with the campus paper, *The Houstonian*, and later with *The Huntsville Item*.

Burson and his wife, Vannessa, have three children—son Payton (named after NFL Hall of Famer Walter Payton); daughter Kyleigh (named after Kyle Field); and daughter Summer (named after former Olympics swimmer Summer Sanders).

In addition to his work with Miramont, this is Burson's 23rd non-fiction book.

CPSIA information can be obtained
at www.ICGtesting.com
Printed in the USA
BVHW020443200322
631886BV00002B/10